Introduction to
Computation and
Programming Using Python

Introduction to Computation and Programming Using Python

Revised and Expanded Edition

John V. Guttag

The MIT Press
Cambridge, Massachusetts
London, England

MIT Press books may be purchased at special quantity discounts for business or sales promotional use. For information, please email special_sales@mitpress.mit.edu or write to Special Sales Department, The MIT Press, 55 Hayward Street, Cambridge, MA 02142.

Printed and bound in the United Kingdom.

Library of Congress Cataloging-in-Publication Data

Guttag, John.

Introduction to computation and programming using Python / John V. Guttag. — Revised and expanded edition.

 pages   cm

Includes index.

ISBN 978-0-262-52500-8 (pbk. : alk. paper)

1. Python (Computer program language) 2. Computer programming. I. Title.

QA76.73.P48G88   2013

005.13'3—dc23

10 9 8 7 6 5 4 3 2 1

To my family:

Olga

David

Andrea

Michael

Mark

Addie

CONTENTS

PREFACE xiii

ACKNOWLEDGMENTS xv

1   GETTING STARTED 1

2   INTRODUCTION TO PYTHON 7

   2.1   The Basic Elements of Python 8

      2.1.1   Objects, Expressions, and Numerical Types.............................. 9

      2.1.2   Variables and Assignment 11

      2.1.3   IDLE 13

   2.2   Branching Programs 14

   2.3   Strings and Input 16

      2.3.1   Input 18

   2.4   Iteration... 18

3   SOME SIMPLE NUMERICAL PROGRAMS 21

   3.1   Exhaustive Enumeration 21

   3.2   For Loops... 23

   3.3   Approximate Solutions and Bisection Search 25

   3.4   A Few Words About Using Floats 29

   3.5   Newton-Raphson 32

4   FUNCTIONS, SCOPING, and ABSTRACTION 34

   4.1   Functions and Scoping 35

      4.1.1   Function Definitions... 35

      4.1.2   Keyword Arguments and Default Values 36

      4.1.3   Scoping 37

   4.2   Specifications 41

   4.3   Recursion 44

      4.3.1   Fibonacci Numbers 45

      4.3.2   Palindromes 48

   4.4   Global Variables 50

   4.5   Modules.. 51

   4.6   Files 53

5   STRUCTURED TYPES, MUTABILITY, AND HIGHER-ORDER FUNCTIONS.. 56

   5.1   Tuples 56

      5.1.1   Sequences and Multiple Assignment.. 57

   5.2   Lists and Mutability.. 58

      5.2.1   Cloning 63

      5.2.2   List Comprehension 63

   5.3   Functions as Objects 64

   5.4   Strings, Tuples, and Lists 66

   5.5   Dictionaries 67

6   TESTING AND DEBUGGING... 70

   6.1   Testing... 70

      6.1.1   Black-Box Testing 71

      6.1.2   Glass-Box Testing 73

      6.1.3   Conducting Tests 74

   6.2   Debugging 76

      6.2.1   Learning to Debug.. 78

      6.2.2   Designing the Experiment 79

      6.2.3   When the Going Gets Tough 81

      6.2.4   And When You Have Found "The" Bug.. 82

7   EXCEPTIONS AND ASSERTIONS 84

   7.1   Handling Exceptions... 84

   7.2   Exceptions as a Control Flow Mechanism 87

   7.3   Assertions.. 90

8   CLASSES AND OBJECT-ORIENTED PROGRAMMING 91

   8.1   Abstract Data Types and Classes 91

      8.1.1   Designing Programs Using Abstract Data Types........................... 96

      8.1.2   Using Classes to Keep Track of Students and Faculty................... 96

   8.2   Inheritance 99

      8.2.1   Multiple Levels of Inheritance 101

      8.2.2   The Substitution Principle 102

   8.3   Encapsulation and Information Hiding.. 103

      8.3.1   Generators 106

   8.4   Mortgages, an Extended Example 108

9   A SIMPLISTIC INTRODUCTION TO ALGORITHMIC COMPLEXITY 113

   9.1   Thinking About Computational Complexity 113

   9.2   Asymptotic Notation 116

   9.3   Some Important Complexity Classes 118

      9.3.1   Constant Complexity 118

      9.3.2   Logarithmic Complexity 118

      9.3.3   Linear Complexity 119

      9.3.4   Log-Linear Complexity 120

      9.3.5   Polynomial Complexity 120

      9.3.6   Exponential Complexity 121

      9.3.7   Comparisons of Complexity Classes 123

10 SOME SIMPLE ALGORITHMS AND DATA STRUCTURES 125

   10.1   Search Algorithms 126

      10.1.1   Linear Search and Using Indirection to Access Elements 126

      10.1.2   Binary Search and Exploiting Assumptions 128

   10.2   Sorting Algorithms 131

      10.2.1   Merge Sort 132

      10.2.2   Exploiting Functions as Parameters 135

      10.2.3   Sorting in Python 136

   10.3   Hash Tables 137

11 PLOTTING AND MORE ABOUT CLASSES 141

   11.1   Plotting Using PyLab 141

   11.2   Plotting Mortgages, an Extended Example 146

12 STOCHASTIC PROGRAMS, PROBABILITY, AND STATISTICS 152

   12.1   Stochastic Programs 153

   12.2   Inferential Statistics and Simulation 155

   12.3   Distributions 166

      12.3.1   Normal Distributions and Confidence Levels 168

      12.3.2   Uniform Distributions 170

      12.3.3   Exponential and Geometric Distributions 171

      12.3.4   Benford's Distribution 173

   12.4   How Often Does the Better Team Win? 174

   12.5   Hashing and Collisions 177

13 RANDOM WALKS AND MORE ABOUT DATA VISUALIZATION 179

  13.1 The Drunkard's Walk 179

  13.2 Biased Random Walks 186

  13.3 Treacherous Fields 191

14 MONTE CARLO SIMULATION 193

  14.1 Pascal's Problem 194

  14.2 Pass or Don't Pass? 195

  14.3 Using Table Lookup to Improve Performance 199

  14.4 Finding π 200

  14.5 Some Closing Remarks About Simulation Models 204

15 UNDERSTANDING EXPERIMENTAL DATA 207

  15.1 The Behavior of Springs 207

    15.1.1 Using Linear Regression to Find a Fit 210

  15.2 The Behavior of Projectiles 214

    15.2.1 Coefficient of Determination 216

    15.2.2 Using a Computational Model 217

  15.3 Fitting Exponentially Distributed Data 218

  15.4 When Theory Is Missing 221

16 LIES, DAMNED LIES, AND STATISTICS 222

  16.1 Garbage In Garbage Out (GIGO) 222

  16.2 Pictures Can Be Deceiving 223

  16.3 *Cum Hoc Ergo Propter Hoc* 225

  16.4 Statistical Measures Don't Tell the Whole Story 226

  16.5 Sampling Bias 228

  16.6 Context Matters 229

  16.7 Beware of Extrapolation 229

  16.8 The Texas Sharpshooter Fallacy 230

  16.9 Percentages Can Confuse 232

  16.10 Just Beware 233

17 KNAPSACK AND GRAPH OPTIMIZATION PROBLEMS 234

  17.1 Knapsack Problems 234

    17.1.1 Greedy Algorithms 235

    17.1.2 An Optimal Solution to the 0/1 Knapsack Problem 238

17.2   Graph Optimization Problems 240

    17.2.1   Some Classic Graph-Theoretic Problems.................................. 244

    17.2.2   The Spread of Disease and Min Cut 245

    17.2.3   Shortest Path: Depth-First Search and Breadth-First Search 246

18   DYNAMIC PROGRAMMING 252

18.1   Fibonacci Sequences, Revisited 252

18.2   Dynamic Programming and the 0/1 Knapsack Problem................... 254

18.3   Dynamic Programming and Divide-and-Conquer............................ 261

19   A QUICK LOOK AT MACHINE LEARNING 262

19.1   Feature Vectors 264

19.2   Distance Metrics 266

19.3   Clustering.. 270

19.4   Types Example and Cluster... 272

19.5   K-means Clustering 274

19.6   A Contrived Example 276

19.7   A Less Contrived Example.. 280

19.8   Wrapping Up.. 286

PYTHON 2.7 QUICK REFERENCE 287

INDEX 289

PREFACE

This book is based on an MIT course that has been offered twice a year since 2006. The course is aimed at students with little or no prior programming experience who have desire to understand computational approaches to problem solving. Each year, a few of the students in the class use the course as a stepping stone to more advanced computer science courses. But for most of the students it will be their only computer science course.

Because the course will be the only computer science course for most of the students, we focus on breadth rather than depth. The goal is to provide students with a brief introduction to many topics, so that they will have an idea of what's possible when the time comes to think about how to use computation to accomplish a goal. That said, it is not a "computation appreciation" course. It is a challenging and rigorous course in which the students spend a lot of time and effort learning to bend the computer to their will.

The main goal of this book is to help you, the reader, become skillful at making productive use of computational techniques. You should learn to apply computational modes of thoughts to frame problems and to guide the process of extracting information from data in a computational manner. The primary knowledge you will take away from this book is the art of computational problem solving.

The book is a bit eccentric. Part 1 (Chapters 1-8) is an unconventional introduction to programming in Python. We braid together four strands of material:

- The basics of programming,
- The Python programming language,
- Concepts central to understanding computation, and
- Computational problem solving techniques.

We cover most of Python's features, but the emphasis is on what one can do with a programming language, not on the language itself. For example, by the end of Chapter 3 the book has covered only a small fraction of Python, but it has already introduced the notions of exhaustive enumeration, guess-and-check algorithms, bisection search, and efficient approximation algorithms. We introduce features of Python throughout the book. Similarly, we introduce aspects of programming methods throughout the book. The idea is to help you learn Python and how to be a good programmer in the context of using computation to solve interesting problems.

Part 2 (Chapters 9-16) is primarily about using computation to solve problems. It assumes no knowledge of mathematics beyond high school algebra, but it does assume that the reader is comfortable with rigorous thinking and not intimidated by mathematical concepts. It covers some of the usual topics found in an introductory text, e.g., computational complexity and simple algorithms.

But the bulk of this part of the book is devoted to topics not found in most introductory texts: data visualization, probabilistic and statistical thinking, simulation models, and using computation to understand data.

Part 3 (Chapters 17-19) looks at three slightly advanced topics—optimization problems, dynamic programming, and clustering.

Part 1 can form the basis of a self-contained course that can be taught in a quarter or half a semester. Experience suggests that it is quite comfortable to fit both Parts 1 and 2 of this book into a full-semester course. When the material in Part 3 is included, the course becomes more demanding than is comfortable for many students.

The book has two pervasive themes: systematic problem solving and the power of abstraction. When you have finished this book you should have:

- Learned a language, Python, for expressing computations,

- Learned a systematic approach to organizing, writing and debugging medium-sized programs,

- Developed an informal understanding of computational complexity,

- Developed some insight into the process of moving from an ambiguous problem statement to a computational formulation of a method for solving the problem,

- Learned a useful set of algorithmic and problem reduction techniques,

- Learned how to use randomness and simulations to shed light on problems that don't easily succumb to closed-form solutions, and

- Learned how to use computational tools, including simple statistical and visualization tools, to model and understand data.

Programming is an intrinsically difficult activity. Just as "there is no royal road to geometry,"[1] there is no royal road to programming. It is possible to deceive students into thinking that they have learned how to program by having them complete a series of highly constrained "fill in the blank" programming problems. However, this does not prepare students for figuring out how to harness computational thinking to solve problems.

If you really want to learn the material, reading the book will not be enough. At the very least you should try running some of the code in the book. All of the code in the book can be found at http://mitpress.mit.edu/ICPPRE. Various versions of the course have been available on MIT's OpenCourseWare (OCW) Web site since 2008. The site includes video recordings of lectures and a complete set of problem sets and exams. Since the fall of 2012, edX and MITx, have offered an online version of this course. We strongly recommend that you do the problem sets associated with one of the OCW or edX offerings.

---

[1] This was Euclid's purported response, circa 300 BC, to King Ptolemy's request for an easier way to learn mathematics.

ACKNOWLEDGMENTS

This book grew out of a set of lecture notes that I prepared while teaching an undergraduate course at MIT. The course, and therefore this book, benefited from suggestions from faculty colleagues (especially Eric Grimson, Srinivas Devadas, and Fredo Durand), teaching assistants, and the students who took the course.

The process of transforming my lecture notes into a book proved far more onerous than I had expected. Fortunately, this misguided optimism lasted long enough to keep me from giving up. The encouragement of colleagues and family also helped keep me going.

Eric Grimson, Chris Terman, and David Guttag provided vital help. Eric, who is MIT's Chancellor, managed to find the time to read almost the entire book with great care. He found numerous errors (including an embarrassing, to me, number of technical errors) and pointed out places where necessary explanations were missing. Chris also read parts of the manuscript and discovered errors. He also helped me battle Microsoft Word, which we eventually persuaded to do most of what we wanted. David overcame his aversion to computer science, and proofread multiple chapters.

Preliminary versions of this book were used in the MIT course 6.00 and the MITx course 6.00x. A number of students in these courses pointed out errors. One 6.00x student, J.C. Cabrejas, was particularly helpful. He found a large number of typos, and more than a few technical errors.

Like all successful professors, I owe a great deal to my graduate students. The photo on the back cover of this book depicts me supporting some of my current students. In the lab, however, it is they who support me. In addition to doing great research (and letting me take some of the credit for it), Guha Balakrishnan, Joel Brooks, Ganeshapillai Gartheeban, Jen Gong, Yun Liu, Anima Singh, Jenna Wiens, and Amy Zhao all provided useful comments on this manuscript.

I owe a special debt of gratitude to Julie Sussman, P.P.A. Until I started working with Julie, I had no idea how much difference an editor could make. I had worked with capable copy editors on previous books, and thought that was what I needed for this book. I was wrong. I needed a collaborator who could read the book with the eyes of a student, and tell me what needed to be done, what should be done, and what could be done if I had the time and energy to do it. Julie buried me in "suggestions" that were too good to ignore. Her combined command of both the English language and programming is quite remarkable.

Finally, thanks to my wife, Olga, for pushing me to finish and for pitching in at critical times.

1 GETTING STARTED

A computer does two things, and two things only: it performs calculations and it remembers the results of those calculations. But it does those two things extremely well. The typical computer that sits on a desk or in a briefcase performs a billion or so calculations a second. It's hard to image how truly fast that is. Think about holding a ball a meter above the floor, and letting it go. By the time it reaches the floor, your computer could have executed over a billion instructions. As for memory, a typical computer might have hundreds of gigabytes of storage. How big is that? If a byte (the number of bits, typically eight, required to represent one character) weighed one ounce (which it doesn't), 100 gigabytes would weigh more than 3,000,000 tons. For comparison, that's roughly the weight of all the coal produced in a year in the U.S.

For most of human history, computation was limited by the speed of calculation of the human brain and the ability to record computational results with the human hand. This meant that only the smallest problems could be attacked computationally. Even with the speed of modern computers, there are still problems that are beyond modern computational models (e.g., understanding climate change), but more and more problems are proving amenable to computational solution. It is our hope that by the time you finish this book, you will feel comfortable bringing computational thinking to bear on solving many of the problems you encounter during your studies, work, and even everyday life.

What do we mean by computational thinking?

All knowledge can be thought of as either declarative or imperative. **Declarative knowledge** is composed of statements of fact. For example, "the square root of x is a number y such that y*y = x." This is a statement of fact. Unfortunately it doesn't tell us how to find a square root.

Imperative knowledge is "how to" knowledge, or recipes for deducing information. Heron of Alexandria was the first to document a way to compute the square root of a number.[2] His method can be summarized as:

- Start with a guess, g.
- If g*g is close enough to x, stop and say that g is the answer.
- Otherwise create a new guess by averaging g and x/g, i.e., (g + x/g)/2.
- Using this new guess, which we again call g, repeat the process until g*g is close enough to x.

---

[2] Many believe that Heron was not the inventor of this method, and indeed there is some evidence that it was well known to the ancient Babylonians.

Consider, for example, finding the square root of 25.

1. Set g to some arbitrary value, e.g., 3.
2. We decide that $3*3 = 9$ is not close enough to 25.
3. Set g to $(3 + 25/3)/2 = 5.67$.[3]
4. We decide that $5.67*5.67 = 32.15$ is still not close enough to 25.
5. Set g to $(5.67 + 25/5.67)/2 = 5.04$
6. We decide that $5.04*5.04 = 25.4$ is close enough, so we stop and declare 5.04 to be an adequate approximation to the square root of 25.

Note that the description of the method is a sequence of simple steps, together with a flow of control that specifies when each step is to be executed. Such a description is called an **algorithm**.[4] This algorithm is an example of a guess-and-check algorithm. It is based on the fact that it is easy to check whether or not a guess is a good one.

A bit more formally, an algorithm is a finite list of instructions that describe a **computation** that when executed on a provided set of inputs will proceed through a set of well-defined states and eventually produce an output.

An algorithm is a bit like a recipe from a cookbook:

1. Put custard mixture over heat.
2. Stir.
3. Dip spoon in custard.
4. Remove spoon and run finger across back of spoon.
5. If clear path is left, remove custard from heat and let cool.
6. Otherwise repeat.

It includes some tests for deciding when the process is complete, as well as instructions about the order in which to execute instructions, sometimes jumping to some instruction based on a test.

So how does one capture this idea of a recipe in a mechanical process? One way would be to design a machine specifically intended to compute square roots. Odd as this may sound, the earliest computing machines were, in fact, **fixed-program computers**, meaning they were designed to do very specific things, and were mostly tools to solve a specific mathematical problem, e.g., to compute the trajectory of an artillery shell. One of the first computers (built in 1941 by Atanasoff and Berry) solved systems of linear equations, but could do nothing else. Alan Turing's bombe machine, developed during World War II, was designed strictly for the purpose of breaking German Enigma codes. Some very simple computers still use this approach. For example, a four-function calculator is a fixed-program computer. It can do basic arithmetic, but it cannot

---

[3] For simplicity, we are rounding results.

[4] The word "algorithm" is derived from the name of the Persian mathematician Muhammad ibn Musa al-Khwarizmi.

be used as a word processor or to run video games. To change the program of such a machine, one has to replace the circuitry.

The first truly modern computer was the Manchester Mark 1.[5] It was distinguished from its predecessors by the fact that it was a **stored-program computer**. Such a computer stores (and manipulates) a sequence of instructions, and has a set of elements that will execute any instruction in that sequence. By creating an instruction-set architecture and detailing the computation as a sequence of instructions (i.e., a program), we make a highly flexible machine. By treating those instructions in the same way as data, a stored-program machine can easily change the program, and can do so under program control. Indeed, the heart of the computer then becomes a program (called an **interpreter**) that can execute any legal set of instructions, and thus can be used to compute anything that one can describe using some basic set of instructions.

Both the program and the data it manipulates reside in memory. Typically there is a program counter that points to a particular location in memory, and computation starts by executing the instruction at that point. Most often, the interpreter simply goes to the next instruction in the sequence, but not always. In some cases, it performs a test, and on the basis of that test, execution may jump to some other point in the sequence of instructions. This is called **flow of control,** and is essential to allowing us to write programs that perform complex tasks.

Returning to the recipe metaphor, given a fixed set of ingredients a good chef can make an unbounded number of tasty dishes by combining them in different ways. Similarly, given a small fixed set of primitive elements a good programmer can produce an unbounded number of useful programs. This is what makes programming such an amazing endeavor.

To create recipes, or sequences of instructions, we need a **programming language** in which to describe these things, a way to give the computer its marching orders.

In 1936, the British mathematician Alan Turing described a hypothetical computing device that has come to be called a **Universal Turing Machine**. The machine had an unbounded memory in the form of tape on which one could write zeros and ones, and some very simple primitive instructions for moving, reading, and writing to the tape. The **Church-Turing thesis** states that if a function is computable, a Turing Machine can be programmed to compute it.

The "if" in the Church-Turing thesis is important. Not all problems have computational solutions. For example, Turing showed that it is impossible to write a program that given an arbitrary program, call it P, prints true if and only if P will run forever. This is known as the **halting problem**.

---

[5] This computer was built at the University of Manchester, and ran its first program in 1949. It implemented ideas previously described by John von Neumann and was anticipated by the theoretical concept of the Universal Turing Machine described by Alan Turing in 1936.

The Church-Turing thesis leads directly to the notion of **Turing completeness**. A programming language is said to be Turing complete if it can be used to simulate a universal Turing Machine. All modern programming languages are Turing complete. As a consequence, anything that can be programmed in one programming language (e.g., Python) can be programmed in any other programming language (e.g., Java). Of course, some things may be easier to program in a particular language, but all languages are fundamentally equal with respect to computational power.

Fortunately, no programmer has to build programs out of Turing's primitive instructions. Instead, modern programming languages offer a larger, more convenient set of primitives. However, the fundamental idea of programming as the process of assembling a sequence of operations remains central.

Whatever set of primitives one has, and whatever methods one has for using them, the best thing and the worst thing about programming are the same: the computer will do exactly what you tell it to do. This is a good thing because it means that you can make it do all sorts of fun and useful things. It is a bad thing because when it doesn't do what you want it to do, you usually have nobody to blame but yourself.

There are hundreds of programming languages in the world. There is no best language (though one could nominate some candidates for worst). Different languages are better or worse for different kinds of applications. MATLAB, for example, is an excellent language for manipulating vectors and matrices. C is a good language for writing the programs that control data networks. PHP is a good language for building Web sites. And Python is a good general-purpose language.

Each programming language has a set of primitive constructs, a syntax, a static semantics, and a semantics. By analogy with a natural language, e.g., English, the primitive constructs are words, the syntax describes which strings of words constitute well-formed sentences, the static semantics defines which sentences are meaningful, and the semantics defines the meaning of those sentences. The primitive constructs in Python include **literals** (e.g., the number 3.2 and the string 'abc') and **infix operators** (e.g., + and /).

The **syntax** of a language defines which strings of characters and symbols are well formed. For example, in English the string "Cat dog boy." is not a syntactically valid sentence, because the syntax of English does not accept sentences of the form <noun> <noun> <noun>. In Python, the sequence of primitives 3.2 + 3.2 is syntactically well formed, but the sequence 3.2 3.2 is not.

The **static semantics** defines which syntactically valid strings have a meaning. In English, for example, the string "I are big," is of the form <pronoun> <linking verb> <adjective>, which is a syntactically acceptable sequence. Nevertheless, it is not valid English, because the noun "I" is singular and the verb "are" is plural. This is an example of a static semantic error. In Python, the sequence 3.2/'abc' is syntactically well formed (<literal> <operator> <literal>), but produces a static semantic error since it is not meaningful to divide a number by a string of characters.

The **semantics** of a language associates a meaning with each syntactically correct string of symbols that has no static semantic errors. In natural languages, the semantics of a sentence can be ambiguous. For example, the sentence "I cannot praise this student too highly," can be either flattering or damning. Programming languages are designed so that each legal program has exactly one meaning.

Though syntax errors are the most common kind of error (especially for those learning a new programming language), they are the least dangerous kind of error. Every serious programming language does a complete job of detecting syntactic errors, and will not allow users to execute a program with even one syntactic error. Furthermore, in most cases the language system gives a sufficiently clear indication of the location of the error that it is obvious what needs to be done to fix it.

The situation with respect to static semantic errors is a bit more complex. Some programming languages, e.g., Java, do a lot of static semantic checking before allowing a program to be executed. Others, e.g., C and Python (alas), do relatively less static semantic checking. Python does do a considerable amount of static semantic checking while running a program. However, it does not catch all static semantic errors. When these errors are not detected, the behavior of a program is often unpredictable. We will see examples of this later in the book.

One doesn't usually speak of a program as having a semantic error. If a program has no syntactic errors and no static semantic errors, it has a meaning, i.e., it has semantics. Of course, that isn't to say that it has the semantics that its creator intended it to have. When a program means something other than what its creator thinks it means, bad things can happen.

What might happen if the program has an error, and behaves in an unintended way?

- It might crash, i.e., stop running and produce some sort of obvious indication that it has done so. In a properly designed computing system, when a program crashes it does not do damage to the overall system. Of course, some very popular computer systems don't have this nice property. Almost everyone who uses a personal computer has run a program that has managed to make it necessary to restart the whole computer.

- Or it might keep running, and running, and running, and never stop. If one has no idea of approximately how long the program is supposed to take to do its job, this situation can be hard to recognize.

- Or it might run to completion and produce an answer that might, or might not, be correct.

Each of these is bad, but the last of them is certainly the worst, When a program appears to be doing the right thing but isn't, bad things can follow. Fortunes can be lost, patients can receive fatal doses of radiation therapy, airplanes can crash, etc.

Whenever possible, programs should be written in such a way that when they don't work properly, it is self-evident. We will discuss how to do this throughout the book.

Finger Exercise: Computers can be annoyingly literal. If you don't tell them exactly what you want them to do, they are likely to do the wrong thing. Try writing an algorithm for driving between two destinations. Write it the way you would for a person, and then imagine what would happen if that person executed the algorithm exactly as written. For example, how many traffic tickets might they get?

2 INTRODUCTION TO PYTHON

Though each programming language is different (though not as different as their designers would have us believe), there are some dimensions along which they can be related.

- **Low-level versus high-level** refers to whether we program using instructions and data objects at the level of the machine (e.g., move 64 bits of data from this location to that location) or whether we program using more abstract operations (e.g., pop up a menu on the screen) that have been provided by the language designer.

- **General versus targeted to an application domain** refers to whether the primitive operations of the programming language are widely applicable or are fine-tuned to a domain. For example Adobe Flash is designed to facilitate adding animation and interactivity to Web pages, but you wouldn't want to use it build a stock portfolio analysis program.

- **Interpreted versus compiled** refers to whether the sequence of instructions written by the programmer, called **source code**, is executed directly (by an interpreter) or whether it is first converted (by a compiler) into a sequence of machine-level primitive operations. (In the early days of computers, people had to write source code in a language that was very close to the **machine code** that could be directly interpreted by the computer hardware.) There are advantages to both approaches. It is often easier to debug programs written in languages that are designed to be interpreted, because the interpreter can produce error messages that are easy to correlate with the source code. Compiled languages usually produce programs that run more quickly and use less space.

In this book, we use **Python**. However, this book is not about Python. It will certainly help readers learn Python, and that's a good thing. What is much more important, however, is that careful readers will learn something about how to write programs that solve problems. This skill can be transferred to any programming language.

Python is a general-purpose programming language that can be used effectively to build almost any kind of program that does not need direct access to the computer's hardware. Python is not optimal for programs that have high reliability constraints (because of its weak static semantic checking) or that are built and maintained by many people or over a long period of time (again because of the weak static semantic checking).

However, Python does have several advantages over many other languages. It is a relatively simple language that is easy to learn. Because Python is designed to be interpreted, it can provide the kind of runtime feedback that is especially helpful to novice programmers. There are also a large number of freely available libraries that interface to Python and provide useful extended functionality. Several of those are used in this book.

Now we are ready to start learning some of the basic elements of Python. These are common to almost all programming languages in concept, though not necessarily in detail.

The reader should be forewarned that this book is by no means a comprehensive introduction to Python. We use Python as a vehicle to present concepts related to computational problem solving and thinking. The language is presented in dribs and drabs, as needed for this ulterior purpose. Python features that we don't need for that purpose are not presented at all. We feel comfortable about not covering the entire language because there are excellent online resources describing almost every aspect of the language. When we teach the course on which this book is based, we suggest to the students that they rely on these free online resources for Python reference material.

Python is a living language. Since its introduction by Guido von Rossum in 1990, it has undergone many changes. For the first decade of its life, Python was a little known and little used language. That changed with the arrival of Python 2.0 in 2000. In addition to incorporating a number of important improvements to the language itself, it marked a shift in the evolutionary path of the language. A large number of people began developing libraries that interfaced seamlessly with Python, and continuing support and development of the Python ecosystem became a community-based activity. Python 3.0 was released at the end of 2008. This version of Python cleaned up many of the inconsistencies in the design of the various releases of Python 2 (often referred to as Python 2.x). However, it was not backward compatible. That meant that most programs written for earlier versions of Python could not be run using implementations of Python 3.0.

The backward incompatibility presents a problem for this book. In our view, Python 3.0 is clearly superior to Python 2.x. However, at the time of this writing, some important Python libraries still do not work with Python 3. We will, therefore, use Python 2.7 (into which many of the most important features of Python 3 have been "back ported") throughout this book.

2.1 The Basic Elements of Python

A Python **program**, sometimes called a **script**, is a sequence of definitions and commands. These definitions are evaluated and the commands are executed by the Python interpreter in something called the **shell**. Typically, a new shell is created whenever execution of a program begins. In most cases, a window is associated with the shell.

We recommend that you start a Python shell now, and use it to try the examples contained in the remainder of the chapter. And, for that matter, later in the book as well.

A **command**, often called a **statement**, instructs the interpreter to do something. For example, the statement `print 'Yankees rule!'` instructs the interpreter to output the string `Yankees rule!` to the window associated with the shell.

The sequence of commands

```
print 'Yankees rule!'
print 'But not in Boston!'
print 'Yankees rule,', 'but not in Boston!'
```

causes the interpreter to produce the output

```
Yankees rule!
But not in Boston!
Yankees rule, but not in Boston!
```

Notice that two values were passed to print in the third statement. The print command takes a variable number of values and prints them, separated by a space character, in the order in which they appear.[6]

2.1.1 Objects, Expressions, and Numerical Types

Objects are the core things that Python programs manipulate. Every object has a **type** that defines the kinds of things that programs can do with objects of that type.

Types are either scalar or non-scalar. **Scalar** objects are indivisible. Think of them as the atoms of the language.[7] Non-scalar objects, for example strings, have internal structure.

Python has four types of scalar objects:

- int is used to represent integers. Literals of type int are written in the way we typically denote integers (e.g., -3 or 5 or 10002).

- float is used to represent real numbers. Literals of type float always include a decimal point (e.g., 3.0 or 3.17 or -28.72). (It is also possible to write literals of type float using scientific notation. For example, the literal 1.6E3 stands for $1.6*10^3$, i.e., it is the same as 1600.0.) You might wonder why this type is not called real. Within the computer, values of type float are stored in the computer as **floating point numbers**. This representation, which is used by all modern programming languages, has many advantages. However, under some situations it causes floating point arithmetic to behave in ways that are slightly different from arithmetic on real numbers. We discuss this in Section 3.4.

- bool is used to represent the Boolean values True and False.

- None is a type with a single value. We will say more about this when we get to variables.

Objects and **operators** can be combined to form **expressions**, each of which evaluates to an object of some type. We will refer to this as the **value** of the expression. For example, the expression 3 + 2 denotes the object 5 of type int, and the expression 3.0 + 2.0 denotes the object 5.0 of type float.

---

[6] In Python 3, print is a function rather than a command. One would therefore write print('Yankees rule!', 'but not in Boston').

[7] Yes, atoms are not truly indivisible. However, splitting them is not easy, and doing so can have consequences that are not always desirable.

The == operator is used to test whether two expressions evaluate to the same value, and the != operator is used to test whether two expressions evaluate to different values.

The symbol >>> is a **shell prompt** indicating that the interpreter is expecting the user to type some Python code into the shell. The line below the line with the prompt is produced when the interpreter evaluates the Python code entered at the prompt, as illustrated by the following interaction with the interpreter:

```
>>> 3 + 2
5
>>> 3.0 + 2.0
5.0
>>> 3 != 2
True
```

The built-in Python function type can be used to find out the type of an object:

```
>>> type(3)
<type 'int'>
>>> type(3.0)
<type 'float'>
```

The operators on types int and float are listed in Figure 2.1.

- **i+j** is the sum of i and j. If i and j are both of type int, the result is an int. If either of them is a float, the result is a float.

- **i-j** is i minus j. If i and j are both of type int, the result is an int. If either of them is a float, the result is a float.

- **i*j** is the product of i and j. If i and j are both of type int, the result is an int. If either of them is a float, the result is a float.

- **i//j** is integer division. For example, the value of 6//2 is the int 3 and the value of 6//4 is the int 1. The value is 1 because integer division returns the quotient and ignores the remainder.

- **i/j** is i divided by j. In Python 2.7, when i and j are both of type int, the result is also an int, otherwise the result is a float. In this book, we will never use / to divide one int by another. We will use // to do that. (In Python 3, the / operator, thank goodness, always returns a float. For example, in Python 3 the value of 6/4 is 1.5.)

- **i%j** is the remainder when the int i is divided by the int j. It is typically pronounced "i mod j," which is short for "i modulo j."

- **i**j** is i raised to the power j. If i and j are both of type int, the result is an int. If either of them is a float, the result is a float.

- The comparison operators are == (equal), != (not equal), > (greater), >= (at least), <, (less) and <= (at most).

Figure 2.1 Operators on types int and float

The arithmetic operators have the usual precedence. For example, * binds more tightly than +, so the expression x+y*2 is evaluated by first multiplying y by 2, and then adding the result to x. The order of evaluation can be changed by using parentheses to group subexpressions, e.g., (x+y)*2 first adds x and y, and then multiplies the result by 2.

The operators on type `bool` are:

- **a and b** is True if both a and b are True, and False otherwise.

- **a or b** is True if at least one of a or b is True, and False otherwise.

- **not a** is True if a is False, and False if a is True.

2.1.2 Variables and Assignment

Variables provide a way to associate names with objects. Consider the code

```
pi = 3
radius = 11
area = pi * (radius**2)
radius = 14
```

It first binds the names pi[8] and `radius` to different objects of type `int`. It then binds the name `area` to a third object of type `int`. This is depicted in the left panel of Figure 2.2.

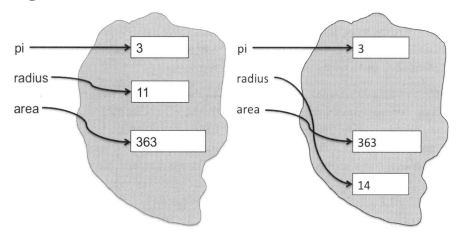

Figure 2.2 Binding of variables to objects

If the program then executes `radius = 11`, the name `radius` is rebound to a different object of type `int`, as shown in the right panel of Figure 2.2. Note that this assignment has no effect on the value to which `area` is bound. It is still bound to the object denoted by the expression 3*(11**2).

In Python, **a variable is just a name,** nothing more. Remember this—it is important. An **assignment** statement associates the name to the left of the = symbol with the object denoted by the expression to the right of the =. Remember this too. An object can have one, more than one, or no name associated with it.

---

[8] If you believe that the actual value of π is not 3, you're right. We even demonstrate that fact in Chapter 15.

Perhaps we shouldn't have said, "a variable is just a name." Despite what Juliet said,[9] names matter. Programming languages let us describe computations in a way that allows machines to execute them. This does not mean that only computers read programs.

As you will soon discover, it's not always easy to write programs that work correctly. Experienced programmers will confirm that they spend a great deal of time reading programs in an attempt to understand why they behave as they do. It is therefore of critical importance to write programs in such way that they are easy to read. Apt choice of variable names plays an important role in enhancing readability.

Consider the two code fragments

```
a = 3.14159        pi = 3.14159
b = 11.2           diameter = 11.2
c = a*(b**2)       area = pi*(diameter**2)
```

As far as Python is concerned, they are not different. When executed, they will do the same thing. To a human reader, however, they are quite different. When we read the fragment on the left, there is no *a priori* reason to suspect that anything is amiss. However, a quick glance at the code on the right should prompt us to be suspicious that something is wrong. Either the variable should have been named `radius` rather than `diameter`, or `diameter` should have been divided by `2.0` in the calculation of the area.

In Python, variable names can contain uppercase and lowercase letters, digits (but they cannot start with a digit), and the special character `_`. Python variable names are case-sensitive e.g., Julie and julie are different names. Finally, there are a small number of **reserved words** (sometimes called **keywords**) in Python that have built-in meanings and cannot be used as variable names. Different versions of Python have slightly different lists of reserved words. The reserved words in Python 2.7 are and, as, assert, break, class, continue, def, del, elif, else, except, exec, finally, for, from, global, if, import, in, is, lambda, not, or, pass, print, raise, return, try, with, while, and yield.

Another good way to enhance the readability of code is to add **comments**. Text following the symbol # is not interpreted by Python. For example, one might write

```
#subtract area of square s from area of circle c
areaC = pi*radius**2
areaS = side*side
difference = areaC-areaS
```

Python allows multiple assignment. The statement

```
x, y = 2, 3
```

binds x to 2 and y to 3. All of the expressions on the right-hand side of the assignment are evaluated before any bindings are changed. This is convenient

---

[9] "What's in a name? That which we call a rose by any other name would smell as sweet."

since it allows you to use multiple assignment to swap the bindings of two variables.

For example, the code

```
x, y = 2, 3
x, y = y, x
print 'x =', x
print 'y =', y
```

will print

```
x = 3
y = 2
```

2.1.3 IDLE

Typing programs directly into the shell is highly inconvenient. Most programmers prefer to use some sort of text editor that is part of an **integrated development environment (IDE)**.

In this book, we will use **IDLE**,[10] the IDE that comes as part of the standard Python installation package. IDLE is an application, just like any other application on your computer. Start it the same way you would start any other application, e.g., by double-clicking on an icon.

IDLE provides

- a text editor with syntax highlighting, autocompletion, and smart indentation,
- a shell with syntax highlighting, and
- an integrated debugger, which you should ignore for now.

When IDLE starts it will open a shell window into which you can type Python commands. It will also provide you with a file menu and an edit menu (as well as some other menus, which you can safely ignore for now).

The **file menu** includes commands to

- create a new editing window into which you can type a Python program,
- open a file containing an existing Python program, and
- save the contents of the current editing window into a file (with file extension .py).

The **edit menu** includes standard text-editing commands (e.g., copy, paste, and find) plus some commands specifically designed to make it easy to edit Python code (e.g., indent region and comment out region).

---

[10] Allegedly, the name Python was chosen as a tribute to the British comedy troupe Monty Python. This leads one to think that the name IDLE is a pun on Eric Idle, a member of the troupe.

For a complete description of IDLE, see
`http://docs.python.org/library/idle.html`.

2.2 Branching Programs

The kinds of computations we have been looking at thus far are called **straight-line programs**. They execute one statement after another in the order in which they appear, and stop when they run out of statements. The kinds of computations we can describe with straight-line programs are not very interesting. In fact, they are downright boring.

Branching programs are more interesting. The simplest branching statement is a **conditional**. As depicted in Figure 2.3, a conditional statement has three parts:

- a test, i.e., an expression that evaluates to either True or False;
- a block of code that is executed if the test evaluates to True; and
- an optional block of code that is executed if the test evaluates to False.

After a conditional statement is executed, execution resumes at the code following the statement.

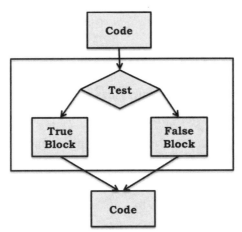

Figure 2.3 Flow chart for conditional statement

In Python, a conditional statement has the form

```
if Boolean expression:
    block of code
else:
    block of code
```

In describing the form of Python statements we use italics to describe the kinds of code that could occur at that point in a program. For example, *Boolean expression* indicates that any expression that evaluates to True or False can follow the reserved word `if`, and *block of code* indicates that any sequence of Python statements can follow `else:`.

Consider the following program that prints "Even" if the value of the variable x is even and "Odd" otherwise:

```
if x%2 == 0:
    print 'Even'
else:
    print 'Odd'
print 'Done with conditional'
```

The expression x%2 == 0 evaluates to True when the remainder of x divided by 2 is 0, and False otherwise. Remember that == is used for comparison, since = is reserved for assignment.

Indentation is semantically meaningful in Python. For example, if the last statement in the above code were indented it would be part of the block of code associated with the else, rather than with the block of code following the conditional statement.

Python is unusual in using indentation this way. Most other programming languages use some sort of bracketing symbols to delineate blocks of code, e.g., C encloses blocks in braces, { }. An advantage of the Python approach is that it ensures that the visual structure of a program is an accurate representation of the semantic structure of that program.

When either the true block or the false block of a conditional contains another conditional, the conditional statements are said to be **nested**. In the code below, there are nested conditionals in both branches of the top-level if statement.

```
if x%2 == 0:
    if x%3 == 0:
        print 'Divisible by 2 and 3'
    else:
        print 'Divisible by 2 and not by 3'
elif x%3 == 0:
    print 'Divisible by 3 and not by 2'
```

The elif in the above code stands for "else if."

It is often convenient to use compound Boolean expressions in the test of a conditional, for example,

```
if x < y and x < z:
    print 'x is least'
elif y < z:
    print 'y is least'
else:
    print 'z is least'
```

Conditionals allow us to write programs that are more interesting than straight-line programs, but the class of branching programs is still quite limited. One way to think about the power of a class of programs is in terms of how long they can take to run. Assume that each line of code takes one unit of time to execute. If a straight-line program has n lines of code, it will take n units of time to run. What about a branching program with n lines of code? It might take less than n units of time to run, but it cannot take more, since each line of code is executed at most once.

A program for which the maximum running time is bounded by the length of the program is said to run in **constant time**. This does not mean that each time it is run it executes the same number of steps. It means that there exists a constant, k, such that the program is guaranteed to take no more than k steps to run. This implies that the running time does not grow with the size of the input to the program.

Constant-time programs are quite limited in what they can do. Consider, for example, writing a program to tally the votes in an election. It would be truly surprising if one could write a program that could do this in a time that was independent of the number of votes cast. In fact, one can prove that it is impossible to do so. The study of the intrinsic difficulty of problems is the topic of **computational complexity**. We will return to this topic several times in this book.

Fortunately, we need only one more programming language construct, iteration, to be able to write programs of arbitrary complexity. We get to that in Section 2.4.

Finger exercise: Write a program that examines three variables—x, y, and z—and prints the largest odd number among them. If none of them are odd, it should print a message to that effect.

2.3 Strings and Input

Objects of type str are used to represent strings of characters.[11] Literals of type str can be written using either single or double quotes, e.g., 'abc' or "abc". The literal '123' denotes a string of characters, not the number one hundred twenty-three.

Try typing the following expressions in to the Python interpreter (remember that the >>> is a prompt, not something that you type):

```
>>> 'a'
>>> 3*4
>>> 3*'a'
>>> 3+4
>>> 'a'+'a'
```

The operator + is said to be **overloaded**: It has different meanings depending upon the types of the objects to which it is applied. For example, it means addition when applied to two numbers and concatenation when applied to two strings. The operator * is also overloaded. It means what you expect it to mean when its operands are both numbers. When applied to an int and a str, it duplicates the str. For example, the expression 2*'John' has the value

---

[11] Unlike many programming languages, Python has no type corresponding to a character. Instead, it uses strings of length 1.

'JohnJohn'. There is a logic to this. Just as the expression 3*2 is equivalent to 2+2+2, the expression 3*'a' is equivalent to 'a'+'a'+'a'.

Now try typing

```
>>> a
>>> 'a'*'a'
```

Each of these lines generates an error message.

The first line produces the message

```
NameError: name 'a' is not defined
```

Because a is not a literal of any type, the interpreter treats it as a name. However, since that name is not bound to any object, attempting to use it causes a runtime error.

The code 'a'*'a' produces the error message

```
TypeError: can't multiply sequence by non-int of type 'str'
```

That **type checking** exists is a good thing. It turns careless (and sometimes subtle) mistakes into errors that stop execution, rather than errors that lead programs to behave in mysterious ways. The type checking in Python is not as strong as in some other programming languages (e.g., Java). For example, it is pretty clear what < should mean when it is used to compare two strings or two numbers. But what should the value of '4' < 3 be? Rather arbitrarily, the designers of Python decided that it should be False, because all numeric values should be less than all values of type str. The designers of some other languages decided that since such expressions don't have an obvious meaning, they should generate an error message.

Strings are one of several sequence types in Python. They share the following operations with all sequence types.

The **length** of a string can be found using the len function. For example, the value of len('abc') is 3.

Indexing can be used to extract individual characters from a string. In Python, all indexing is zero-based. For example, typing 'abc'[0] into the interpreter will cause it to display the string 'a'. Typing 'abc'[3] will produce the error message IndexError: string index out of range. Since Python uses 0 to indicate the first element of a string, the last element of a string of length 3 is accessed using the index 2. Negative numbers are used to index from the end of a string. For example, the value of 'abc'[-1] is 'c'.

Slicing is used to extract substrings of arbitrary length. If s is a string, the expression s[start:end] denotes the substring of s that starts at index start and ends at index end-1. For example, 'abc'[1:3] = 'bc'. Why does it end at index end-1 rather than end? So that expressions such as 'abc'[0:len('abc')] have the value one might expect. If the value before the colon is omitted, it defaults to 0. If the value after the colon is omitted, it defaults to the length of the string. Consequently, the expression 'abc'[:] is semantically equivalent to the more verbose 'abc'[0:len('abc')].

2.3.1 Input

Python 2.7 has two functions (see Chapter 4 for a discussion of functions in Python) that can be used to get input directly from a user, `input` and `raw_input`.[12] Each takes a string as an argument and displays it as a prompt in the shell. It then waits for the user to type something, followed by hitting the enter key. For `raw_input`, the input line is treated as a string and becomes the value returned by the function; `input` treats the typed line as a Python expression and infers a type. In this book, we use only `raw_input`, which is less likely to lead to programs that behave in unexpected ways.

Consider the code

```
>>> name = raw_input('Enter your name: ')
Enter your name: George Washington
>>> print 'Are you really', name, '?'
Are you really George Washington ?
>>> print 'Are you really ' + name + '?'
Are you really George Washington?
```

Notice that the first `print` statement introduces a blank before the "?" It does this because when `print` is given multiple arguments it places a blank space between the values associated with the arguments. The second `print` statement uses concatenation to produce a string that does not contain the superfluous blank and passes this as the only argument to `print`.

Now consider,

```
>>> n = raw_input('Enter an int: ')
Enter an int: 3
>>> print type(n)
<type 'str'>
```

Notice that the variable n is bound to the `str` '3' not the `int` 3. So, for example, the value of the expression n*4 is '3333' rather than 12. The good news is that whenever a string is a valid literal of some type, a type conversion can be applied to it.

Type conversions (also called **type casts**) are used often in Python code. We use the name of a type to convert values to that type. So, for example, the value of int('3')*4 is 12. When a `float` is converted to an `int`, the number is truncated (not rounded), e.g., the value of int(3.9) is the `int` 3.

2.4   Iteration

A generic **iteration** (also called **looping**) mechanism is depicted in Figure 2.4. Like a conditional statement it begins with a test. If the test evaluates to `True`, the program executes the **loop body** once, and then goes back to reevaluate the test. This process is repeated until the test evaluates to `False`, after which control passes to the code following the iteration statement.

---

[12] Python 3 has only one command, `input`. Somewhat confusingly, Python 3's `input` has the same semantics as `raw_input` in Python 2.7. Go figure.

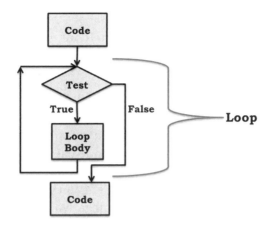

Figure 2.4 Flow chart for iteration

Consider the following example:

```
# Square an integer, the hard way
x = 3
ans = 0
itersLeft = x
while (itersLeft != 0):
    ans = ans + x
    itersLeft = itersLeft - 1
print str(x) + '*' + str(x) + ' = ' + str(ans)
```

The code starts by binding the variable x to the integer 3. It then proceeds to square x by using repetitive addition. The following table shows the value associated with each variable each time the test at the start of the loop is reached. We constructed it by **hand-simulating** the code, i.e., we pretended to be a Python interpreter and executed the program using pencil and paper. Using pencil and paper might seem kind of quaint, but it is an excellent way to understand how a program behaves.[13]

```
test #        x        ans        itersLeft
1             3        0          3
2             3        3          2
3             3        6          1
4             3        9          0
```

The fourth time the test is reached, it evaluates to `False` and flow of control proceeds to the `print` statement following the loop.

For what values of x will this program terminate?

If x `==` 0, the initial value of `itersLeft` will also be 0, and the loop body will never be executed. If x > 0, the initial value of `itersLeft` will be greater than 0, and the loop body will be executed.

---

[13] It is also possible to hand-simulate a program using pen and paper, or even a text editor.

Each time the loop body is executed, the value of itersLeft is decreased by exactly 1. This means that if itersLeft started out greater than 0, after some finite number of iterations of the loop, itersLeft == 0. At this point the loop test evaluates to False, and control proceeds to the code following the while statement.

What if the value of x is -1? Something very bad happens. Control will enter the loop, and each iteration will move itersLeft farther from 0 rather than closer to it. The program will therefore continue executing the loop forever (or until something else bad, e.g., an overflow error, occurs). How might we remove this flaw in the program? Initializing itersLeft to the absolute value of x almost works. The loop terminates, but it prints a negative value. If the assignment statement inside the loop is also changed, to ans = ans+abs(x), the code works properly.

We have now covered pretty much everything about Python that we need to know to start writing interesting programs that deal with numbers and strings. We now take a short break from learning the language. In the next chapter, we use Python to solve some simple problems.

Finger exercise: Write a program that asks the user to input 10 integers, and then prints the largest odd number that was entered. If no odd number was entered, it should print a message to that effect.

3 SOME SIMPLE NUMERICAL PROGRAMS

Now that we have covered some basic Python constructs, it is time to start thinking about how we can combine those constructs to write some simple programs. Along the way, we'll sneak in a few more language constructs and some algorithmic techniques.

3.1 Exhaustive Enumeration

The code in Figure 3.1 prints the integer cube root, if it exists, of an integer. If the input is not a perfect cube, it prints a message to that effect.

```
#Find the cube root of a perfect cube
x = int(raw_input('Enter an integer: '))
ans = 0
while ans**3 < abs(x):
    ans = ans + 1
if ans**3 != abs(x):
    print x, 'is not a perfect cube'
else:
    if x < 0:
        ans = -ans
    print 'Cube root of', x,'is', ans
```

Figure 3.1 Using exhaustive enumeration to find the cube root

For what values of x will this program terminate?

The answer is, "all integers." This can be argued quite simply.

- The value of the expression ans**3 starts at 0, and gets larger each time through the loop.

- When it reaches or exceeds abs(x), the loop terminates.

- Since abs(x) is always positive there are only a finite number of iterations before the loop must terminate.

Whenever you write a loop, you should think about an appropriate **decrementing function**. This is a function that has the following properties:

1. It maps a set of program variables into an integer.

2. When the loop is entered, its value is nonnegative.

3. When its value is <=0, the loop terminates.

4. Its value is decreased every time through the loop.

What is the decrementing function for the loop in Figure 3.1? It is abs(x) - ans**3.

Now, let's insert some errors and see what happens. First, try commenting out the statement ans = 0. The Python interpreter prints the error message, NameError: name 'ans' is not defined, because the interpreter attempts to find the value to which ans is bound before it has been bound to anything. Now, restore the initialization of ans, replace the statement ans = ans + 1 by ans = ans, and try finding the cube root of 8. After you get tired of waiting, enter "control c" (hold down the control key and the c key simultaneously). This will return you to the user prompt in the shell.

Now, add the statement

```
print 'Value of the decrementing function abs(x) - ans**3 is',\
      abs(x) - ans**3
```

at the start of the loop, and try running it again. (The \ at the end of the first line of the print statement is used to indicate that the statement continues on the next line.)

This time it will print

```
Value of the decrementing function abs(x) - ans**3 is 8
```

over and over again.

The program would have run forever because the loop body is no longer reducing the distance between ans**3 and abs(x). When confronted with a program that seems not to be terminating, experienced programmers often insert print statements, such as the one here, to test whether the decrementing function is indeed being decremented.

The algorithmic technique used in this program is a variant of **guess and check** called **exhaustive enumeration**. We enumerate all possibilities until we get to the right answer or exhaust the space of possibilities. At first blush, this may seem like an incredibly stupid way to solve a problem. Surprisingly, however, exhaustive enumeration algorithms are often the most practical way to solve a problem. They are typically easy to implement and easy to understand. And, in many cases, they run fast enough for all practical purposes. Make sure to remove or comment out the print statement that you inserted and reinsert the ans = ans + 1 statement, and then try finding the cube root of 1957816251. The program will seem to finish almost instantaneously. Now, try 7406961012236344616.

As you can see, even if millions of guesses are required, it's not usually a problem. Modern computers are amazingly fast. It takes on the order of one nanosecond—one billionth of a second—to execute an instruction. It's a bit hard to appreciate how fast that is. For perspective, it takes slightly more than a nanosecond for light to travel a single foot (0.3 meters). Another way to think about this is that in the time it takes for the sound of your voice to travel a hundred feet, a modern computer can execute millions of instructions.

Just for fun, try executing the code

```
max = int(raw_input('Enter a postive integer: '))
i = 0
while i < max:
    i = i + 1
print i
```

See how large an integer you need to enter before there is a perceptible pause before the result is printed.

Finger exercise: Write a program that asks the user to enter an integer and prints two integers, root and pwr, such that 0 < pwr < 6 and root**pwr is equal to the integer entered by the user. If no such pair of integers exists, it should print a message to that effect.

3.2 For Loops

The while loops we have used so far are highly stylized. Each iterates over a sequence of integers. Python provides a language mechanism, the **for loop**, that can be used to simplify programs containing this kind of iteration.

The general form of a for statement is (recall that the words in italics are descriptions of what can appear, not actual code):

```
for variable in sequence:
    code block
```

The variable following for is bound to the first value in the sequence, and the code block is executed. The variable is then assigned the second value in the sequence, and the code block is executed again. The process continues until the sequence is exhausted or a **break** statement is executed within the code block.

The sequence of values bound to variable is most commonly generated using the built-in function **range**, which returns a sequence containing an arithmetic progression. The range function takes three integer arguments: start, stop, and step. It produces the progression start, start + step, start + 2*step, etc. If step is positive, the last element is the largest integer start + i*step less than stop. If step is negative, the last element is the smallest integer start + i*step greater than stop. For example, range(5, 40, 10) produces the sequence [5, 15, 25, 35], and range(40, 5, -10) produces the sequence [40, 30, 20, 10]. If the first argument is omitted it defaults to 0, and if the last argument (the step size) is omitted it defaults to 1. For example, range(0, 3) and range(3) both produce the sequence [0, 1, 2].

Less commonly, we specify the sequence to be iterated over in a for loop by using a literal, e.g., [0, 1, 2]. In Python 2.7, range generates the entire sequence when it is invoked. Therefore, for example, the expression range(1000000) uses quite a lot of memory. This can be avoided by using the built-in function `xrange` instead of `range`, since `xrange` generates the values only as they are needed by the `for` loop.[14]

Consider the code

```
x = 4
for i in range(0, x):
    print i
```

It prints

```
0
1
2
3
```

Now, think about the code

```
x = 4
for i in range(0, x):
    print i
    x = 5
```

It raises the question of whether changing the value of x inside the loop affects the number of iterations. It does not. The `range` function in the line with `for` is evaluated just before the first iteration of the loop, and not reevaluated for subsequent iterations. To see how this works, consider

```
x = 4
for j in range(x):
    for i in range(x):
        print i
        x = 2
```

It prints

```
0
1
2
3
0
1
0
1
0
1
```

because the `range` function in the outer loop is evaluated only once, but the range `function` in the inner loop is evaluated each time the inner `for` statement is reached.

The code in Figure 3.2 reimplements the exhaustive enumeration algorithm for finding cube roots. The `break` statement in the `for` loop causes the loop to terminate before it has been run on each element in the sequence over which it is iterating. When executed, a `break` statement exits the innermost loop in which it is enclosed.

---

[14] In Python 3, `range` behaves the way `xrange` behaves in Python 2.

```
#Find the cube root of a perfect cube
x = int(raw_input('Enter an integer: '))
for ans in range(0, abs(x)+1):
    if ans**3 >= abs(x):
        break
if ans**3 != abs(x):
    print x, 'is not a perfect cube'
else:
    if x < 0:
        ans = -ans
    print 'Cube root of', x,'is', ans
```

Figure 3.2 Using for and break statements

The for statement can be used to conveniently iterate over characters of a string. For example,

```
total = 0
for c in '123456789':
    total = total + int(c)
print total
```

sums the digits in the string denoted by the literal '123456789' and prints the total.

Finger exercise: Let s be a string that contains a sequence of decimal numbers separated by commas, e.g., s = '1.23,2.4,3.123'. Write a program that prints the sum of the numbers in s.

3.3 Approximate Solutions and Bisection Search

Imagine that someone asks you to write a program that finds the square root of any nonnegative number. What should you do?

You should probably start by saying that you need a better problem statement. For example, what should the program do if asked to find the square root of 2? The square root of 2 is not a rational number. This means that there is no way to precisely represent its value as a finite string of digits (or as a float), so the problem as initially stated cannot be solved.

The right thing to have asked for is a program that finds an **approximation** to the square root—i.e., an answer that is close enough to the actual square root to be useful. We will return to this issue in considerable detail later in the book. But for now, let's think of "close enough" as an answer that lies within some constant, call it epsilon, of the actual answer.

The code in Figure 3.3 implements an algorithm that finds an approximation to a square root. It uses an operator, +=, that we have not previously used. The code ans += step is semantically equivalent to the more verbose code ans = ans+step. The operators -= and *= work similarly.

```
x = 25
epsilon = 0.01
step = epsilon**2
numGuesses = 0
ans = 0.0
while abs(ans**2 - x) >= epsilon and ans <= x:
    ans += step
    numGuesses += 1
print 'numGuesses =', numGuesses
if abs(ans**2 - x) >= epsilon:
    print 'Failed on square root of', x
else:
    print ans, 'is close to square root of', x
```

Figure 3.3 Approximating the square root using exhaustive enumeration

Once again, we are using exhaustive enumeration. Notice that this method for finding the square root has nothing in common with the way of finding square roots using a pencil that you might have learned in middle school. It is often the case that the best way to solve a problem with a computer is quite different from how one would approach the problem by hand.

When the code is run, it prints

```
numGuesses = 49990
4.999 is close to square root of 25
```

Should we be disappointed that the program didn't figure out that 25 is a perfect square and print 5? No. The program did what it was intended to do. Though it would have been OK to print 5, doing so is no better than printing any value close enough to 5.

What do you think will happen if we set x = 0.25? Will it find a root close to 0.5? Nope. Exhaustive enumeration is a search technique that works only if the set of values being searched includes the answer. In this case, we are enumerating the values between 0 and x. When x is between 0 and 1, the square root of x does not lie in this interval. One way to fix this is to change the first line of the while loop to

```
while abs(ans**2 - x) >= epsilon and ans*ans <= x:
```

Now, let's think about how long the program will take to run. The number of iterations depends upon how close the answer is to zero and on the size of the steps. Roughly speaking, the program will execute the while loop at most x/step times.

Let's try the code on something bigger, e.g., x = 123456. It will run for a bit, and then print

```
numGuesses = 3513631
Failed on square root of 123456
```

What do you think happened? Surely there exists a floating point number that approximates the square root of 123456 to within 0.01. Why didn't our program find it? The problem is that our step size was too large, and the program skipped over all the suitable answers. Try making step equal to epsilon**3 and running the program. It will eventually find a suitable answer, but you might not have the patience to wait for it to do so.

Roughly how many guesses will it have to make? The step size will be 0.000001 and the square root of 123456 is around 351.36. This means that the program will have to make in the neighborhood of 351,000,000 guesses to find a satisfactory answer. We could try to speed it up by starting closer to the answer, but that presumes that we know the answer.

The time has come to look for a different way to attack the problem. We need to choose a better algorithm rather than fine tune the current one. But before doing so, let's look at a problem that, at first blush, appears to be completely different from root finding.

Consider the problem of discovering whether a word starting with a given sequence of letters appears in some hard-copy dictionary of the English language. Exhaustive enumeration would, in principle, work. You could start at the first word and examine each word until either you found a word starting with the sequence of letters or you ran out of words to examine. If the dictionary contained n words, it would, on average, take n/2 probes to find the word. If the word were not in the dictionary, it would take n probes. Of course, those who have had the pleasure of actually looking a word up in a physical (rather than online) dictionary would never proceed in this way.

Fortunately, the folks who publish dictionaries go to the trouble of putting the words in lexicographical order. This allows us to open the book to a page where we think the word might lie (e.g., near the middle for words starting with the letter m). If the sequence of letters lexicographically precedes the first word on the page, we know to go backwards. If the sequence of letters follows the last word on the page, we know to go forwards. Otherwise, we check whether the sequence of letters matches a word on the page.

Now let's take the same idea and apply it the problem of finding the square root of x. Suppose we know that a good approximation to the square root of x lies somewhere between 0 and max. We can exploit the fact that numbers are **totally ordered**. That is to say, for any pair of distinct numbers, n1 and n2, either n1 < n2 or n1 > n2. So, we can think of the square root of x as lying somewhere on the line

0_____max

and start searching that interval. Since we don't necessarily know where to start searching, let's start in the middle.

0_____guess_____max

If that is not the right answer (and it won't be most of the time), ask whether it is too big or too small. If it is too big, we know that the answer must lie to the left. If it is too small, we know that the answer must lie to the right. We then repeat the process on the smaller interval. Figure 3.4 contains an implementation and test of this algorithm.

```
x = 25
epsilon = 0.01
numGuesses = 0
low = 0.0
high = max(1.0, x)
ans = (high + low)/2.0
while abs(ans**2 - x) >= epsilon:
    print 'low =', low, 'high =', high, 'ans =', ans
    numGuesses += 1
    if ans**2 < x:
        low = ans
    else:
        high = ans
    ans = (high + low)/2.0
print 'numGuesses =', numGuesses
print ans, 'is close to square root of', x
```

Figure 3.4 Using bisection search to approximate square root

When run, it prints

```
low = 0.0 high = 25 ans = 12.5
low = 0.0 high = 12.5 ans = 6.25
low = 0.0 high = 6.25 ans = 3.125
low = 3.125 high = 6.25 ans = 4.6875
low = 4.6875 high = 6.25 ans = 5.46875
low = 4.6875 high = 5.46875 ans = 5.078125
low = 4.6875 high = 5.078125 ans = 4.8828125
low = 4.8828125 high = 5.078125 ans = 4.98046875
low = 4.98046875 high = 5.078125 ans = 5.029296875
low = 4.98046875 high = 5.029296875 ans = 5.0048828125
low = 4.98046875 high = 5.0048828125 ans = 4.99267578125
low = 4.99267578125 high = 5.0048828125 ans = 4.99877929688
low = 4.99877929688 high = 5.0048828125 ans = 5.00183105469
numGuesses = 13
5.00030517578 is close to square root of 25
```

Notice that it finds a different answer than our earlier algorithm. That is perfectly fine, since it still meets the problem statement.

More important, notice that at each iteration the size of the space to be searched is cut in half. Because it divides the search space in half at each step, it is called a **bisection search**. Bisection search is a huge improvement over our earlier algorithm, which reduced the search space by only a small amount at each iteration.

Let us try x = 123456 again. This time the program takes only thirty guesses to find an acceptable answer. How about x = 123456789 ? It takes only forty-five guesses.

There is nothing special about the fact that we are using this algorithm to find square roots. For example, by changing a couple of 2's to 3's, we can use it to approximate a cube root of a nonnegative number. In the next chapter we will introduce a language mechanism that allows us to generalize this code to find any root.

Finger exercise: What would the code in Figure 3.4 do if the statement x = 25 were replaced by x = -25?

Finger exercise: What would have to be changed to make the code in Figure 3.4 work for finding an approximation to the cube root of both negative and positive numbers? (Hint: think about changing low to ensure that the answer lies within the region being searched.)

3.4   A Few Words About Using Floats

Most of the time, numbers of type float provide a reasonably good approximation to real numbers. But "most of the time" is not all of the time, and when they don't it can lead to surprising consequences. For example, try running the code

```
x = 0.0
for i in range(10):
    x = x + 0.1
if x == 1.0:
    print x, '= 1.0'
else:
    print x, 'is not 1.0'
```

Perhaps you, like most people, find it doubly surprising that it prints,

```
1.0 is not 1.0
```

Why does it get to the else clause in the first place? And if it somehow does get there, why is it printing such a nonsensical phrase?

To understand why this happens, we need to understand how floating point numbers are represented in the computer during a computation. To understand that, we need to understand binary numbers.

When you first learned about decimal numbers, i.e., numbers base 10, you learned that a decimal number is represented by a sequence of the digits 0123456789. The rightmost digit is the 10^0 place, the next digit towards the left the 10^1 place, etc. For example, the sequence of decimal digits 302 represents $3*100 + 0*10 + 2*1$. How many different numbers can be represented by a sequence of length n? A sequence of length one can represent any one of ten numbers (0 - 9). A sequence of length two can represent one hundred different numbers (0-99). More generally, with a sequence of length n, one can represent 10^n different numbers.

Binary numbers—numbers base 2—work similarly. A binary number is represented by a sequence of digits each of which is either 0 or 1. These digits are often called **bits**. The rightmost digit is the 2^0 place, the next digit towards the left the 2^1 place, etc. For example, the sequence of binary digits 101 represents $1*4 + 0*2 + 1*1 = 5$. How many different numbers can be represented by a sequence of length n? 2^n.

Finger exercise: What is the decimal equivalent of the binary number 10011?

Perhaps because most people have ten fingers, we seem to like to use decimals to represent numbers. On the other hand, all modern computer systems represent numbers in binary. This is not because computers are born with two fingers. It is because it is easy to build hardware switches, i.e., devices that can be in only one of two states, on or off. That the computer uses a binary representation and people a decimal representation can lead to occasional cognitive dissonance.

In almost modern programming languages non-integer numbers are implemented using a representation called **floating point**. For the moment, let's pretend that the internal representation is in decimal. We would represent a number as a pair of integers—the **significant digits** of the number and an **exponent**. For example, the number 1.949 would be represented as the pair (1949, -3), which stands for the product 1949 X 10^{-3}.

The number of significant digits determines the **precision** with which numbers can be represented. If for example, there were only two significant digits, the number 1.949 could not be represented exactly. It would have to be converted to some approximation of 1.949, in this case 1.9. That approximation is called the **rounded value**.

Modern computers use binary, not decimal, representations. We represent the significant digits and exponents in binary rather than decimal and raise 2 rather than 10 to the exponent. For example, the number 0.625 (5/8) would be represented as the pair (101, -11); because 5/8 is 0.101 in binary and -11 is the binary representation of -3, the pair (101, -11) stands for 5 X 2^{-3} = 5/8 = 0.625.

What about the decimal fraction 1/10, which we write in Python as 0.1? The best we can do with four significant binary digits is (0011, -101). This is equivalent to 3/32, i.e., 0.09375. If we had five significant binary digits, we would represent 0.1 as (11001, -1000), which is equivalent to 25/256, i.e., 0.09765625. How many significant digits would we need to get an exact floating point representation of 0.1? An infinite number of digits! There do not exist integers sig and exp such that sig * 2^{-exp} equals 0.1. So no matter how many bits Python (or any other language) chooses to use to represent floating point numbers, it will be able to represent only an approximation to 0.1. In most Python implementations, there are 53 bits of precision available for floating point numbers, so the significant digits stored for the decimal number 0.1 will be

    11001100110011001100110011001100110011001100110011001

This is equivalent to the decimal number

    0.1000000000000000055511151231257827021181583404541015625

Pretty close to 1/10, but not exactly 1/10.

Returning to the original mystery, why does

```
x = 0.0
for i in range(10):
    x = x + 0.1
if x == 1.0:
    print x, '= 1.0'
else:
    print x, 'is not 1.0'
```

print

```
1.0 is not 1.0
```

We now see that the test x == 1.0 produces the result False because the value to which x is bound is not exactly 1.0. What gets printed if we add to the end of the else clause the code print x == 10.0*0.1? It prints False because during at least one iteration of the loop Python ran out of significant digits and did some rounding. It's not what our elementary school teachers taught us, but adding 0.1 ten times does not produce the same value as multiplying 0.1 by 10.

Finally, why does the code

```
print x
```

print 1.0 rather than the actual value of the variable x? Because the designers of Python thought that would be convenient for users if print did some automatic rounding. This is probably an accurate assumption most of the time. However, it is important to keep in mind that what is being displayed does not necessarily exactly match the value stored in the machine.

By the way, if you want to explicitly round a floating point number, use the round function. The expression round(x, numDigits) returns the floating point number equivalent to rounding the value of x to numDigits decimal digits following the decimal point. For example print round(2**0.5, 3) will print 1.414 as an approximation to the square root of 2.

Does the difference between real and floating point numbers really matter? Most of the time, mercifully, it does not. However, one thing that is almost always worth worrying about is tests for equality. As we have seen, using == to compare two floating point values can produce a surprising result. It is almost always more appropriate to ask whether two floating point values are close enough to each other, not whether they are identical. So, for example, it is better to write abs(x-y) < 0.0001 rather than x == y.

Another thing to worry about is the accumulation of rounding errors. Most of the time things work out OK because sometimes the number stored in the computer is a little bigger than intended, and sometimes it is a little smaller than intended. However, in some programs, the errors will all be in the same direction and accumulate over time.

3.5 Newton-Raphson

The most commonly used approximation algorithm is usually attributed to Isaac Newton. It is typically called Newton's method, but is sometimes referred to as the Newton-Raphson method.[15] It can be used to find the real roots of many functions, but we shall look at it only in the context of finding the real roots of a polynomial with one variable. The generalization to polynomials with multiple variables is straightforward both mathematically and algorithmically.

A **polynomial** with one variable (by convention, we will write the variable as x) is either zero or the sum of a finite number of nonzero terms, e.g., $3x^2 + 2x + 3$. Each term, e.g., $3x^2$, consists of a constant (the **coefficient** of the term, 3 in this case) multiplied by the variable (x in this case) raised to a nonnegative integer exponent (2 in this case). The exponent on a variable in a term is called the **degree** of that term. The degree of a polynomial is the largest degree of any single term. Some examples are, 3 (degree 0), 2.5x + 12 (degree 1), and $3x^2$ (degree 2). In contrast, 2/x and $x^{0.5}$ are not polynomials.

If p is a polynomial and r a real number, we will write p(r) to stand for the value of the polynomial when x = r. A **root** of the polynomial p is a solution to the equation p = 0, i.e., an r such that p(r) = 0. So, for example, the problem of finding an approximation to the square root of 24 can be formulated as finding an x such that $x^2 - 24 \approx 0$.

Newton proved a theorem that implies that if a value, call it guess, is an approximation to a root of a polynomial, then guess – p(guess)/p'(guess), where p' is the first derivative of p, is a better approximation.[16]

For any constant k and any coefficient c, the first derivative of $cx^2 + k$ is $2cx$. For example, the first derivative of $x^2 - k$ is 2x. Therefore, we know that we can improve on the current guess, call it y, by choosing as our next guess y - $(y^2 - k)/2y$. This is called **successive approximation**. Figure 3.5 contains code illustrating how to use this idea to quickly find an approximation to the square root.

[15] Joseph Raphson published a similar method about the same time as Newton.

[16] The first derivative of a function f(x) can be thought of as expressing how the value of f(x) changes with respect to changes in x. If you haven't previously encountered derivatives, don't worry. You don't need to understand them, or for that matter polynomials, to understand the implementation of Newton's method.

```
#Newton-Raphson for square root
#Find x such that x**2 - 24 is within epsilon of 0
epsilon = 0.01
k = 24.0
guess = k/2.0
while abs(guess*guess - k) >= epsilon:
    guess = guess - (((guess**2) - k)/(2*guess))
print 'Square root of', k, 'is about', guess
```

Figure 3.5 Newton-Raphson method

Finger exercise: Add some code to the implementation of Newton-Raphson that keeps track of the number of iterations used to find the root. Use that code as part of a program that compares the efficiency of Newton-Raphson and bisection search. (You should discover that Newton-Raphson is more efficient.)

4 FUNCTIONS, SCOPING, AND ABSTRACTION

So far, we have introduced numbers, assignments, input/output, comparisons, and looping constructs. How powerful is this subset of Python? In a theoretical sense, it is as powerful as you will ever need. Such languages are called **Turing complete**. This means that if a problem can be solved via computation, it can be solved using only those statements you have already seen.

Which isn't to say that you should use only these statements. At this point we have covered a lot of language mechanisms, but the code has been a single sequence of instructions, all merged together. For example, in the last chapter we looked at the code in Figure 4.1.

```
x = 25
epsilon = 0.01
numGuesses = 0
low = 0.0
high = max(1.0, x)
ans = (high + low)/2.0
while abs(ans**2 - x) >= epsilon:
    numGuesses += 1
    if ans**2 < x:
        low = ans
    else:
        high = ans
    ans = (high + low)/2.0
print 'numGuesses =', numGuesses
print ans, 'is close to square root of', x
```

Figure 4.1 Using bisection search to approximate square root

This is a reasonable piece of code, but it lacks general utility. It works only for values denoted by the variables x and epsilon. This means that if we want to reuse it, we need to copy the code, possibly edit the variable names, and paste it where we want it. Because of this we cannot easily use this computation inside of some other, more complex, computation.

Furthermore, if we want to compute cube roots rather than square roots, we have to edit the code. If we want a program that computes both square and cube roots (or for that matter square roots in two different places), the program would contain multiple chunks of almost identical code. This is a very bad thing. The more code a program contains, the more chance there is for something to go wrong, and the harder the code is to maintain. Imagine, for example, that there was an error in the initial implementation of square root, and that the error came to light when testing the program. It would be all too easy to fix the implementation of square root in one place and forget that there was similar code elsewhere that was also in need of repair.

Python provides several linguistic features that make it relatively easy to generalize and reuse code. The most important is the function.

4.1 Functions and Scoping

We've already used a number of built-in functions, e.g., max and abs in Figure 4.1. The ability for programmers to define and then use their own functions, as if they were built-in, is a qualitative leap forward in convenience.

4.1.1 Function Definitions

In Python each **function definition** is of the form[17]

```
def name of function (list of formal parameters):
    body of function
```

For example, we could define the function max[18] by the code

```
def max(x, y):
    if x > y:
        return x
    else:
        return y
```

def is a reserved word that tells Python that a function is about to be defined. The function name (max in this example) is simply a name that is used to refer to the function.

The sequence of names (x, y in this example) within the parentheses following the function name are the **formal parameters** of the function. When the function is used, the formal parameters are bound (as in an assignment statement) to the **actual parameters** (often referred to as **arguments**) of the **function invocation** (also referred to as a **function call**). For example, the invocation

```
max(3, 4)
```

binds x to 3 and y to 4.

The function body is any piece of Python code. There is, however, a special statement, **return**, that can be used only within the body of a function.

A function call is an expression, and like all expressions it has a value. That value is the value returned by the invoked function. For example, the value of the expression max(3,4)*max(3,2) is 12, because the first invocation of max returns the int 4 and the second returns the int 3. Note that execution of a return statement terminates that invocation of the function.

To recapitulate, when a function is called

1. The expressions that make up the actual parameters are evaluated, and the formal parameters of the function are bound to the resulting values. For example, the invocation max(3+4, z) will bind the formal parameter x to 7 and the formal parameter y to whatever value the variable z has when the invocation is evaluated.

---

[17] Recall that italics is used to describe Python code.

[18] In practice, you would probably use the built-in function max, rather than define your own.

2. The **point of execution** (the next instruction to be executed) moves from the point of invocation to the first statement in the body of the function.

3. The code in the body of the function is executed until either a `return` statement is encountered, in which case the value of the expression following the `return` becomes the value of the function invocation, or there are no more statements to execute, in which case the function returns the value None. (If no expression follows the `return`, the value of the invocation is None.)

4. The value of the invocation is the returned value.

5. The point of execution is transferred back to the code immediately following the invocation.

Parameters provide something called **lambda abstraction**,[19] allowing programmers to write code that manipulates not specific objects, but instead whatever objects the caller of the function chooses to use as actual parameters.

Finger exercise: Write a function `isIn` that accepts two strings as arguments and returns True if either string occurs anywhere in the other, and False otherwise. Hint: you might want to use the built-in `str` operation `in`.

4.1.2 Keyword Arguments and Default Values

In Python, there are two ways that formal parameters get bound to actual parameters. The most common method, which is the only one we have used thus far, is called **positional**—the first formal parameter is bound to the first actual parameter, the second formal to the second actual, etc. Python also supports what it calls **keyword arguments**, in which formals are bound to actuals using the name of the formal parameter. Consider the function definition in Figure 4.2. The function `printName` assumes that `firstName` and `lastName` are strings and that `reverse` is a Boolean. If `reverse == True`, it prints `lastName, firstName`, otherwise it prints `firstName lastName`.

```
def printName(firstName, lastName, reverse):
    if reverse:
        print lastName + ', ' + firstName
    else:
        print firstName, lastName
```

Figure 4.2 Function that prints a name

Each of the following is an equivalent invocation of `printName`:

```
printName('Olga', 'Puchmajerova', False)
printName('Olga', 'Puchmajerova', False)
printName('Olga', 'Puchmajerova', reverse = False)
printName('Olga', lastName = 'Puchmajerova', reverse = False)
printName(lastName='Puchmajerova', firstName='Olga', reverse=False)
```

---

[19] The name "lambda abstraction" is derived from some mathematics developed by Alonzo Church in the 1930s and 1940s.

Though the keyword arguments can appear in any order in the list of actual parameters, it is not legal to follow a keyword argument with a non-keyword argument. Therefore, an error message would be produced by

```
printName('Olga', lastName = 'Puchmajerova', False)
```

Keyword arguments are commonly used in conjunction with **default parameter values**. We can, for example, write

```
def printName(firstName, lastName, reverse = False):
    if reverse:
        print lastName + ', ' + firstName
    else:
        print firstName, lastName
```

Default values allow programmers to call a function with fewer than the specified number of arguments. For example,

```
printName('Olga', 'Puchmajerova')
printName('Olga', 'Puchmajerova', True)
printName('Olga', 'Puchmajerova', reverse = True)
```

will print

```
Olga Puchmajerova
Puchmajerova, Olga
Puchmajerova, Olga
```

The last two invocations of `printName` are semantically equivalent. The last one has the advantage of providing some documentation for the perhaps mysterious parameter `True`.

4.1.3 Scoping

Let's look at another small example,

```
def f(x): #name x used as formal parameter
    y = 1
    x = x + y
    print 'x =', x
    return x

x = 3
y = 2
z = f(x) #value of x used as actual parameter
print 'z =', z
print 'x =', x
print 'y =', y
```

When run, this code prints,

```
x = 4
z = 4
x = 3
y = 2
```

What is going on here? At the call of f, the formal parameter x is locally bound to the value of the actual parameter x. It is important to note that though the actual and formal parameters have the same name, they are not the same variable. Each function defines a new **name space**, also called a **scope**. The

formal parameter x and the **local variable** y that are used in f exist only within
the scope of the definition of f. The assignment statement x = x + y within the
function body binds the local name x to the object 4. The assignments in f have
no effect at all on the bindings of the names x and y that exist outside the scope
of f.

Here's one way to think about this:

- At top level, i.e., the level of the shell, a **symbol table** keeps track of all
  names defined at that level and their current bindings.

- When a function is called, a new symbol table (sometimes called a **stack
  frame**) is created. This table keeps track of all names defined within the
  function (including the formal parameters) and their current bindings. If
  a function is called from within the function body, yet another stack
  frame is created.

- When the function completes, its stack frame goes away.

In Python, one can always determine the scope of a name by looking at the
program text. This is called **static** or **lexical scoping**. Figure 4.3 contains a
slightly more elaborate example.

```
def f(x):
    def g():
        x = 'abc'
        print 'x =', x
    def h():
        z = x
        print 'z =', z
    x = x + 1
    print 'x =', x
    h()
    g()
    print 'x =', x
    return g

x = 3
z = f(x)
print 'x =', x
print 'z =', z
z()
```

Figure 4.3 Nested scopes

The history of the stack frames associated with the code in Figure 4.3 is
depicted in Figure 4.4.

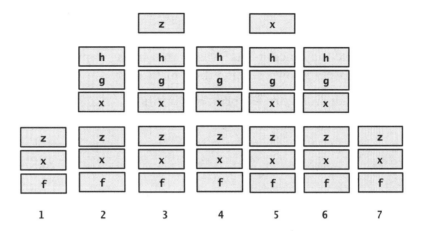

Figure 4.4 Stack frames

The first column contains the set of names known outside the body of the function f, i.e., the variables x and z, and the function name f. The first assignment statement binds x to 3.

The assignment statement z = f(x) first evaluates the expression f(x) by invoking the function f with the value to which x is bound. When f is entered, a stack frame is created, as shown in column 2. The names in the stack frame are x (the formal parameter, not the x in the calling context), g and h. The variables g and h are bound to objects of type function. The properties of each of these functions are given by the function definitions within f.

When h is invoked from within f, yet another stack frame is created, as shown in column 3. This frame contains only the local variable z. Why does it not also contain x? A name is added to the scope associated with a function only if that name is either a formal parameter of the function or a variable that is bound to an object within the body of the function. In the body of h, x occurs only on the right-hand side of an assignment statement. The appearance of a name (x in this case) that is not bound anywhere in the function body (the body of h) causes the interpreter to search the previous stack frame associated with the scope within which the function is defined (the stack frame associated with f). If the name is found (which it is in this case) the value to which it is bound (4) is used. If it is not found there, an error message is produced.

When h returns, the stack frame associated with the invocation of h goes away (i.e., it is **popped** off the top of the stack), as depicted in column 4. Note that we never remove frames from the middle of the stack, but only the most recently added frame. It is because it has this "last in first out" behavior that we refer to it as a **stack** (think of a stack of trays waiting to be taken in a cafeteria).

Next g is invoked, and a stack frame containing g's local variable x is added (column 5). When g returns, that frame is popped (column 6). When f returns, the stack frame containing the names associated with f is popped, getting us back to the original stack frame (column 7).

Notice that when f returns, even though the variable g no longer exists, the object of type function to which that name was once bound still exists. This is because functions are objects, and can be returned just like any other kind of object. So, z can be bound to the value returned by f, and the function call z() can be used to invoke the function that was bound to the name g within f—even though the name g is not known outside the context of f.

So, what does the code in Figure 4.3 print? It prints

```
x = 4
z = 4
x = abc
x = 4
x = 3
z = <function g at 0x15b43b0>
x = abc
```

The order in which references to a name occur is not germane. If an object is bound to a name anywhere in the function body (even if it occurs in an expression before it appears as the left-hand-side of an assignment), it is treated as local to that function.[20]

Consider, for example, the code

```
def f():
    print x

def g():
    print x
    x = 1

x = 3
f()
x = 3
g()
```

It prints 3 when f is invoked, but an error message is printed when it encounters the print statement in g because the assignment statement following the print statement causes x to be local to g. And because x is local to g, it has no value when the print statement is executed.

Confused yet? It takes most people a bit of time to get their head around scope rules. Don't let this bother you. For now, charge ahead and start using functions. Most of the time you will find that you only want to use variables that are local to a function, and the subtleties of scoping will be irrelevant.

---

[20] The wisdom of this language design decision is debatable.

4.2 Specifications

Figure 4.5 defines a function, `findRoot`, that generalizes the bisection search we used to find square roots in Figure 4.1. It also contains a function, `testFindRoot`, that can be used to test whether or not `findRoot` works as intended.

The function `testFindRoot` is almost as long as `findRoot` itself. To inexperienced programmers, writing **test functions** such as this often seems to be a waste of effort. Experienced programmers know, however, that an investment in writing testing code often pays big dividends. It certainly beats typing test cases into the shell over and over again during **debugging** (the process of finding out why a program does not work, and then fixing it). It also forces us to think about which tests are likely to be most illuminating.

The text between the triple quotation marks is called a **docstring** in Python. By convention, Python programmers use docstrings to provide specifications of functions. These docstrings can be accessed using the built-in function **help**.

If we enter the shell and type `help(abs)`, the system will display

```
Help on built-in function abs in module __builtin__:
abs(...)
    abs(number) -> number
        Return the absolute value of the argument.
```

If the code in Figure 4.5 (below) has been loaded into IDLE, typing `help(findRoot)` in the shell will display

```
Help on function findRoot in module __main__:

findRoot(x, power, epsilon)
    Assumes x and epsilon int or float, power an int,
        epsilon > 0 & power >= 1
    Returns float y such that y**power is within epsilon of x.
        If such a float does not exist, it returns None
```

If we type

```
findRoot(
```

in either the shell or the editor, the list of formal parameters and the first line of the docstring will be displayed.

```
def findRoot(x, power, epsilon):
    """Assumes x and epsilon int or float, power an int,
          epsilon > 0 & power >= 1
       Returns float y such that y**power is within epsilon of x.
          If such a float does not exist, it returns None"""
    if x < 0 and power%2 == 0:
        return None
    low = min(-1.0, x)
    high = max(1.0, x)
    ans = (high + low)/2.0
    while abs(ans**power - x) >= epsilon:
        if ans**power < x:
            low = ans
        else:
            high = ans
        ans = (high + low)/2.0
    return ans

def testFindRoot():
    epsilon = 0.0001
    for x in (0.25, -0.25, 2, -2, 8, -8):
        for power in range(1, 4):
            print 'Testing x = ' + str(x) +\
                  ' and power = ' + str(power)
            result = findRoot(x, power, epsilon)
            if result == None:
                print '   No root'
            else:
                print '   ', result**power, '~=', x
```

Figure 4.5 Finding an approximation to a root

A **specification** of a function defines a contract between the implementer of a function and those who will be writing programs that use the function. We will refer to the users of a function as its **clients**. This contract can be thought of as containing two parts:

1. **Assumptions**: These describe conditions that must be met by clients of the function. Typically, they describe constraints on the actual parameters. Almost always, they specify the acceptable set of types for each parameter, and not infrequently some constraints on the value of one or more of the parameters. For example, the first two lines of the docstring of findRoot describe the assumptions that must be satisfied by clients of findRoot.

2. **Guarantees**: These describe conditions that must be met by the function, provided that it has been called in a way that satisfies the assumptions. The last two lines of the docstring of findRoot describe the guarantees that the implementation of the function must meet.

Functions are a way of creating computational elements that we can think of as primitives. Just as we have the built-in functions max and abs, we would like to have the equivalent of a built-in function for finding roots and for many other complex operations. Functions facilitate this by providing decomposition and abstraction.

Decomposition creates structure. It allows us to break a problem into modules that are reasonably self-contained, and that may be reused in different settings.

Abstraction hides detail. It allows us to use a piece of code as if it were a black box—that is, something whose interior details we cannot see, don't need to see, and shouldn't even want to see.[21] The essence of abstraction is preserving information that is relevant in a given context, and forgetting information that is irrelevant in that context. The key to using abstraction effectively in programming is finding a notion of relevance that is appropriate for both the builder of an abstraction and the potential clients of the abstraction. That is the true art of programming.

Abstraction is all about forgetting. There are lots of ways to model this, for example, the auditory apparatus of most teenagers.

Teenager says: *May I borrow the car tonight?*

Parent says: *Yes, but be back before midnight, and make sure that the gas tank is full.*

Teenager hears: *Yes.*

The teenager has ignored all of those pesky details that he or she considers irrelevant. Abstraction is a many-to-one process. Had the parent said *Yes, but be back before 2:00 a.m., and make sure that the car is clean*, it would also have been abstracted to *Yes*.

By way of analogy, imagine that you were asked to produce an introductory computer science course containing twenty-five lectures. One way to do this would be to recruit twenty-five professors, and ask each of them to prepare a fifty-minute lecture on their favorite topic. Though you might get twenty-five wonderful hours, the whole thing is likely to feel like a dramatization of Pirandello's "Six Characters in Search of an Author" (or that political science course you took with fifteen guest lecturers). If each professor worked in isolation, they would have no idea how to relate the material in their lecture to the material covered in other lectures.

Somehow, one needs to let everyone know what everyone else is doing, without generating so much work that nobody is willing to participate. This is where abstraction comes in. You could write twenty-five specifications, each saying what material the students should learn in each lecture, but not giving any detail about how that material should be taught. What you got might not be pedagogically wonderful, but at least it might make sense.

This is the way organizations go about using teams of programmers to get things done. Given a specification of a module, a programmer can work on implementing that module without worrying unduly about what the other programmers on the team are doing. Moreover, the other programmers can use the specification to start writing code that uses that module without worrying unduly about how that module is to be implemented.

---

[21] "Where ignorance is bliss, 'tis folly to be wise."—Thomas Gray

The specification of findRoot is an abstraction of all the possible implementations that meet the specification. Clients of findRoot can assume that the implementation meets the specification, but they should assume nothing more. For example, clients can assume that the call findRoot(4.0, 2, 0.01) returns some value whose square is between 3.99 and 4.01. The value returned could be positive or negative, and even though 4.0, is a perfect square the value returned might not be 2.0 or -2.0.

4.3 Recursion

You may have heard of **recursion**, and in all likelihood think of it as a rather subtle programming technique. That's an urban legend spread by computer scientists to make people think that we are smarter than we really are. Recursion is a very important idea, but it's not so subtle, and it is more than a programming technique.

As a descriptive method recursion is widely used, even by people who would never dream of writing a program.

Consider part of the legal code of the United States defining the notion of a "natural-born" citizen. Roughly speaking, the definition is as follows

1. Any child born inside the United States,

2. Any child born in wedlock outside the United States both of whose parents are citizens of the U.S., as long as one parent has lived in the U.S. prior to the birth of the child, and

3. Any child born in wedlock outside the United States one of whose parents is a U.S. citizen who has lived at least five years in the U.S. prior to the birth of the child, provided that at least two of those years were after the citizen's fourteenth birthday.

The first part is simple; if you are born in the United States, you are a natural-born citizen (such as Barack Obama). If you are not born in the U.S., then one has to decide if your parents are U.S. citizens (either natural born or naturalized). To determine if your parents are U.S. citizens, you might have to look at your grandparents, and so on.

In general, a recursive definition is made up of two parts. There is at least one **base case** that directly specifies the result for a special case (case 1 in the example above), and there is at least one **recursive (inductive) case** (cases 2 and 3 in the example above) that defines the answer in terms of the answer to the question on some other input, typically a simpler version of the same problem.

The world's simplest recursive definition is probably the factorial function (typically written in mathematics using !) on natural numbers.[22] The classic **inductive definition** is,

1! = 1

(n + 1)! = (n + 1) * n!

The first equation defines the base case. The second equation defines factorial for all natural numbers, except the base case, in terms of the factorial of the previous number.

Figure 4.6 contains both an iterative (factI) and a recursive (factR) implementation of factorial.

```python
def factI(n):
    """Assumes that n is an int > 0
        Returns n!"""
    result = 1
    while n > 1:
        result = result * n
        n -= 1
    return result

def factR(n):
    """Assumes that n is an int > 0
        Returns n!"""
    if n == 1:
        return n
    else:
        return n*factR(n - 1)
```

Figure 4.6 Iterative and recursive implementations of factorial

This function is sufficiently simple that neither implementation is hard to follow. Still, the second is a more obvious translation of the original recursive definition.

It almost seems like cheating to implement factR by calling factR from within the body of factR. It works for the same reason that the iterative implementation works. We know that the iteration in factI will terminate because n starts out positive and each time around the loop it is reduced by 1. This means that it cannot be greater than 1 forever. Similarly, if factR is called with 1, it returns a value without making a recursive call. When it does make a recursive call, it always does so with a value one less than the value with which it was called. Eventually, the recursion terminates with the call factR(1).

4.3.1 Fibonacci Numbers

The Fibonacci sequence is another common mathematical function that is usually defined recursively. "They breed like rabbits," is often used to describe a population that the speaker thinks is growing too quickly. In the year 1202, the

---

[22] The exact definition of "natural number" is subject to debate. Some define it as the positive integers and others as the nonnegative integers. That's why we were explicit about the possible values of n in the docstring in Figure 4.6.

Italian mathematician Leonardo of Pisa, also known as Fibonacci, developed a formula designed to quantify this notion, albeit with some not terribly realistic assumptions.

Suppose a newly born pair of rabbits, one male and one female, are put in a pen (or worse, released in the wild). Suppose further that the rabbits are able to mate at the age of one month (which, astonishingly, some breeds can) and have a one-month gestation period (which, astonishingly, some breeds do). Finally, suppose that these mythical rabbits never die, and that the female always produces one new pair (one male, one female) every month from its second month on. How many pregnant rabbits will there be at the end of six months?

On the last day of the first month (call it month 0), there will be one female (ready to conceive on the first day of the next month). On the last day of the second month, there will still be only one female (since she will not give birth until the first day of the next month). On the last day of the next month, there will be two females (one pregnant and one not). On the last day of the next month, there will be three females (two pregnant and one not). And so on. Let's look at this progression in tabular form.

Notice that in this table, for month n > 1, females(n) = females(n-1) + females(n-2). This is not an accident. Each female that was alive in month n-1 will still be alive in month n. In addition, each female that was alive in month n-2 will produce one new female in month n. The new females can be added to the females alive in month n-1 to get the number of females in month n.

Month	Females
0	1
1	1
2	2
3	3
4	5
5	8
6	13

The growth in population is described naturally by the **recurrence**:

```
females(0) = 1
females(1) = 1
females(n + 2) = females(n+1) + females(n)
```

This definition is a little different from the recursive definition of factorial:

• It has two base cases, not just one. In general, you can have as many base cases as you need.

• In the recursive case, there are two recursive calls, not just one. Again, there can be as many as you need.

Figure 4.7 contains a straightforward implementation of the Fibonacci recurrence,[23] along with a function that can be used to test it.

---

[23] While obviously correct, this is a terribly inefficient implementation of the Fibonacci function. There is a simple iterative implemenenation that is much better.

```
def fib(n):
    """Assumes n an int >= 0
        Returns Fibonacci of n"""
    if n == 0 or n == 1:
        return 1
    else:
        return fib(n-1) + fib(n-2)

def testFib(n):
    for i in range(n+1):
        print 'fib of', i, '=', fib(i)
```

Figure 4.7 Recursive implementation of Fibonacci sequence

Writing the code is the easy part of solving this problem. Once we went from the vague statement of a problem about bunnies to a set of recursive equations, the code almost wrote itself. Finding some kind of abstract way to express a solution to the problem at hand is very often the hardest step in building a useful program. We will talk much more about this later in the book.

As you might guess, this is not a perfect model for the growth of rabbit populations in the wild. In 1859, Thomas Austin, an Australian farmer, imported twenty-four rabbits from England, to be used as targets in hunts. Ten years later, approximately two million rabbits were shot or trapped each year in Australia, with no noticeable impact on the population. That's a lot of rabbits, but not anywhere close to the 120th Fibonacci number.[24]

Though the Fibonacci sequence[25] does not actually provide a perfect model of the growth of rabbit populations, it does have many interesting mathematical properties. Fibonacci numbers are also quite common in nature.[26]

Finger exercise: When the implementation of fib in Figure 4.7 is used to compute fib(5), how many times does it compute the value fib(2)?

---

[24] The damage done by the descendants of those twenty-four cute bunnies has been estimated to be $600 million per year, and they are in the process of eating many native plants into extinction.

[25] That we call this a Fibonacci sequence is an example of a Eurocentric interpretation of history. Fibonacci's great contribution to European mathematics was his book *Liber Abaci*, which introduced to European mathematicians many concepts already well known to Indian and Arabic scholars. These concepts included Hindu-Arabic numerals and the decimal system. What we today call the Fibonacci sequence was taken from the work of the Sanskrit mathematician Pingala.

[26] If you are feeling especially geeky, try writing a Fibonacci poem. This is a form of poetry in which the number of syllables in each line is equal to the total number of syllables in the previous two lines. Think of the first line (which has zero syllables) as a place to take a deep breath before starting to read your poem.

4.3.2 Palindromes

Recursion is also useful for many problems that do not involve numbers. Figure 4.8 contains a function, isPalindrome, that checks whether a string reads the same way backwards and forwards.

```
def isPalindrome(s):
    """Assumes s is a str
        Returns True if the letters in s form a palindrome;
            False otherwise. Non-letters and capitalization are ignored."""

    def toChars(s):
        s = s.lower()
        letters = ''
        for c in s:
            if c in 'abcdefghijklmnopqrstuvwxyz':
                letters = letters + c
        return letters

    def isPal(s):
        if len(s) <= 1:
            return True
        else:
            return s[0] == s[-1] and isPal(s[1:-1])

    return isPal(toChars(s))
```

Figure 4.8 Palindrome testing

The function isPalindrome contains two internal **helper functions**. This should be of no interest to clients of the function, who should care only that isPalindrome meets its specification. But you should care, because there are things to learn by examining the implementation.

The helper function toChars converts all letters to lowercase and removes all non-letters. It starts by using a built-in method on strings to generate a string that is identical to s, except that all uppercase letters have been converted to lowercase. We will talk a lot more about **method invocation** when we get to classes. For now, think of it as a peculiar syntax for a function call. Instead of putting the first (and in this case only) argument inside parentheses following the function name, we use **dot notation** to place that argument before the function name.

The helper function isPal uses recursion to do the real work. The two base cases are strings of length zero or one. This means that the recursive part of the implementation is reached only on strings of length two or more. The conjunction[27] in the else clause is evaluated from left to right. The code first checks whether the first and last characters are the same, and if they are goes on to check whether the string minus those two characters is a palindrome. That the second conjunct is not evaluated unless the first conjunct evaluates to

---

[27] When two Boolean-valued expressions are connected by "and," each expression is called a **conjunct**. If they are connected by "or," they are called **disjuncts**.

True is semantically irrelevant in this example. However, later in the book we will see examples where this kind of **short-circuit evaluation** of Boolean expressions is semantically relevant.

This implementation of isPalindrome is an example of a problem-solving principle known as **divide-and-conquer**. (This principle is related to but different from divide-and-conquer algorithms, which are discussed in Chapter 10.) The problem-solving principle is to conquer a hard problem by breaking it into a set of subproblems with the properties that

- the subproblems are easier to solve than the original problem, and

- solutions of the subproblems can be combined to solve the original problem.

In this case, we solve the problem by breaking the original problem into a simpler version of the same problem (checking whether a shorter string is a palindrome), plus some simple things we know how to do (comparing single characters). Figure 4.9 contains some code that can be used to visualize how this works.

```
def isPalindrome(s):
    """Assumes s is a str
        Returns True if s is a palindrome; False otherwise.
        Punctuation marks, blanks, and capitalization are
        ignored."""

    def toChars(s):
        s = s.lower()
        letters = ''
        for c in s:
          if c in 'abcdefghijklmnopqrstuvwxyz':
              letters = letters + c
        return letters

    def isPal(s):
        print '  isPal called with', s
        if len(s) <= 1:
            print '  About to return True from base case'
            return True
        else:
            answer = s[0] == s[-1] and isPal(s[1:-1])
            print '  About to return', answer, 'for', s
            return answer

    return isPal(toChars(s))

def testIsPalindrome():
    print 'Try dogGod'
    print isPalindrome('dogGod')
    print 'Try doGood'
    print isPalindrome('doGood')
```

Figure 4.9 Code to visualize palindrome testing

When the code in Figure 4.9 is run, it will print

```
Try dogGod
  isPal called with doggod
  isPal called with oggo
  isPal called with gg
  isPal called with
  About to return True from base case
  About to return True for gg
  About to return True for oggo
  About to return True for doggod
True
Try doGood
  isPal called with dogood
  isPal called with ogoo
  isPal called with go
  About to return False for go
  About to return False for ogoo
  About to return False for dogood
False
```

Divide-and-conquer is a very old idea. Julius Caesar practiced what the Romans referred to as *divide et impera* (divide and rule). The British practiced it brilliantly to control the Indian subcontinent. Benjamin Franklin was well aware of the British expertise in using this technique, prompting him to say at the signing of the U.S. Declaration of Independence, "We must all hang together, or assuredly we shall all hang separately."

4.4 Global Variables

If you tried calling fib with a large number, you probably noticed that it took a very long time to run. Suppose we want to know how many recursive calls are made? We could do a careful analysis of the code and figure it out, and in Chapter 9 we will talk about how to do that. Another approach is to add some code that counts the number of calls. One way to do that uses **global variables**.

Until now, all of the functions we have written communicate with their environment solely through their parameters and return values. For the most part, this is exactly as it should be. It typically leads to programs that are relatively easy to read, test, and debug. Every once in a while, however, global variables come in handy. Consider the code in Figure 4.10.

```
def fib(x):
    """Assumes x an int >= 0
       Returns Fibonacci of x"""
    global numFibCalls
    numFibCalls += 1
    if x == 0 or x == 1:
        return 1
    else:
        return fib(x-1) + fib(x-2)

def testFib(n):
    for i in range(n+1):
        global numFibCalls
        numFibCalls = 0
        print 'fib of', i, '=', fib(i)
        print 'fib called', numFibCalls, 'times.'
```

Figure 4.10 Using a global variable

In each function, the line of code global numFibCalls tells Python that the name numCalls should be defined at the outermost scope of the module (see Section 4.5) in which the line of code appears rather than within the scope of the function in which the line of code appears—despite the fact that numFibCalls occurs on the left-hand side of an assignment statement in both fib and testFib. (Had we not included the code global numFibCalls, the name numFibCalls would have been local to each of fib and testFib.) The functions fib and testFib both have unfettered access to the object referenced by the variable numFibCalls. The function testFib binds numFibCalls to 0 each time it calls fib, and fib increments the value of numFibCalls each time fib is entered.

It is with some trepidation that we introduce the topic of global variables. Since the 1970s card-carrying computer scientists have inveighed against them. The indiscriminate use of global variables can lead to lots of problems. The key to making programs readable is locality. One reads a program a piece at a time, and the less context needed to understand each piece, the better. Since global variables can be modified or read in a wide variety of places, the sloppy use of them can destroy locality. Nevertheless, there are times when they are just what is needed.

4.5 Modules

So far, we have operated under the assumption that our entire program is stored in one file. This is perfectly reasonable as long as programs are small. As programs get larger, however, it is typically more convenient to store different parts of them in different files. Imagine, for example, that multiple people are working on the same program. It would be a nightmare if they were all trying to update the same file. Python modules allow us to easily construct a program from code in multiple files.

A **module** is a .py file containing Python definitions and statements. We could create, for example, a file circle.py containing

```
pi = 3.14159

def area(radius):
    return pi*(radius**2)

def circumference(radius):
    return 2*pi*radius

def sphereSurface(radius):
    return 4.0*area(radius)

def sphereVolume(radius):
    return (4.0/3.0)*pi*(radius**3)
```

A program gets access to a module through an `import` statement. So, for example, the code

```
import circle
print circle.pi
print circle.area(3)
print circle.circumference(3)
print circle.sphereSurface(3)
```

will print

```
3.14159
28.27431
18.84954
113.09724
```

Modules are typically stored in individual files. Each module has its own private symbol table. Consequently, within `circle.py` we access objects (e.g., `pi` and `area`) in the usual way. Executing `import M` creates a binding for module `M` in the scope in which the importation occurs. Therefore, in the importing context we use dot notation to indicate that we are referring to a name defined in the imported module.[28] For example, outside of `circle.py`, the references `pi` and `circle.pi` can (and in this case do) refer to different objects.

At first glance, the use of dot notation may seem cumbersome. On the other hand, when one imports a module one often has no idea what local names might have been used in the implementation of that module. The use of dot notation to fully qualify names avoids the possibility of getting burned by an accidental name clash. For example, the assignment statement `pi = 3.0` does not change the value of `pi` used within the `circle` module.

There is a variant of the `import` statement that allows the importing program to omit the module name when accessing names defined inside the imported module. Executing the statement `from M import *` creates bindings in the current scope to all objects defined within M, but not to M itself. For example, the code

```
from circle import *
print pi
print circle.pi
```

---

[28] Superficially, this may seem unrelated to the use of dot notation in method invocation. However, as we will see in Chapter 8, there is a deep connection.

will first print 3.14159, and then produce the error message

```
NameError: name 'circle' is not defined
```

Some Python programmers frown upon using this form of import because they believe that it makes code more difficult to read.

As we have seen, a module can contain executable statements as well as function definitions. Typically, these statements are used to initialize the module. For this reason, the statements in a module are executed only the first time a module is imported into a program. On a related note, a module is imported only once per interpreter session. If you start up IDLE, import a module, and then change the contents of that module, the interpreter will still be using the original version of the module. This can lead to puzzling behavior when debugging. You can force the interpreter to reload all imported modules by executing reload().

There are lots of useful modules that come as part of the standard Python library. For example, it is rarely necessary to write your own implementations of common mathematical or string functions. A description of this library can be found at http://docs.python.org/2/library/.

4.6 Files

Every computer system uses **files** to save things from one computation to the next. Python provides many facilities for creating and accessing files. Here we illustrate some of the basic ones.

Each operating system (e.g., Windows and MAC OS) comes with its own file system for creating and accessing files. Python achieves operating-system independence by accessing files through something called a **file handle**. The code

```
nameHandle = open('kids', 'w')
```

instructs the operating system to create a file with the name kids, and return a file handle for that file. The argument 'w' to open indicates that the file is to be opened for writing. The following code opens a file, uses the **write** method to write two lines, and then closes the file. It is important to remember to close the file when the program is finished using it. Otherwise there is a risk that some or all of the writes may not be saved.

```
nameHandle = open('kids', 'w')
for i in range(2):
    name = raw_input('Enter name: ')
    nameHandle.write(name + '\n')
nameHandle.close()
```

In a string, the character "\" is an escape character used to indicate that the next character should be treated in a special way. In this example, the string '\n' indicates a new line character.

We can now open the file for **reading** (using the argument `'r'`), and print its contents. Since Python treats a file as a sequence of lines, we can use a `for` statement to iterate over the file's contents.

```
nameHandle = open('kids', 'r')
for line in nameHandle:
    print line
nameHandle.close()
```

If we had typed in the names David and Andrea, this will print

```
David

Andrea
```

The extra line between David and Andrea is there because print starts a new line each time it encounters the `'\n'` at the end of each line in the file. We could have avoided printing that by writing `print line[:-1]`. Now consider

```
nameHandle = open('kids', 'w')
nameHandle.write('Michael\n')
nameHandle.write('Mark\n')
nameHandle.close()
nameHandle = open('kids', 'r')
for line in nameHandle:
    print line[:-1]
nameHandle.close()
```

It will print

```
Michael
Mark
```

Notice that we have overwritten the previous contents of the file `kids`. If we don't want to do that we can open the file for **appending** (instead of writing) by using the argument `'a'`.

For example, if we now run the code

```
nameHandle = open('kids', 'a')
nameHandle.write('David\n')
nameHandle.write('Andrea\n')
nameHandle.close()
nameHandle = open('kids', 'r')
for line in nameHandle:
    print line[:-1]
nameHandle.close()
```

it will print

```
Michael
Mark
David
Andrea
```

Some of the common operations on files are summarized in Figure 4.11.

---

open(fn, 'w') fn is a string representing a file name. Creates a file for writing and returns a file handle.

open(fn, 'r') fn is a string representing a file name. Opens an existing file for reading and returns a file handle.

open(fn, 'a') fn is a string representing a file name. Opens an existing file for appending and returns a file handle.

fh.read() returns a string containing the contents of the file associated with the file handle fh.

fh.readline() returns the next line in the file associated with the file handle fh.

fh.readlines() returns a list each element of which is one line of the file associated with the file handle fh.

fh.write(s) write the string s to the end of the file associated with the file handle fh.

fh.writeLines(S) S is a sequence of strings. Writes each element of S to the file associated with the file handle fh.

fh.close() closes the file associated with the file handle fh.

Figure 4.11 Common functions for accessing files

5 STRUCTURED TYPES, MUTABILITY, AND HIGHER-ORDER FUNCTIONS

The programs we have looked at thus far have dealt with three types of objects: `int`, `float`, and `str`. The numeric types `int` and `float` are scalar types. That is to say, objects without accessible internal structure. In contrast, `str` can be thought of as a structured, or non-scalar, type. One can use indexing to extract individual characters from a string and slicing to extract substrings.

In this chapter, we introduce three structured types. One, `tuple`, is a rather simple generalization of `str`. The other two, `list` and `dict`, are more interesting—in part because they are mutable. We also return to the topic of functions with some examples that illustrate the utility of being able to treat functions in the same way as other types of objects.

5.1 Tuples

Like strings, **tuples** are ordered sequences of elements. The difference is that the elements of a tuple need not be characters. The individual elements can be of any type, and need not be of the same type as each other.

Literals of type `tuple` are written by enclosing a comma-separated list of elements within parentheses. For example, we can write

```
t1 = ()
t2 = (1, 'two', 3)
print t1
print t2
```

Unsurprisingly, the `print` statements produce the output

```
()
(1, 'two', 3)
```

Looking at this example, you might naturally be led to believe that the tuple containing the single value 1 would be written (1). But, to quote Richard Nixon, "that would be wrong." Since parentheses are used to group expressions, (1) is merely a verbose way to write the integer 1. To denote the singleton tuple containing this value, we write (1,). Almost everybody who uses Python has at one time or another accidentally omitted that annoying comma.

Like strings, tuples can be concatenated, indexed, and sliced. Consider

```
t1 = (1, 'two', 3)
t2 = (t1, 3.25)
print t2
print (t1 + t2)
print (t1 + t2)[3]
print (t1 + t2)[2:5]
```

The second assignment statement binds the name t2 to a tuple that contains the tuple to which t1 is bound and the floating point number 3.25. This is possible because a tuple, like everything else in Python, is an object, so tuples can contain tuples. Therefore, the first `print` statement produces the output,

```
((1, 'two', 3), 3.25)
```

The second `print` statement prints the value generated by concatenating the values bound to t1 and t2, which is a tuple with five elements. It produces the output

```
(1, 'two', 3, (1, 'two', 3), 3.25)
```

The next statement selects and prints the fourth element of the concatenated tuple (as always in Python, indexing starts at 0), and the statement after that creates and prints a slice of that tuple, producing the output

```
(1, 'two', 3)
(3, (1, 'two', 3), 3.25)
```

A for statement can be used to iterate over the elements of a tuple. For example, the following code prints the common divisors of 20 and 100 and then the sum of all the divisors.

```
def findDivisors (n1, n2):
    """Assumes that n1 and n2 are positive ints
       Returns a tuple containing all common divisors of n1 & n2"""
    divisors = () #the empty tuple
    for i in range(1, min (n1, n2) + 1):
        if n1%i == 0 and n2%i == 0:
            divisors = divisors + (i,)
    return divisors

divisors = findDivisors(20, 100)
print divisors
total = 0
for d in divisors:
    total += d
print total
```

5.1.1 Sequences and Multiple Assignment

If you know the length of a sequence (e.g., a tuple or a string), it can be convenient to use Python's multiple assignment statement to extract the individual elements. For example, after executing the statement x, y = (3, 4), x will be bound to 3 and y to 4. Similarly, the statement a, b, c = 'xyz' will bind a to 'x', b to 'y', and c to 'z'.

This mechanism is particularly convenient when used in conjunction with functions that return fixed-size sequences.

Consider, for example the function

```
def findExtremeDivisors(n1, n2):
    """Assumes that n1 and n2 are positive ints
       Returns a tuple containing the smallest common
       divisor > 1 and the largest common divisor of n1
       and n2"""
    divisors = () #the empty tuple
    minVal, maxVal = None, None
    for i in range(2, min(n1, n2) + 1):
        if n1%i == 0 and n2%i == 0:
            if minVal == None or i < minVal:
                minVal = i
            if maxVal == None or i > maxVal:
                maxVal = i
    return (minVal, maxVal)
```

The multiple assignment statement

```
    minDivisor, maxDivisor = findExtremeDivisors(100, 200)
```

will bind `minDivisor` to 2 and `maxDivisor` to 100.

5.2 Lists and Mutability

Like a tuple, a **list** is an ordered sequence of values, where each value is identified by an index. The syntax for expressing literals of type `list` is similar to that used for tuples; the difference is that we use square brackets rather than parentheses. The empty list is written as [], and singleton lists are written without that (oh so easy to forget) comma before the closing bracket. So, for example, the code,

```
L = ['I did it all', 4, 'love']
for i in range(len(L)):
    print L[i]
```

produces the output,

```
I did it all
4
love
```

Occasionally, the fact that square brackets are used for literals of type `list`, indexing into lists, and slicing lists can lead to some visual confusion. For example, the expression [1,2,3,4][1:3][1], which evaluates to 3, uses the square brackets in three different ways. This is rarely a problem in practice, because most of the time lists are built incrementally rather than written as literals.

Lists differ from tuples in one hugely important way: lists are **mutable**. In contrast, tuples and strings are **immutable**. There are many operators that can be used to create objects of these immutable types, and variables can be bound to objects of these types. But objects of immutable types cannot be modified. On the other hand, objects of type `list` can be modified after they are created.

The distinction between mutating an object and assigning an object to a variable may, at first, appear subtle. However, if you keep repeating the mantra, "In

Python a variable is merely a name, i.e., a label that can be attached to an object," it will bring you clarity.

When the statements

```
Techs = ['MIT', 'Caltech']
Ivys = ['Harvard', 'Yale', 'Brown']
```

are executed, the interpreter creates two new lists and binds the appropriate variables to them, as pictured below.

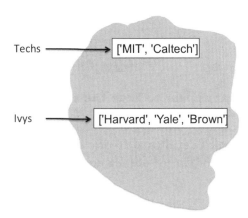

Figure 5.1 Two lists

The assignment statements

```
Univs = [Techs, Ivys]
Univs1 = [['MIT', 'Caltech'], ['Harvard', 'Yale', 'Brown']]
```

also create new lists and bind variables to them. The elements of these lists are themselves lists. The three print statements

```
print 'Univs =', Univs
print 'Univs1 =', Univs1
print Univs == Univs1
```

produce the output

```
Univs = [['MIT', 'Caltech'], ['Harvard', 'Yale', 'Brown']]
Univs1 = [['MIT', 'Caltech'], ['Harvard', 'Yale', 'Brown']]
True
```

It appears as if Univs and Univs1 are bound to the same value. But appearances can be deceiving. As the following picture illustrates, Univs and Univs1 are bound to quite different values.

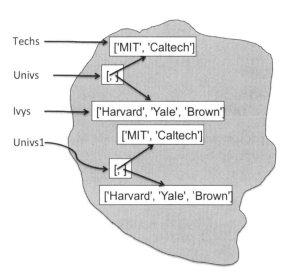

Figure 5.2 Two lists that appear to have the same value, but don't

That `Univs` and `Univs1` are bound to different objects can be verified using the built-in Python function **id**, which returns a unique integer identifier for an object. This function allows us to test for **object equality**. When we run the code

```
print Univs == Univs1 #test value equality
print id(Univs) == id(Univs1) #test object equality
print 'Id of Univs =', id(Univs)
print 'Id of Univs1 =', id(Univs1)
```

it prints

```
True
False
Id of Univs = 24499264
Id of Univs1 = 24500504
```

(Don't expect to see the same unique identifiers if you run this code. The semantics of Python says nothing about what identifier is associated with each object; it merely requires that no two objects have the same identifier.)

Notice that in Figure 5.2 the elements of `Univs` are not copies of the lists to which `Techs` and `Ivys` are bound, but are rather the lists themselves. The elements of `Univs1` are lists that contain the same elements as the lists in `Univs`, but they are not the same lists. We can see this by running the code

```
print 'Ids of Univs[0] and Univs[1]', id(Univs[0]), id(Univs[1])
print 'Ids of Univs1[0] and Univs1[1]', id(Univs1[0]), id(Univs1[1])
```

which prints

```
Ids of Univs[0] and Univs[1] 22287944 22286464
Ids of Univs1[0] and Univs1[1] 22184184 22287984
```

Why does this matter? It matters because lists are mutable.

Consider the code

```
Techs.append('RPI')
```

The **append** method has a **side effect**. Rather than create a new list, it mutates the existing list Techs by adding a new element, the string 'RPI', to the end of it.

After append is executed, the state of the computation looks like

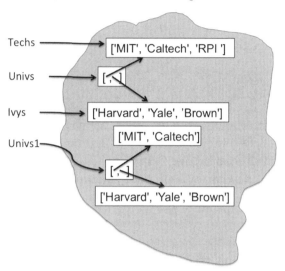

Figure 5.3 Demonstration of mutability

Univs still contains the same two lists, but the contents of one of those lists has been changed. Consequently, the print statements

```
print 'Univs =', Univs
print 'Univs1 =', Univs1
```

now produce the output

```
Univs = [['MIT', 'Caltech', 'RPI'], ['Harvard', 'Yale', 'Brown']]
Univs1 = [['MIT', 'Caltech'], ['Harvard', 'Yale', 'Brown']]
```

What we have here is something called **aliasing**. There are two distinct paths to the same list object. One path is through the variable Techs and the other through the first element of the list object to which Univs is bound. One can mutate the object via either path, and the effect of the mutation will be visible through both paths. This can be convenient, but it can also be treacherous. Unintentional aliasing leads to programming errors that are often enormously hard to track down.

As with tuples, a for statement can be used to iterate over the elements of a list. For example,

```
for e in Univs:
    print 'Univs contains', e
    print '  which contains'
    for u in e:
        print '    ', u
```

will print

```
Univs contains ['MIT', 'Caltech', 'RPI']
   which contains
      MIT
      Caltech
      RPI
Univs contains ['Harvard', 'Yale', 'Brown']
   which contains
      Harvard
      Yale
      Brown
```

When we append one list to another, e.g., `Techs.append(Ivys)`, the original structure is maintained. I.e., the result is a list that contains a list. Suppose we do not want to maintain this structure, but want to add the elements of one list into another list. We can do that by using list concatenation or the `extend` method, e.g.,

```
L1 = [1,2,3]
L2 = [4,5,6]
L3 = L1 + L2
print 'L3 =', L3
L1.extend(L2)
print 'L1 =', L1
L1.append(L2)
print 'L1 =', L1
```

will print

```
L3 = [1, 2, 3, 4, 5, 6]
L1 = [1, 2, 3, 4, 5, 6]
L1 = [1, 2, 3, 4, 5, 6, [4, 5, 6]]
```

Notice that the operator + does not have a side effect. It creates a new list and returns it. In contrast, `extend` and `append` each mutated L1.

Figure 5.4 contains short descriptions of some of the methods associated with lists. Note that all of these except `count` and `index` mutate the list.

L.append(e) adds the object e to the end of L.

L.count(e) returns the number of times that e occurs in L.

L.insert(i, e) inserts the object e into L at index i.

L.extend(L1) adds the items in list L1 to the end of L.

L.remove(e) deletes the first occurrence of e from L.

L.index(e) returns the index of the first occurrence of e in L. It raises an exception (see Chapter 7) if e is not in L.

L.pop(i) removes and returns the item at index i in L. If i is omitted, it defaults to -1, to remove and return the last element of L.

L.sort() sorts the elements of L in ascending order.

L.reverse() reverses the order of the elements in L.

Figure 5.4 Methods associated with lists

5.2.1 Cloning

Though allowed, it is usually prudent to avoid mutating a list over which one is iterating. Consider, for example, the code

```
def removeDups(L1, L2):
    """Assumes that L1 and L2 are lists.
       Removes any element from L1 that also occurs in L2"""
    for e1 in L1:
        if e1 in L2:
            L1.remove(e1)
L1 = [1,2,3,4]
L2 = [1,2,5,6]
removeDups(L1, L2)
print 'L1 =', L1
```

You might be surprised to discover that the `print` statement produces the output

```
L1 = [2, 3, 4]
```

During a `for` loop, the implementation of Python keeps track of where it is in the list using an internal counter that is incremented at the end of each iteration. When the value of the counter reaches the current length of the list, the loop terminates. This works as one might expect if the list is not mutated within the loop, but can have surprising consequences if the list is mutated. In this case, the hidden counter starts out at 0, discovers that `L1[0]` is in `L2`, and removes it—reducing the length of `L1` to 3. The counter is then incremented to 1, and the code proceeds to check if the value of `L1[1]` is in `L2`. Notice that this is not the original value of `L1[1]` (i.e., 2), but rather the current value of `L1[1]` (i.e., 3). As you can see, it is possible to figure out what happens when the list is modified within the loop. However, it is not easy. And what happens is likely to be unintentional, as in this example.

One way to avoid this kind of problem is to use slicing to **clone** (i.e., make a copy of) the list and write `for e1 in L1[:]`. Notice that writing `newL1 = L1` followed by `for e1 in newL1` would not have solved the problem. It would not have created a copy of `L1`, but would merely have introduced a new name for the existing list.

Slicing is not the only way to clone lists in Python. The expression `list(l)` returns a copy of the list `l`. If the list to be copied contains mutable objects that you want to copy as well, import the standard library module `copy` and use the function `copy.deepcopy`.

5.2.2 List Comprehension

List comprehension provides a concise way to apply an operation to the values in a sequence. It creates a new list in which each element is the result of applying a given operation to a value from a sequence (e.g., the elements in another list). For example,

```
L = [x**2 for x in range(1,7)]
print L
```

will print the list

```
[1, 4, 9, 16, 25, 36]
```

The `for` clause in a list comprehension can be followed by one or more `if` and `for` statements that are applied to the values produced by the `for` clause. These additional clauses modify the sequence of values generated by the first `for` clause and produce a new sequence of values, to which the operation associated with the comprehension is applied.

For example, the code

```
mixed = [1, 2, 'a', 3, 4.0]
print [x**2 for x in mixed if type(x) == int]
```

squares the integers in `mixed`, and then prints [1, 4, 9].

Some Python programmers use list comprehensions in marvelous and subtle ways. That is not always a great idea. Remember that somebody else may need to read your code, and "subtle" is not usually a desirable property.

5.3 Functions as Objects

In Python, functions are **first-class objects**. That means that they can be treated like objects of any other type, e.g., `int` or `list`. They have types, e.g., the expression `type(fact)` has the value `<type 'function'>`; they can appear in expressions, e.g., as the right-hand side of an assignment statement or as an argument to a function; they can be elements of lists; etc.

Using functions as arguments can be particularly convenient in conjunction with lists. It allows a style of coding called **higher-order programming**. Consider the code in Figure 5.5.

```
def applyToEach(L, f):
    """Assumes L is a list, f a function
       Mutates L by replacing each element, e, of L by f(e)"""
    for i in range(len(L)):
        L[i] = f(L[i])

L = [1, -2, 3.33]
print 'L =', L
print 'Apply abs to each element of L.'
applyToEach(L, abs)
print 'L =', L
print 'Apply int to each element of', L
applyToEach(L, int)
print 'L =', L
print 'Apply factorial to each element of', L
applyToEach(L, factR)
print 'L =', L
print 'Apply Fibonnaci to each element of', L
applyToEach(L, fib)
print 'L =', L
```

Figure 5.5 Applying a function to elements of a list

The function applyToEach is called **higher-order** because it has an argument that is itself a function. The first time it is called, it mutates L by applying the unary built-in function abs to each element. The second time it is called, it applies a type conversion to each element. The third time it is called, it replaces each element by the result of applying the function factR (defined in Figure 4.6) to each element. And the fourth time it is called, it replaces each element by the result of applying the function fib (defined in Figure 4.7) to each element. It prints

```
L = [1, -2, 3.3300000000000001]
Apply abs to each element of L.
L = [1, 2, 3.3300000000000001]
Apply int to each element of [1, 2, 3.3300000000000001]
L = [1, 2, 3]
Apply factorial to each element of [1, 2, 3]
L = [1, 2, 6]
Apply Fibonnaci to each element of [1, 2, 6]
L = [1, 2, 13]
```

Python has a built-in higher-order function, map, that is similar to, but more general than, the applyToEach function defined in Figure 5.5. In its simplest form the first argument to map is a unary function (i.e., a function that has only one parameter) and the second argument is any ordered collection of values suitable as arguments to the first argument. It returns a list generated by applying the first argument to each element of the second argument. For example, the expression map(fact, [1, 2, 3]) has the value [1, 2, 6].

More generally, the first argument to map can be of function of n arguments, in which case it must be followed by n subsequent ordered collections. For example, the code

```
L1 = [1, 28, 36]
L2 = [2, 57, 9]
print map(min, L1, L2)
```

prints the list

```
[1, 28, 9]
```

5.4   Strings, Tuples, and Lists

We have looked at three different sequence types: `str`, `tuple`, and `list`. They are similar in that objects of all of these types can be operated upon as described in Figure 5.6.

---

seq[i] returns the ith element in the sequence.

len(seq) returns the length of the sequence.

seq1 + seq2 returns the concatenation of the two sequences.

n * seq returns a sequence that repeats seq n times.

seq[start:end] returns a slice of the sequence.

e in seq is True if e is contained in the sequence and False otherwise.

e not in seq is True if e is not in the sequence and False otherwise.

for e in seq iterates over the elements of the sequence.

Figure 5.6 Common operations on sequence types

Some of their other similarities and differences are summarized in Figure 5.7.

Type	Type of elements	Examples of literals	Mutable
str	characters	`''`, `'a'`, `'abc'`	No
tuple	any type	`()`, `(3,)`, `('abc', 4)`	No
list	any type	`[]`, `[3]`, `['abc', 4]`	Yes

Figure 5.7 Comparison of sequence types

Python programmers tend to use lists far more often than tuples. Since lists are mutable, they can be constructed incrementally during a computation.

For example, the following code incrementally builds a list containing all of the even numbers in another list.

```
evenElems = []
for e in L:
    if e%2 == 0:
        evenElems.append(e)
```

One advantage of tuples is that because they are immutable, aliasing is never a worry. Another advantage of their being immutable is that tuples, unlike lists, can be used as keys in dictionaries, as we will see in the next section.

Since strings can contain only characters, they are considerably less versatile than tuples or lists. On the other hand, when you are working with a string of characters there are many built-in methods that make life easy. Figure 5.8 contains short descriptions of a few of them. Keep in mind that since strings are immutable these all return values and have no side effect.

---

s.count(s1) counts how many times the string s1 occurs in s.

s.find(s1) returns the index of the first occurrence of the substring s1 in s, and -1 if s1 is not in s.

s.rfind(s1) same as find, but starts from the end of s (the "r" in rfind stands for reverse).

s.index(s1) same as find, but raises an exception (see Chapter 7) if s1 is not in s.

s.rindex(s1) same as index, but starts from the end of s.

s.lower() converts all uppercase letters in s to lowercase.

s.replace(old, new) replaces all occurrences of the string old in s with the string new.

s.rstrip() removes trailing white space from s.

s.split(d) Splits s using d as a delimiter. Returns a list of substrings of s. For example, the value of 'David Guttag plays basketball'.split(' ') is ['David', 'Guttag', 'plays', 'basketball']. If d is omitted, the substrings are separated by arbitrary strings of whitespace characters (space, tab, newline, return, and formfeed).

Figure 5.8 Some methods on strings

5.5 Dictionaries

Objects of type **dict** (short for dictionary) are like lists except that "indices" need not be integers—they can be values of any immutable type. Since they are not ordered, we call them **keys** rather than indices. Think of a dictionary as a set of key/value pairs. Literals of type dict are enclosed in curly braces, and each element is written as a key followed by a colon followed by a value.

For example, the code,

```
monthNumbers = {'Jan':1, 'Feb':2, 'Mar':3, 'Apr':4, 'May':5,
                1:'Jan', 2:'Feb', 3:'Mar', 4:'Apr', 5:'May'}
print 'The third month is ' + monthNumbers[3]
dist = monthNumbers['Apr'] - monthNumbers['Jan']
print 'Apr and Jan are', dist, 'months apart'
```

will print

```
The third month is Mar
Apr and Jan are 3 months apart
```

The entries in a dict are unordered and cannot be accessed with an index. That's why monthNumbers[1] unambiguously refers to the entry with the key 1 rather than the second entry.

The method keys returns a list containing the keys of a dictionary. The order in which the keys appear is not defined. So, for example, the code
print monthNumbers.keys() might print

```
[1, 2, 'Mar', 'Feb', 5, 'Apr', 'Jan', 'May', 3, 4]
```

When a for statement is used to iterate over a dictionary, the value assigned to the iteration variable is a key, not a key/value pair. For example, the code

```
keys = []
for e in monthNumbers:
    keys.append(e)
keys.sort()
print keys
```

prints [1, 2, 3, 4, 5, 'Apr', 'Feb', 'Jan', 'Mar', 'May'].

Dictionaries are one of the great things about Python. They greatly reduce the difficulty of writing a variety of programs. For example, in Figure 5.9 we use dictionaries to write a (pretty horrible) program to translate between languages.

```
EtoF = {'bread':'pain', 'wine':'vin', 'with':'avec', 'I':'Je',
        'eat':'mange', 'drink':'bois', 'John':'Jean',
        'friends':'amis', 'and': 'et', 'of':'du','red':'rouge'}
FtoE = {'pain':'bread', 'vin':'wine', 'avec':'with', 'Je':'I',
        'mange':'eat', 'bois':'drink', 'Jean':'John',
        'amis':'friends', 'et':'and', 'du':'of', 'rouge':'red'}
dicts = {'English to French':EtoF, 'French to English':FtoE}

def translateWord(word, dictionary):
    if word in dictionary.keys():
        return dictionary[word]
    elif word != '':
        return '"' + word + '"'
    return word

def translate(phrase, dicts, direction):
    UCLetters = 'ABCDEFGHIJKLMNOPQRSTUVWXYZ'
    LCLetters = 'abcdefghijklmnopqrstuvwxyz'
    letters = UCLetters + LCLetters
    dictionary = dicts[direction]
    translation = ''
    word = ''
    for c in phrase:
        if c in letters:
            word = word + c
        else:
            translation = translation\
                          + translateWord(word, dictionary) + c
            word = ''
    return translation + ' ' + translateWord(word, dictionary)

print translate('I drink good red wine, and eat bread.',
                dicts,'English to French')
print translate('Je bois du vin rouge.',
                dicts, 'French to English')
```

Figure 5.9 Translating text (badly)

The code in the figure prints,

```
Je bois "good" rouge vin, et mange pain.
I drink of wine red.
```

Like lists, dictionaries are mutable. So, one must be careful about side effects. For example,

```
FtoE['bois'] = 'wood'
print translate('Je bois du vin rouge.', dicts, 'French to English')
```

will print

```
I wood of wine red.
```

We add elements to a dictionary by assigning a value to an unused key, e.g.,

```
FtoE['blanc'] = 'white'
```

As with lists, there are many useful methods, including some for removing elements, associated with dictionaries. We do not enumerate them here, but will use them as convenient in examples later in the book. Figure 5.10 contains some of the more useful operations on dictionaries.

---

len(d) returns the number of items in d.

d.keys() returns a list containing the keys in d.

d.values() returns a list containing the values in d.

k in d returns True if key k is in d.

d[k] returns the item in d with key k.

d.get(k, v) returns d[k] if k is in d, and v otherwise.

d[k] = v associates the value v with the key k in d. If there is already a value associated with k, that value is replaced.

del d[k] removes the key k from d.

for k in d iterates over the keys in d.

Figure 5.10 Some common operations on dicts

Objects of any immutable type, e.g., type tuple, may be used as dictionary keys. Imagine for example using a tuple of the form (flightNumber, day) to represent airline flights. It would then be easy to use such tuples as keys in a dictionary implementing a mapping from flights to arrival times.

Most programming languages do not contain a built-in type that provides a mapping from keys to values. Instead, programmers use other types to provide similar functionality. It is, for example, relatively easy to implement a dictionary using a list in which each element is a key/value pair. One can then write a simple function that does the associative retrieval, e.g.,

```
def keySearch(L, k):
    for elem in L:
        if elem[0] == k:
            return elem[1]
    return None
```

The problem with such an implementation is that it is computationally inefficient. In the worst case, a program might have to examine each element in the list to perform a single retrieval. In contrast, the built-in implementation is quite fast. It uses a technique called hashing, described in Chapter 10, to do the lookup in time that is nearly independent of the size of the dictionary.

6 TESTING AND DEBUGGING

We hate to bring this up, but Dr. Pangloss was wrong. We do not live in "the best of all possible worlds." There are some places where it rains too little, and others where it rains too much. Some places are too cold, some too hot, and some too hot in the summer and too cold in the winter. Sometimes the stock market goes down—a lot. And, perhaps worst of all, our programs don't always function properly the first time we run them.

Books have been written about how to deal with this last problem, and there is a lot to be learned from reading these books. However, in the interest of providing you with some hints that might help you get that next problem set in on time, this chapter provides a highly condensed discussion of the topic. While all of the programming examples are in Python, the general principles are applicable to getting any complex system to work.

Testing is the process of running a program to try and ascertain whether or not it works as intended. **Debugging** is the process of trying to fix a program that you already know does not work as intended.

Testing and debugging are not processes that you should begin to think about after a program has been built. Good programmers design their programs in ways that make them easier to test and debug. The key to doing this is breaking the program up into separate components that can be implemented, tested, and debugged independently of other components. At this point in the book, we have discussed only one mechanism for modularizing programs, the function. So, for now, all of our examples will be based around functions. When we get to other mechanisms, in particular classes, we will return to some of the topics covered in this chapter.

The first step in getting a program to work is getting the language system to agree to run it—that is, eliminating syntax errors and static semantic errors that can be detected without running the program. If you haven't gotten past that point in your programming, you're not ready for this chapter. Spend a bit more time working on small programs, and then come back.

6.1 Testing

The most important thing to say about testing is that its purpose is to show that bugs exist, not to show that a program is bug-free. To quote Edsger Dijkstra, "Program testing can be used to show the presence of bugs, but never to show their absence!"[29] Or, as Albert Einstein reputedly once said, "No amount of experimentation can ever prove me right; a single experiment can prove me wrong."

---

[29] "Notes On Structured Programming," Technical University Eindhoven, T.H. Report 70-WSK-03, April 1970.

Why is this so? Even the simplest of programs has billions of possible inputs. Consider, for example, a program that purports to meet the specification:

```
def isBigger(x, y):
    """Assumes x and y are ints
       Returns True if x is less than y and False otherwise."""
```

Running it on all pairs of integers would be, to say the least, tedious. The best we can do is to run it on pairs of integers that have a reasonable probability of producing the wrong answer if there is a bug in the program.

The key to testing is finding a collection of inputs, called a **test suite**, that has a high likelihood of revealing bugs, yet does not take too long to run. The key to doing this is partitioning the space of all possible inputs into subsets that provide equivalent information about the correctness of the program, and then constructing a test suite that contains one input from each partition. (Usually, constructing such a test suite is not actually possible. Think of this as an unachievable ideal.)

A **partition** of a set divides that set into a collection of subsets such that each element of the original set belongs to exactly one of the subsets. Consider, for example, isBigger(x, y). The set of possible inputs is all pairwise combinations of integers. One way to partition this set is into these seven subsets:

- x positive, y positive
- x negative, y negative
- x positive, y negative
- x negative, y positive
- x = 0, y = 0
- x = 0, y ≠ 0
- x ≠ 0, y = 0

If one tested the implementation on at least one value from each of these subsets, there would be reasonable probability (but no guarantee) of exposing a bug if one exists.

For most programs, finding a good partitioning of the inputs is far easier said than done. Typically, people rely on heuristics based on exploring different paths through some combination of the code and the specifications. Heuristics based on exploring paths through the code fall into a class called **glass-box testing**. Heuristics based on exploring paths through the specification fall into a class called **black-box testing**.

6.1.1 Black-Box Testing

In principle, black-box tests are constructed without looking at the code to be tested. Black-box testing allows testers and implementers to be drawn from separate populations. When those of us who teach programming courses generate test cases for the problem sets we assign students, we are developing black-box test suites. Developers of commercial software often have quality assurance groups that are largely independent of development groups.

This independence reduces the likelihood of generating test suites that exhibit mistakes that are correlated with mistakes in the code. Suppose, for example, that the author of a program made the implicit, but invalid, assumption that a function would never be called with a negative number. If the same person constructed the test suite for the program, he would likely repeat the mistake, and not test the function with a negative argument.

Another positive feature of black-box testing is that it is robust with respect to implementation changes. Since the test data is generated without knowledge of the implementation, it need not be changed when the implementation is changed.

As we said earlier, a good way to generate black-box test data is to explore paths through a specification. Consider, the specification

```
def sqrt(x, epsilon):
    """Assumes x, epsilon floats
            x >= 0
            epsilon > 0
       Returns result such that
            x-epsilon <= result*result <= x+epsilon"""
```

There seem to be only two distinct paths through this specification: one corresponding to x = 0 and one corresponding to x > 0. However, common sense tells us that while it is necessary to test these two cases, it is hardly sufficient.

Boundary conditions should also be tested. When looking at lists, this often means looking at the empty list, a list with exactly one element, and a list containing lists. When dealing with numbers, it typically means looking at very small and very large values as well as "typical" values. For sqrt, it might make sense to try values of x and epsilon similar to those in the following table.

The first four rows are intended to represent typical cases. Notice that the values for x include a perfect square, a number less than one, and a number with an irrational square root. If any of these tests fail, there is a bug in the program that needs to be fixed.

x	epsilon
0.0	0.0001
25.0	0.0001
0.5	0.0001
2.0	0.0001
2.0	1.0/2.0**64.0
1.0/2.0**64	1.0/2.0**64.0
2.0**64.0	1.0/2.0**64.0
1.0/2.0**64.0	2.0**64.0
2.0**64.0	2.0**64.0

The remaining rows test extremely large and small values of x and epsilon. If any of these tests fail, something needs to be fixed. Perhaps there is a bug in the code that needs to be fixed, or perhaps the specification needs to be changed so that it is easier to meet. It might, for example, be unreasonable to expect to find an approximation of a square root when epsilon is ridiculously small.

Another important boundary condition to think about is aliasing. Consider, for example, the code

```
def copy(L1, L2):
    """Assumes L1, L2 are lists
        Mutates L2 to be a copy of L1"""
    while len(L2) > 0: #remove all elements from L2
        L2.pop() #remove last element of L2
    for e in L1: #append L1's elements to initially empty L2
        L2.append(e)
```

It will work most of the time, but not when L1 and L2 refer to the same list. Any test suite that did not include a call of the form copy(L, L), would not reveal the bug.

6.1.2 Glass-Box Testing

Black-box testing should never be skipped, but it is rarely sufficient. Without looking at the internal structure of the code, it is impossible to know which test cases are likely to provide new information. Consider the following trivial example:

```
def isPrime(x):
    """Assumes x is a nonnegative int
        Returns True if x is prime; False otherwise"""
    if x <= 2:
        return False
    for i in range(2, x):
        if x%i == 0:
            return False
    return True
```

Looking at the code, we can see that because of the test if x <= 2, the values 0, 1, and 2 are treated as special cases, and therefore need to be tested. Without looking at the code, one might not test isPrime(2), and would therefore not discover that the function call isPrime(2) returns False, erroneously indicating that 2 is not a prime.

Glass-box test suites are usually much easier to construct than black-box test suites. Specifications are usually incomplete and often pretty sloppy, making it a challenge to estimate how thoroughly a black-box test suite explores the space of interesting inputs. In contrast, the notion of a path through code is well defined, and it is relatively easy to evaluate how thoroughly one is exploring the space. There are, in fact, commercial tools that can be used to objectively measure the completeness of glass-box tests.

A glass-box test suite is **path-complete** if it exercises every potential path through the program. This is typically impossible to achieve, because it depends upon the number of times each loop is executed and the depth of each recursion. For example, a recursive implementation of factorial follows a different path for each possible input (because the number of levels of recursion will differ).

Furthermore, even a path-complete test suite does not guarantee that all bugs will be exposed. Consider:

```
def abs(x):
    """Assumes x is an int
       Returns x if x>=0 and -x otherwise"""
    if x < -1:
        return -x
    else:
        return x
```

The specification suggests that there are two possible cases, x is either negative or it isn't. This suggests that the set of inputs {2, -2} is sufficient to explore all paths in the specification. This test suite has the additional nice property of forcing the program through all of its paths, so it looks like a complete glass-box suite as well. The only problem is that this test suite will not expose the fact that abs(-1)will return -1.

Despite the limitations of glass-box testing, there are a few rules of thumb that are usually worth following:

- Exercise both branches of all if statements.

- Make sure that each except clause (see Chapter 7) is executed.

- For each for loop, have test cases in which

    o The loop is not entered (e.g., if the loop is iterating over the elements of a list, make sure that it is tested on the empty list),

    o The body of the loop is executed exactly once, and

    o The body of the loop is executed more than once.

- For each while loop,

    o Look at the same kinds of cases as when dealing with for loops, and

    o Include test cases corresponding to all possible ways of exiting the loop. For example, for a loop starting with

        while len(L) > 0 and not L[i] == e

      find cases where the loop exits because len(L) is greater than zero and cases where it exits because L[i] == e.

- For recursive functions, include test cases that cause the function to return with no recursive calls, exactly one recursive call, and more than one recursive call.

6.1.3 Conducting Tests

Testing is often thought of as occurring in two phases. One should always start with **unit testing**. During this phase testers construct and run tests designed to ascertain whether individual units of code (e.g., functions) work properly. This is followed by **integration testing**, which is designed to ascertain whether the program as a whole behaves as intended. In practice, testers cycle through these two phases, since failures during integration testing lead to making changes to individual units.

Integration testing is almost always more challenging than unit testing. One reason for this is that the intended behavior of an entire program is often considerably harder to characterize than the intended behavior of each of its parts. For example, characterizing the intended behavior of a word processor is considerably more challenging than characterizing the behavior of a function that counts the number of characters in a document. Problems of scale can also make integration testing difficult. It is not unusual for integration tests to take hours or even days to run.

Many industrial software development organizations have a **software quality assurance (SQA)** group that is separate from the group charged with implementing the software. The mission of this group is to insure that before the software is released it is suitable for its intended purpose. In some organizations the development group is responsible for unit testing and the QA group for integration testing.

In industry, the testing process is often highly automated. Testers[30] do not sit at terminals typing inputs and checking outputs. Instead, they use **test drivers** that autonomously

- Set up the environment needed to invoke the program (or unit) to be tested,

- Invoke the program (or unit) to be tested with a predefined or automatically generated sequence of inputs,

- Save the results of these invocations,

- Check the acceptability of the results of the tests, and

- Prepare an appropriate report.

During unit testing, we often need to build **stubs** as well as drivers. Drivers simulate parts of the program that use the unit being tested, whereas stubs simulate parts of the program used by the unit being tested. Stubs are useful because they allow people to test units that depend upon software or sometimes even hardware that does not yet exist. This allows teams of programmers to simultaneously develop and test multiple parts of a system.

Ideally, a stub should

- Check the reasonableness of the environment and arguments supplied by the caller (calling a function with inappropriate arguments is a common error),

- Modify arguments and global variables in a manner consistent with the specification, and

- Return values consistent with the specification.

---

[30] Or, for that matter, those who grade problem sets in very large programming courses.

Building adequate stubs is often a challenge. If the unit the stub is replacing is intended to perform some complex task, building a stub that performs actions consistent with the specification may be tantamount to writing the program that the stub is designed to replace. One way to surmount this problem is to limit the set of arguments accepted by the stub, and create a table that contains the values to be returned for each combination of arguments to be used in the test suite.

One attraction of automating the testing process is that it facilitates **regression testing**. As programmers attempt to debug a program, it is all too common to install a "fix" that breaks something that used to work. Whenever any change is made, no matter how small, you should check that the program still passes all of the tests that it used to pass.

6.2 Debugging

There is a charming urban legend about how the process of fixing flaws in software came to be known as debugging. The photo below is of a September 9, 1947, page in a laboratory book from the group working on the Mark II Aiken Relay Calculator at Harvard University.

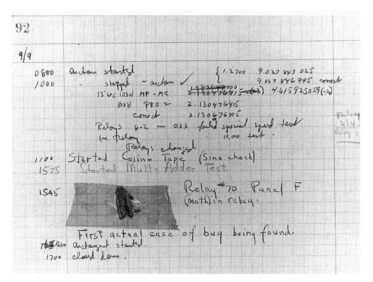

Some have claimed that the discovery of that unfortunate moth trapped in the Mark II led to the use of the phrase debugging. However the wording, "First actual case of a bug being found," suggests that a less literal interpretation of the phrase was already common. Grace Murray Hopper, a leader of the Mark II project, made it clear that the term "bug" was already in wide use to describe problems with electronic systems during World War II. And well prior to that, *Hawkins' New Catechism of Electricity*, an 1896 electrical handbook, included the entry, "The term 'bug' is used to a limited extent to designate any fault or trouble in the connections or working of electric apparatus." In English usage the word "bugbear" means "anything causing seemingly needless or excessive fear or anxiety."[31]   Shakespeare seems to have shortened this to "bug," when he had Hamlet kvetch about "bugs and goblins in my life."[32]

The use of the word "bug" sometimes leads people to ignore the fundamental fact that if you wrote a program and it has a "bug," you messed up. Bugs do not crawl unbidden into flawless programs. If your program has a bug, it is because you put it there. Bugs do not breed in programs. If your program has multiple bugs, it is because you made multiple mistakes.

Runtime bugs can be categorized along two dimensions:

1. **Overt → covert**: An **overt bug** has an obvious manifestation, e.g., the program crashes or takes far longer (maybe forever) to run than it should. A **covert bug** has no obvious manifestation. The program may run to conclusion with no problem—other than providing an incorrect answer. Many bugs fall between the two extremes, and whether or not the bug is overt can depend upon how carefully one examines the behavior of the program.

2. **Persistent → intermittent**: A **persistent bug** occurs every time the program is run with the same inputs. An **intermittent bug** occurs only some of the time, even when the program is run on the same inputs and seemingly under the same conditions. When we get to Chapter 12, we will start writing programs of the kind where intermittent bugs are common.

The best kinds of bugs to have are overt and persistent. Developers can be under no illusion about the advisability of deploying the program. And if someone else is foolish enough to attempt to use it, they will quickly discover their folly. Perhaps the program will do something horrible before crashing, e.g., delete files, but at least the user will have reason to be worried (if not panicked). Good programmers try to write their programs in such a way that programming mistakes lead to bugs that are both overt and persistent. This is often called **defensive programming**.

The next step into the pit of undesirability is bugs that are overt but intermittent. An air traffic control system that computes the correct location for planes almost all of the time would be far more dangerous than one that makes obvious mistakes all the time. One can live in a fool's paradise for a period of time, and maybe get so far are as deploying a system incorporating the flawed program, but sooner or later the bug will become manifest. If the conditions prompting the bug to become manifest are easily reproducible, it is often relatively easy to track down and repair the problem. If the conditions provoking the bug are not clear, life is much harder.

Programs that fail in covert ways are often highly dangerous. Since they are not apparently problematical, people use them and trust them to do the right thing. Increasingly, society relies on software to perform critical computations that are beyond the ability of humans to carry out or even check for correctness.

---

[31] *Webster's New World College Dictionary.*

[32] Act 5, scene 2.

Therefore, a program can provide undetected fallacious answer for long periods of time. Such programs can, and have, caused a lot of damage.[33] A program that evaluates the risk of a mortgage bond portfolio and confidently spits out the wrong answer can get a bank (and perhaps all of society) into a lot of trouble. A radiation therapy machine that delivers a little more or a little less radiation than intended can be the difference between life and death for a person with cancer. A program that makes a covert error only occasionally may or may not wreak less havoc than one that always commits such an error. Bugs that are both covert and intermittent are almost always the hardest to find and fix.

6.2.1 Learning to Debug

Debugging is a learned skill. Nobody does it well instinctively. The good news is that it's not hard to learn, and it is a transferable skill. The same skills used to debug software can be used to find out what is wrong with other complex systems, e.g., laboratory experiments or sick humans.

For at least four decades people have been building tools called debuggers, and there are debugging tools built into IDLE. These are supposed to help people find bugs in their programs. They can help, but only a little. What's much more important is how you approach the problem. Many experienced programmers don't even bother with debugging tools. Most programmers say that the most important debugging tool is the `print` statement.

Debugging starts when testing has demonstrated that the program behaves in undesirable ways. Debugging is the process of searching for an explanation of that behavior. The key to being consistently good at debugging is being systematic in conducting that search.

Start by studying the available data. This includes the test results and the program text. Study all of the test results. Examine not only the tests that revealed the presence of a problem, but also those tests that seemed to work perfectly. Trying to understand why one test worked and another did not is often illuminating. When looking at the program text, keep in mind that you don't completely understand it. If you did, there probably wouldn't be a bug.

Next, form a hypothesis that you believe to be consistent with all the data. The hypothesis could be as narrow as "if I change line 403 from x < y to x <= y, the problem will go away" or as broad as "my program is not terminating because I have the wrong exit condition in some `while` loop."

Next, design and run a repeatable experiment with the potential to refute the hypothesis. For example, you might put a print statement before and after each `while` loop. If these are always paired, then the hypothesis that a `while` loop is causing nontermination has been refuted. Decide before running the experiment how you would interpret various possible results. If you wait until

---

[33] On August 1, 2012, Knight Capital Group, Inc. deployed a new piece of stock-trading software. Within forty-five minutes a bug in that software lost the company $440,000,000. The next day, the CEO of Knight commented that the bug caused the software to enter "a ton of orders, all erroneous."

after you run the experiment, you are more likely to fall prey to wishful thinking.

Finally, it's important to keep a record of what experiments you have tried. When you've spent many hours changing your code trying to track down an elusive bug, it's easy to forget what you have already tried. If you aren't careful, it is easy to waste way too many hours trying the same experiment (or more likely an experiment that looks different but will give you the same information) over and over again. Remember, as many have said, "insanity is doing the same thing, over and over again, but expecting different results."[34]

6.2.2 Designing the Experiment

Think of debugging as a search process, and each experiment as an attempt to reduce the size of the search space. One way to reduce the size of the search space is to design an experiment that can be used to decide whether a specific region of code is responsible for a problem uncovered during integration testing. Another way to reduce the search space is to reduce the amount of test data needed to provoke a manifestation of a bug.

Let's look at a contrived example to see how one might go about debugging it. Imagine that you wrote the palindrome checking code in Figure 6.1 and that you are so confident of your programming skills that you put it up on the Web—without testing it. Suppose further that you receive an email saying, "I tested your !!**! program on the following 1000-string input, and it printed Yes. Yet any fool can see that it is not a palindrome. Fix it!"

```
def isPal(x):
    """Assumes x is a list
        Returns True if the list is a palindrome; False otherwise"""
    temp = x
    temp.reverse
    if temp == x:
        return True
    else:
        return False

def silly(n):
    """Assumes n is an int > 0
        Gets n inputs from user
        Prints 'Yes' if the sequence of inputs forms a palindrome;
            'No' otherwise"""
    for i in range(n):
        result = []
        elem = raw_input('Enter element: ')
        result.append(elem)
    if isPal(result):
        print 'Yes'
    else:
        print 'No'
```

Figure 6.1 Program with bugs

[34] This line appears in Rita Mae Brown's *Sudden Death*. However, it has been variously attributed to many other sources—including Albert Einstein.

You could try and test it on the supplied 1000-string input. But it might be more sensible to begin by trying it on something smaller. In fact, it would make sense to test it on a minimal non-palindrome, e.g.,

```
>>> silly(2)
Enter element: a
Enter element: b
```

The good news is that it fails even this simple test, so you don't have to type in a thousand strings. The bad news is that you have no idea why it failed.

In this case, the code is small enough that you can probably stare at it and find the bug (or bugs). However, let's pretend that it is too large to do this, and start to systematically reduce the search space.

Often the best way to do this is to conduct a binary search. Find some point about halfway through the code, and devise an experiment that will allow you to decide if there is a problem before that point that might be related to the symptom. (Of course, there may be problems after that point as well, but it is usually best to hunt down one problem at a time.) In choosing such a point, look for a place where there are some easily examined intermediate values that provide useful information. If an intermediate value is not what you expected, there is probably a problem that occurred prior to that point in the code. If the intermediate values all look fine, the bug probably lies somewhere later in the code. This process can be repeated until you have narrowed the region in which a problem is located to a few lines of code.

Looking at `silly`, the halfway point is around the line `if isPal(result)`. The obvious thing to check is whether `result` has the expected value, `['a', 'b']`. We check this by inserting the statement `print result` before the `if` statement in `silly`. When the experiment is run, the program prints `['b']`, suggesting that something has already gone wrong. The next step is to print `result` roughly halfway through the loop. This quickly reveals that `result` is never more than one element long, suggesting that the initialization of `result` needs to be moved outside the `for` loop. The corrected code for `silly` is

```
def silly(n):
    """Assumes n is an int > 0
       Gets n inputs from user
       Prints 'Yes' if the sequence of inputs forms a palindrome;
          'No' otherwise"""
    result = []
    for i in range(n):
        elem = raw_input('Enter element: ')
        result.append(elem)
    print result
    if isPal(result):
        print 'Yes'
    else:
        print 'No'
```

Let's try that, and see if `result` has the correct value after the `for` loop. It does, but unfortunately the program still prints `Yes`. Now, we have reason to believe that a second bug lies below the `print` statement. So, let's look at `isPal`. The line `if temp == x:` is about halfway through that function. So, we insert the

line print temp, x before that line. When we run the code, we see that temp
has the expected value, but x does not. Moving up the code, we insert a print
statement after the line temp = x, and discover that both temp and x have the
value ['a', 'b']. A quick inspection of the code reveals that in isPal we wrote
temp.reverse rather than temp.reverse()—the evaluation of temp.reverse
returns the built-in reverse method for lists, but does not invoke it.[35]

We run the test again, and now it seems that both temp and x have the value
['b', 'a']. We have now narrowed the bug to one line. It seems that
temp.reverse() unexpectedly changed the value of x. An aliasing bug has bitten
us: temp and x are names for the same list, both before and after the list gets
reversed. One way to fix it is to replace the first assignment statement in isPal
by temp = x[:], which causes a copy of x to be made. The corrected version of
isPal is

```
def isPal(x):
    """Assumes x is a list
        Returns True if the list is a palindrome; False otherwise"""
    temp = x[:]
    temp.reverse()
    if temp == x:
        return True
    else:
        return False
```

6.2.3 When the Going Gets Tough

Joseph P. Kennedy, father of President Kennedy, reputedly instructed his
children, "When the going gets tough, the tough get going."[36] But he never
debugged a piece of software. This subsection contains a few pragmatic hints
about what do when the debugging gets tough.

- *Look for the usual suspects.* E.g., have you

    o Passed arguments to a function in the wrong order,

    o Misspelled a name, e.g., typed a lowercase letter when you should
      have typed an uppercase one,

    o Failed to reinitialize a variable,

    o Tested that two floating point values are equal (==) instead of
      nearly equal (remember that floating point arithmetic is not the
      same as the arithmetic you learned in school),

    o Tested for value equality (e.g., compared two lists by writing the
      expression L1 == L2) when you meant object equality (e.g.,
      id(L1) == id(L2)),

    o Forgotten that some built-in function has a side effect,

---

[35] One might well wonder why there isn't a static checker that detected the fact that the
line of code temp.reverse doesn't cause any useful computatation to be done, and is
therefore likely to be an error.

[36] He also reputedly told JFK, "Don't buy a single vote more than necessary. I'll be
damned if I'm going to pay for a landslide."

  o   Forgotten the () that turns a reference to an object of type
      `function` into a function invocation,

  o   Created an unintentional alias, or

  o   Made any other mistake that is typical for you.

- *Stop asking yourself why the program isn't doing what you want it to.
  Instead, ask yourself why it is doing what it is.* That should be an easier
  question to answer, and will probably be a good first step in figuring out
  how to fix the program.

- *Keep in mind that the bug is probably not where you think it is.* If it were,
  you would probably have found it long ago. One practical way to go
  about deciding where to look is asking where the bug cannot be. As
  Sherlock Holmes said, "Eliminate all other factors, and the one which
  remains must be the truth."[37]

- *Try to explain the problem to somebody else.* We all develop blind spots.
  It is often the case that merely attempting to explain the problem to
  someone will lead you to see things you have missed. A good thing to try
  to explain is why the bug cannot be in certain places.

- *Don't believe everything you read.* In particular, don't believe the
  documentation. The code may not be doing what the comments suggest.

- *Stop debugging and start writing documentation.* This will help you
  approach the problem from a different perspective.

- *Walk away, and try again tomorrow.* This may mean that bug is fixed
  later in time than if you had stuck with it, but you will probably spend a
  lot less of your time looking for it. That is, it is possible to trade latency
  for efficiency. (Students, this is an excellent reason to start work on
  programming problem sets earlier rather than later!)

6.2.4 And When You Have Found "The" Bug

When you think you have found a bug in your code, the temptation to start
coding and testing a fix is almost irresistible. It is often better, however, to slow
down a little. Remember that the goal is not to fix one bug, but to move rapidly
and efficiently towards a bug-free program.

Ask yourself if this bug explains all the observed symptoms, or whether it is just
the tip of the iceberg. If the latter, it may be better to think about taking care of
this bug in concert with other changes. Suppose, for example, that you have
discovered that the bug is the result of having accidentally mutated a list. You
could circumvent the problem locally (perhaps by making a copy of the list), or
you could consider using a tuple instead of a list (since tuples are immutable),
perhaps eliminating similar bugs elsewhere in the code.

Before making any change, try and understand the ramification of the proposed
"fix." Will it break something else? Does it introduce excessive complexity?
Does it offer the opportunity to tidy up other parts of the code?

---

[37] Arthur Conan Doyle, "The Sign of the Four."

Always make sure that you can get back to where you are. There is nothing more frustrating than realizing that a long series of changes have left you further from the goal than when you started, and having no way to get back to where you started. Disk space is usually plentiful. Use it to store old versions of your program.

Finally, if there are many unexplained errors, you might consider whether finding and fixing bugs one at a time is even the right approach. Maybe you would be better off thinking about whether there is some better way to organize your program or some simpler algorithm that will be easier to implement correctly.

7 EXCEPTIONS AND ASSERTIONS

An "exception" is usually defined as "something that does not conform to the norm," and is therefore somewhat rare. There is nothing rare about **exceptions** in Python. They are everywhere. Virtually every module in the standard Python library uses them, and Python itself will raise them in many different circumstances. You've already seen some of them.

Open a Python shell and enter,

```
test = [1,2,3]
test[3]
```

and the interpreter will respond with something like

```
Traceback (most recent call last):
  File "<pyshell#1>", line 1, in <module>
    test[3]
IndexError: list index out of range
```

IndexError is the type of exception that Python **raises** when a program tries to access an element that is not within the bounds of an indexable type. The string following IndexError provides additional information about what caused the exception to occur.

Most of the built-in exceptions of Python deal with situations in which a program has attempted to execute a statement with no appropriate semantics. (We will deal with the exceptional exceptions—those that do not deal with errors—later in this chapter.) Those readers (all of you, we hope) who have attempted to write and run Python programs will already have encountered many of these. Among the most commonly occurring types of exceptions are TypeError, NameError, and ValueError.

7.1 Handling Exceptions

Up to now, we have treated exceptions as fatal events. When an exception is raised, the program terminates (crashes might be a more appropriate word in this case), and we go back to our code and attempt to figure out what went wrong. When an exception is raised that causes the program to terminate, we say that an **unhandled exception** has been raised.

An exception does not need to lead to program termination. Exceptions, when raised, can and should be **handled** by the program. Sometimes an exception is raised because there is a bug in the program (like accessing a variable that doesn't exist), but many times, an exception is something the programmer can and should anticipate. A program might try to open a file that does not exist. If an interactive program asks a user for input, the user might enter something inappropriate.

If you know that a line of code might raise an exception when executed, you should handle the exception. In a well-written program, unhandled exceptions should be the exception.

Consider the code

```
successFailureRatio = numSuccesses/float(numFailures)
print 'The success/failure ratio is', successFailureRatio
print 'Now here'
```

Most of the time, this code will work just fine, but it will fail if `numFailures` happens to be zero. The attempt to divide by zero will cause the Python runtime system to raise a `ZeroDivisionError` exception, and the `print` statements will never be reached.

It would have been better to have written something along the lines of

```
try:
    successFailureRatio = numSuccesses/float(numFailures)
    print 'The success/failure ratio is', successFailureRatio
except ZeroDivisionError:
    print 'No failures so the success/failure ratio is undefined.'
print 'Now here'
```

Upon entering the **try block**, the interpreter attempts to evaluate the expression `numSuccesses/float(numFailures)`. If expression evaluation is successful, the program assigns the value of the expression to the variable `successFailureRatio`, executes the `print` statement at the end of the `try` block, and proceeds to the `print` statement following the try-except. If, however, a `ZeroDivisionError` exception is raised during the expression evaluation, control immediately jumps to the **except block** (skipping the assignment and the `print` statement in the `try` block), the `print` statement in the `except` block is executed, and then execution continues at the `print` statement following the `try-except` block.

Finger exercise: Implement a function that meets the specification below. Use a try-except block.

```
def sumDigits(s):
    """Assumes s is a string
       Returns the sum of the decimal digits in s
          For example, if s is 'a2b3c' it returns 5"""
```

Let's look at another example. Consider the code

```
val = int(raw_input('Enter an integer: '))
print 'The square of the number you entered is', val**2
```

If the user obligingly types a string that can be converted to an integer, everything will be fine. But suppose the user types abc? Executing the line of code will cause the Python runtime system to raise a `ValueError` exception, and the `print` statement will never be reached.

What the programmer should have written would look something like

```
while True:
    val = raw_input('Enter an integer: ')
    try:
        val = int(val)
        print 'The square of the number you entered is', val**2
        break #to exit the while loop
    except ValueError:
        print val, 'is not an integer'
```

After entering the loop, the program will ask the user to enter an integer. Once the user has entered something, the program executes the `try-except` block. If neither of the first two statements in the `try` block causes a `ValueError` exception to be raised, the `break` statement is executed and the `while` loop is exited. However, if executing the code in the `try` block raises a `ValueError` exception, control is immediately transferred to the code in the `except` block. Therefore, if the user enters a string that does not represent an integer, the program will ask the user to try again. No matter what text the user enters, it will not cause an unhandled exception.

The downside of this change is that the program text has grown from two lines to eight. If there are many places where the user is asked to enter an integer, this can be problematical. Of course, this problem can be solved by introducing a function:

```
def readInt():
    while True:
        val = raw_input('Enter an integer: ')
        try:
            val = int(val)
            return val
        except ValueError:
            print val, 'is not an integer'
```

Better yet, this function can be generalized to ask for any type of input,

```
def readVal(valType, requestMsg, errorMsg):
  while True:
      val = raw_input(requestMsg + ' ')
      try:
          val = valType(val)
          return val
      except ValueError:
          print val, errorMsg
```

The function `readVal` is **polymorphic**, i.e., it works for arguments of many different types. Such functions are easy to write in Python, since types are first-class values. We can now ask for an integer using the code

```
val = readVal(int, 'Enter an integer:', 'is not an integer')
```

Exceptions may seem unfriendly (after all, if not handled, an exception will cause the program to crash), but consider the alternative. What should the type conversion `int` do, for example, when asked to convert the string `'abc'` to an object of type `int`? It could return an integer corresponding to the bits used to encode the string, but this is unlikely to have any relation to the intent of the programmer. Alternatively, it could return the special value `None`. If it did that, the programmer would need to insert code to check whether the type conversion had returned `None`. A programmer who forgot that check would run the risk of getting some strange error during program execution.

With exceptions, the programmer still needs to include code dealing with the exception. However, if the programmer forgets to include such code and the exception is raised, the program will halt immediately. This is a good thing. It alerts the user of the program to the fact that something troublesome has happened. (And, as we discussed in the last chapter, overt bugs are much better than covert bugs.) Moreover, it gives someone debugging the program a clear indication of where things went awry.

If it is possible for a block of program code to raise more than one kind of exception, the reserved word `except` can be followed by a tuple of exceptions, e.g.,

```
except (ValueError, TypeError):
```

in which case the `except` block will be entered if any of the listed exceptions is raised within the `try` block. Alternatively, we can write a separate `except` block for each kind of exception, which allows the program to choose an action based upon which exception was raised. If the programmer writes

```
except:
```

the `except` block will be entered if any kind of exception is raised within the `try` block. These features are shown in Figure 7.1.

7.2 Exceptions as a Control Flow Mechanism

Don't think of exceptions as purely for errors. They are a convenient flow-of-control mechanism that can be used to simplify programs.

In many programming languages, the standard approach to dealing with errors is to have functions return a value (often something analogous to Python's `None`) indicating that something has gone amiss. Each function invocation has to check whether that value has been returned. In Python, it is more usual to have a function raise an exception when it cannot produce a result that is consistent with the function's specification.

The Python **raise** statement forces a specified exception to occur. The form of a raise statement is

```
raise exceptionName(arguments)
```

The *exceptionName* is usually one of the built-in exceptions, e.g., `ValueError`. However, programmers can define new exceptions by creating a subclass (see Chapter 8) of the built-in class `Exception`. Different types of exceptions can have different types of arguments, but most of the time the argument is a single string, which is used to describe the reason the exception is being raised.

Finger Exercise: Implement a function that satisfies the specification

```
def findAnEven(l):
    """Assumes l is a list of integers
       Returns the first even number in l
       Raises ValueError if l does not contain an even number"""
```

Consider the function definition in Figure 7.1.

```
def getRatios(vect1, vect2):
    """Assumes: vect1 and vect2 are lists of equal length of numbers
       Returns: a list containing the meaningful values of
             vect1[i]/vect2[i]"""
    ratios = []
    for index in range(len(vect1)):
        try:
            ratios.append(vect1[index]/float(vect2[index]))
        except ZeroDivisionError:
            ratios.append(float('nan')) #nan = Not a Number
        except:
            raise ValueError('getRatios called with bad arguments')
    return ratios
```

Figure 7.1 Using exceptions for control flow

There are two except blocks associated with the try block. If an exception is raised within the try block, Python first checks to see if it is a ZeroDivisionError. If so, it appends a special value, nan, of type float to ratios. (The value nan stands for "not a number." There is no literal for it, but it can be denoted by converting the string 'nan' or the string 'NaN' to type float. When nan is used as an operand in an expression of type float, the value of that expression is also nan.) If the exception is anything other than a ZeroDivisionError, the code executes the second except block, which raises a ValueError exception with an associated string.

In principle, the second except block should never be entered, because the code invoking getRatios should respect the assumptions in the specification of getRatios. However, since checking these assumptions imposes only an insignificant computational burden, it is probably worth practicing defensive programming and checking anyway.

The following code illustrates how a program might use getRatios. The name msg in the line except ValueError, msg: is bound to the argument (a string in this case) associated with ValueError when it was raised. When executed

```
try:
    print getRatios([1.0,2.0,7.0,6.0], [1.0,2.0,0.0,3.0])
    print getRatios([], [])
    print getRatios([1.0, 2.0], [3.0])
except ValueError, msg:
    print msg
```

prints

```
[1.0, 1.0, nan, 2.0]
[]
getRatios called with bad arguments
```

Figure 7.2 contains an implementation of the same specification, but without using a try-except.

```
def getRatios(vect1, vect2):
    """Assumes: vect1 and vect2 are lists of equal length of numbers
       Returns: a list containing the meaningful values of
                vect1[i]/vect2[i]"""
    ratios = []
    if len(vect1) != len(vect2):
        raise ValueError('getRatios called with bad arguments')
    for index in range(len(vect1)):
        vect1Elem = vect1[index]
        vect2Elem = vect2[index]
        if (type(vect1Elem) not in (int, float))\
           or (type(vect2Elem) not in (int, float)):
            raise ValueError('getRatios called with bad arguments')
        if vect2Elem == 0.0:
            ratios.append(float('NaN')) #NaN = Not a Number
        else:
            ratios.append(vect1Elem/vect2Elem)
    return ratios
```

Figure 7.2 Control flow without a try-except

The code in Figure 7.2 is longer and more difficult to read than the code in Figure 7.1. It is also less efficient. (The code in Figure 7.2 could be slightly shortened by eliminating the local variables vect1Elem and vect2Elem, but only at the cost of introducing yet more inefficiency by accessing each element repeatedly.)

Let us look at one more example.

```
def getGrades(fname):
    try:
        gradesFile = open(fname, 'r') #open file for reading
    except IOError:
        raise ValueError('getGrades could not open ' + fname)
    grades = []
    for line in gradesFile:
        try:
            grades.append(float(line))
        except:
            raise ValueError('Unable to convert line to float')
    return grades

try:
    grades = getGrades('quiz1grades.txt')
    grades.sort()
    median = grades[len(grades)//2]
    print 'Median grade is', median
except ValueError, errorMsg:
    print 'Whoops.', errorMsg
```

Figure 7.3 Get grades

The function getGrades either returns a value or raises an exception with which it has associated a value. It raises a ValueError exception if the call to open raises an IOError. It could have ignored the IOError and let the part of the program calling getGrades deal with it, but that would have provided less information to the calling code about what went wrong. The code that uses getGrades either uses the returned value to compute another value or handles the exception and prints a useful error message.

7.3 Assertions

The Python assert statement provides programmers with a simple way to confirm that the state of the computation is as expected. An assert statement can take one of two forms:

    assert *Boolean expression*

or

    assert *Boolean expression, argument*

When an assert statement is encountered, the Boolean expression is evaluated. If it evaluates to True, execution proceeds on its merry way. If it evaluates to False, an AssertionError exception is raised.

Assertions are a useful defensive programming tool. They can be used to confirm that the arguments to a function are of appropriate types. They are also a useful debugging tool. The can be used, for example, to confirm that intermediate values have the expected values or that a function returns an acceptable value.

8 CLASSES AND OBJECT-ORIENTED PROGRAMMING

We now turn our attention to our last major topic related to writing programs in Python: using classes to organize programs around modules and data abstractions.

Classes can be used in many different ways. In this book we emphasize using them in the context of **object-oriented programming**. The key to object-oriented programming is thinking about objects as collections of both data and the methods that operate on that data.

The ideas underlying object-oriented programming are about forty years old, and have been widely accepted and practiced over the last twenty years or so. In the mid-1970s people began to write articles explaining the benefits of this approach to programming. About the same time, the programming languages SmallTalk (at Xerox PARC) and CLU (at MIT) provided linguistic support for the ideas. But it wasn't until the arrival of C++ and Java that it really took off in practice.

We have been implicitly relying on object-oriented programming throughout most of this book. Back in Section 2.1.1 we said "Objects are the core things that Python programs manipulate. Every object has a type that defines the kinds of things that programs can do with objects of that type." Since Chapter 5, we have relied heavily upon built-in types such as `list` and `dict` and the methods associated with those types. But just as the designers of a programming language can build in only a small fraction of the useful functions, they can only build in only a small fraction of the useful types. We have already looked at a mechanism that allows programmers to define new functions; we now look at a mechanism that allows programmers to define new types.

8.1 Abstract Data Types and Classes

The notion of an abstract data type is quite simple. An **abstract data type** is a set of objects and the operations on those objects. These are bound together so that one can pass an object from one part of a program to another, and in doing so provide access not only to the data attributes of the object but also to operations that make it easy to manipulate that data.

The specifications of those operations define an **interface** between the abstract data type and the rest of the program. The interface defines the behavior of the operations—what they do, but not how they do it. The interface thus provides an **abstraction barrier** that isolates the rest of the program from the data structures, algorithms, and code involved in providing a realization of the type abstraction.

Programming is about managing complexity in a way that facilitates change. There are two powerful mechanisms available for accomplishing this: decomposition and abstraction. Decomposition creates structure in a program, and abstraction suppresses detail. The key is to suppress the appropriate details. This is where data abstraction hits the mark. One can create domain-specific types that provide a convenient abstraction. Ideally, these types capture concepts that will be relevant over the lifetime of a program. If one starts the programming process by devising types that will be relevant months and even decades later, one has a great leg up in maintaining that software.

We have been using abstract data types (without calling them that) throughout this book. We have written programs using integers, lists, floating point numbers, strings, and dictionaries without giving any thought to how these types might be implemented. To paraphrase Molière's *Bourgeois Gentilhomme*, *"Par ma foi, il y a plus de quatre-vingt pages que nous avons utilisé ADTs, sans que nous le sachions."*[38]

In Python, one implements data abstractions using **classes**. Figure 8.1 contains a **class definition** that provides a straightforward implementation of a set-of-integers abstraction called `IntSet`.

A class definition creates an object of type `type` and associates with that object a set of objects of type `instancemethod`. For example, the expression `IntSet.insert` refers to the method `insert` defined in the definition of the class `IntSet`. And the code

```
print type(IntSet), type(IntSet.insert)
```

will print

```
<type 'type'> <type 'instancemethod'>
```

Notice that the docstring (the comment enclosed in """) at the top of the class definition describes the abstraction provided by the class, not information about how the class is implemented. The comment below the docstring does contain information about the implementation. That information is aimed at programmers who might want to modify the implementation or build subclasses (see Section 8.2) of the class, not at programmers who might want to use the abstraction.

―――――――――――――――――

[38] "Good heavens, for more than eighty pages we have been using ADTs without knowing it."

```
class IntSet(object):
    """An intSet is a set of integers"""
    #Information about the implementation (not the abstraction)
    #The value of the set is represented by a list of ints, self.vals.
    #Each int in the set occurs in self.vals exactly once.

    def __init__(self):
        """Create an empty set of integers"""
        self.vals = []

    def insert(self, e):
        """Assumes e is an integer and inserts e into self"""
        if not e in self.vals:
            self.vals.append(e)

    def member(self, e):
        """Assumes e is an integer
           Returns True if e is in self, and False otherwise"""
        return e in self.vals

    def remove(self, e):
        """Assumes e is an integer and removes e from self
           Raises ValueError if e is not in self"""
        try:
            self.vals.remove(e)
        except:
            raise ValueError(str(e) + ' not found')

    def getMembers(self):
        """Returns a list containing the elements of self.
           Nothing can be assumed about the order of the elements"""
        return self.vals[:]

    def __str__(self):
        """Returns a string representation of self"""
        self.vals.sort()
        result = ''
        for e in self.vals:
            result = result + str(e) + ','
        return '{' + result[:-1] + '}' #-1 omits trailing comma
```

Figure 8.1 Class `IntSet`

When a function definition occurs within a class definition, the defined function is called a **method** and is associated with the class. These methods are sometimes referred to as **method attributes** of the class. If this seems confusing at the moment, don't worry about it. We will have lots more to say about this topic later in this chapter.

Classes support two kinds of operations:

- **Instantiation** is used to create instances of the class. For example, the statement `s = IntSet()` creates a new object of type `IntSet`. This object is called an **instance** of `IntSet`.

- **Attribute references** use dot notation to access attributes associated with the class. For example, `s.member` refers to the method `member` associated with the instance `s` of type `IntSet`.

Each class definition begins with the reserved word `class` followed by the name of the class and some information about how it relates to other classes. In this case, the first line indicates that `IntSet` is a subclass of `object`. For now, ignore what it means to be a subclass. We will get to that shortly.

As we will see, Python has a number of special method names that start and end with two underscores. The first of these we will look at is `__init__`. Whenever a class is instantiated, a call is made to the `__init__` method defined in that class. When the line of code

```
s = IntSet()
```

is executed, the interpreter will create a new instance of type `IntSet`, and then call `IntSet.__init__` with the newly created object as the actual parameter that is bound to the formal parameter `self`. When invoked, `IntSet.__init__` creates `vals`, an object of type `list`, which becomes part of the newly created instance of type `IntSet`. (The list is created using the by now familiar notation `[]`, which is simply an abbreviation for `list()`.) This list is called a **data attribute** of the instance of `IntSet`. Notice that each object of type `IntSet` will have a different `vals` list, as one would expect.

As we have seen, methods associated with an instance of a class can be invoked using dot notation. For example, the code,

```
s = IntSet()
s.insert(3)
print s.member(3)
```

creates a new instance of `IntSet`, inserts the integer 3 into that `IntSet`, and then prints `True`.

At first blush there appears to be something inconsistent here. It looks as if each method is being called with one argument too few. For example, `member` has two formal parameters, but we appear to be calling it with only one actual parameter. This is an artifact of the dot notation. The object associated with the expression preceding the dot is implicitly passed as the first parameter to the method. Throughout this book, we follow the convention of using `self` as the name of the formal parameter to which this actual parameter is bound. Python programmers observe this convention almost universally, and we strongly suggest that you use it as well.

A class should not be confused with instances of that class, just as an object of type `list` should not be confused with the `list` type. Attributes can be associated either with a class itself or with instances of a class:

- Method attributes are defined in a class definition, for example `IntSet.member` is an attribute of the class `IntSet`. When the class is instantiated, e.g., by `s = IntSet()`, instance attributes, e.g., `s.member`, are created. Keep in mind that `IntSet.member` and `s.member` are different objects. While `s.member` is initially bound to the `member` method defined in the class `IntSet`, that binding can be changed during the course of a computation. For example, you could (but shouldn't!) write `s.member = IntSet.insert`.

- When data attributes are associated with a class we call them **class variables**. When they are associated with an instance we call them **instance variables**. For example, vals is an instance variable because for each instance of class IntSet, vals is bound to a different list. So far, we haven't seen a class variable. We will use one in Figure 8.3.

Data abstraction achieves representation-independence. Think of the implementation of an abstract type as having several components:

- Implementations of the methods of the type,

- Data structures that together encode values of the type, and

- Conventions about how the implementations of the methods are to use the data structures. A key convention is captured by the representation invariant.

The **representation invariant** defines which values of the data attributes correspond to valid representations of class instances. The representation invariant for IntSet is that vals contains no duplicates. The implementation of __init__ is responsible for establishing the invariant (which holds on the empty list), and the other methods are responsible for maintaining that invariant. That is why insert appends e only if it is not already in self.vals.

The implementation of remove exploits the assumption that the representation invariant is satisfied when remove is entered. It calls list.remove only once, since the representation invariant guarantees that there is at most one occurrence of e in self.vals.

The last method defined in the class, __str__, is another one of those special __ methods. When the print command is used, the __str__ function associated with the object to be printed is automatically invoked. For example, the code

```
s = IntSet()
s.insert(3)
s.insert(4)
print s
```

will print,

```
{3,4}
```

(If no __str__ method were defined, print s would cause something like <__main__.IntSet object at 0x1663510> to be printed.) We could also print the value of s by writing print s.__str__() or even print IntSet.__str__(s), but using those forms is less convenient. The __str__ method of a class is also invoked when a program converts an instance of that class to a string by calling str.

8.1.1 Designing Programs Using Abstract Data Types

Abstract data types are a big deal. They lead to a different way of thinking about organizing large programs. When we think about the world, we rely on abstractions. In the world of finance people talk about stocks and bonds. In the world of biology people talk about proteins and residues. When trying to understand these concepts, we mentally gather together some of the relevant data and features of these kinds of objects into one intellectual package. For example, we think of bonds as having an interest rate and a maturity date as data attributes. We also think of bonds as having operations such as "set price" and "calculate yield to maturity." Abstract data types allow us to incorporate this kind of organization into the design of programs.

Data abstraction encourages program designers to focus on the centrality of data objects rather than functions. Thinking about a program more as a collection of types than as a collection of functions leads to a profoundly different organizing principle. Among other things, it encourages one to think about programming as a process of combining relatively large chunks, since data abstractions typically encompass more functionality than do individual functions. This, in turn, leads us to think of the essence of programming as a process not of writing individual lines of code, but of composing abstractions.

The availability of reusable abstractions not only reduces development time, but also usually leads to more reliable programs, because mature software is usually more reliable than new software. For many years, the only program libraries in common use were statistical or scientific. Today, however, there is a great range of available program libraries (especially for Python), often based on a rich set of data abstractions, as we shall see later in this book.

8.1.2 Using Classes to Keep Track of Students and Faculty

As an example use of classes, imagine that you are designing a program to help keep track of all the students and faculty at a university. It is certainly possible to write such a program without using data abstraction. Each student would have a family name, a given name, a home address, a year, some grades, etc. This could all be kept in some combination of lists and dictionaries. Keeping track of faculty and staff would require some similar data structures and some different data structures, e.g., data structures to keep track of things like salary history.

Before rushing in to design a bunch of data structures, let's think about some abstractions that might prove useful. Is there an abstraction that covers the common attributes of students, professors, and staff? Some would argue that they are all human. Figure 8.2 contains a class that incorporates some of the common attributes (name and birthdate) of humans. It makes use of the standard Python library module `datetime`, which provides many convenient methods for creating and manipulating dates.

```
import datetime

class Person(object):

    def __init__(self, name):
        """Create a person"""
        self.name = name
        try:
            lastBlank = name.rindex(' ')
            self.lastName = name[lastBlank+1:]
        except:
            self.lastName = name
        self.birthday = None

    def getName(self):
        """Returns self's full name"""
        return self.name

    def getLastName(self):
        """Returns self's last name"""
        return self.lastName

    def setBirthday(self, birthdate):
        """Assumes birthdate is of type datetime.date
           Sets self's birthday to birthdate"""
        self.birthday = birthdate

    def getAge(self):
        """Returns self's current age in days"""
        if self.birthday == None:
            raise ValueError
        return (datetime.date.today() - self.birthday).days

    def __lt__(self, other):
        """Returns True if self's name is lexicographically
           less than other's name, and False otherwise"""
        if self.lastName == other.lastName:
            return self.name < other.name
        return self.lastName < other.lastName

    def __str__(self):
        """Returns self's name"""
        return self.name
```

Figure 8.2 Class Person

The following code makes use of Person.

```
me = Person('Michael Guttag')
him = Person('Barack Hussein Obama')
her = Person('Madonna')
print him.getLastName()
him.setBirthday(datetime.date(1961, 8, 4))
her.setBirthday(datetime.date(1958, 8, 16))
print him.getName(), 'is', him.getAge(), 'days old'
```

Notice that whenever Person is instantiated an argument is supplied to the
__init__ function. In general, when instantiating a class we need to look at the

specification of the __init__ function for that class to know what arguments to supply and what properties those arguments should have.

After this code is executed, there will be three instances of class `Person`. One can then access information about these instances using the methods associated with them. For example, `him.getLastName()` will return `'Obama'`. The expression `him.lastName` will also return `'Obama'`; however, for reasons discussed later in this chapter, writing expressions that directly access instance variables is considered poor form, and should be avoided. Similarly, there is no appropriate way for a user of the `Person` abstraction to extract a person's birthday, despite the fact that the implementation contains an attribute with that value. There is, however, a way to extract information that depends upon the person's birthday, as illustrated by the last `print` statement in the above code.

Class `Person` defines yet another specially named method, __lt__. This method overloads the < operator. The method `Person.__lt__` gets called whenever the first argument to the < operator is of type `Person`. The __lt__ method in class `Person` is implemented using the < operator of type `str`. The expression `self.Name < other.name` is shorthand for `self.name.__lt__(self.other)`. Since `self.name` is of type `str`, the __lt__ method is the one associated with type `str`.

In addition to providing the syntactic convenience of writing infix expressions that use <, this overloading provides automatic access to any polymorphic method defined using __lt__. The built-in method `sort` is one such method. So, for example, if `pList` is a list composed of elements of type `Person`, the call `pList.sort()` will sort that list using the __lt__ method defined in class `Person`. The code

```
pList = [me, him, her]
for p in pList:
    print p
pList.sort()
for p in pList:
    print p
```

will first print

```
Michael Guttag
Barack Hussein Obama
Madonna
```

and then print

```
Michael Guttag
Madonna
Barack Hussein Obama
```

8.2 Inheritance

Many types have properties in common with other types. For example, types
list and str each have len functions that mean the same thing. **Inheritance**
provides a convenient mechanism for building groups of related abstractions. It
allows programmers to create a type hierarchy in which each type inherits
attributes from the types above it in the hierarchy.

The class object is at the top of the hierarchy. This makes sense, since in
Python everything that exists at runtime is an object. Because Person inherits
all of the properties of objects, programs can bind a variable to a Person, append
a Person to a list, etc.

The class MITPerson in Figure 8.3 inherits attributes from its parent class,
Person, including all of the attributes that Person inherited from its parent class,
object.

```
class MITPerson(Person):

    nextIdNum = 0 #identification number

    def __init__(self, name):
        Person.__init__(self, name)
        self.idNum = MITPerson.nextIdNum
        MITPerson.nextIdNum += 1

    def getIdNum(self):
        return self.idNum

    def __lt__(self, other):
        return self.idNum < other.idNum
```

Figure 8.3 Class MITPerson

In the jargon of object-oriented programming, MITPerson is a **subclass** of Person,
and therefore **inherits** the attributes of its **superclass**. In addition to what it
inherits, the subclass can:

- Add new attributes. For example, MITPerson has added the class
  variable nextIdNum, the instance variable idNum, and the method
  getIdNum.

- **Override** attributes of the superclass. For example, MITPerson has
  overridden __init__ and __lt__.

The method MITPerson.__init__ first invokes Person.__init__ to initialize the
inherited instance variable self.name. It then initializes self.idNum, an instance
variable that instances of MITPerson have but instances of Person do not.

The instance variable self.idNum is initialized using a **class variable**, nextIdNum,
that belongs to the class MITPerson, rather than to instances of the class. When
an instance of MITPerson is created, a new instance of nextIdNum is not created.
This allows __init__ to ensure that each instance of MITPerson has a unique
idNum.

Consider the code

```
p1 = MITPerson('Barbara Beaver')
print str(p1) + '\'s id number is ' + str(p1.getIdNum())
```

The first line creates a new MITPerson. The second line is a bit more
complicated. When it attempts to evaluate the expression str(p1), the runtime
system first checks to see if there is an __str__ method associated with class
MITPerson. Since there is not, it next checks to see if there is an __str__ method
associated with the superclass, Person, of MITPerson. There is, so it uses that.
When the runtime system attempts to evaluate the expression p1.getidNum(), it
first checks to see if there is a getIdNum method associated with class MITPerson.
There is, so it invokes that method and prints

```
Barbara Beaver's id number is 0
```

(Recall that in a string, the character "\" is an escape character used to indicate
that the next character should be treated in a special way. In the string

```
'\'s id number is '
```

the "\" indicates that the apostrophe is part of the string, not a delimiter
terminating the string.)

Now consider the code

```
p1 = MITPerson('Mark Guttag')
p2 = MITPerson('Billy Bob Beaver')
p3 = MITPerson('Billy Bob Beaver')
p4 = Person('Billy Bob Beaver')
```

We have created four virtual people, three of whom are named Billy Bob Beaver.
Two of the Billy Bobs are of type MITPerson, and one merely a Person. If we
execute the lines of code

```
print 'p1 < p2 =', p1 < p2
print 'p3 < p2 =', p3 < p2
print 'p4 < p1 =', p4 < p1
```

the interpreter will print

```
p1 < p2 = True
p3 < p2 = False
p4 < p1 = True
```

Since p1, p2, and p3 are all of type MITPerson, the interpreter will use the __lt__
method defined in class MITPerson when evaluating the first two comparisons, so
the ordering will be based on identification numbers. In the third comparison,
the < operator is applied to operands of different types. Since the first argument
of the expression is used to determine which __lt__ method to invoke, p4 < p1
is shorthand for p4.__lt__(p1). Therefore, the interpreter uses the __lt__
method associated with the type of p4, Person, and the "people" will be ordered by
name.

What happens if we try

```
print 'p1 < p4 =', p1 < p4
```

The interpreter will invoke the __lt__ operator associated with the type of p1, i.e., the one defined in class MITPerson. This will lead to the exception

```
AttributeError: 'Person' object has no attribute 'idNum'
```

because the object to which p4 is bound does not have an attribute idNum.

8.2.1 Multiple Levels of Inheritance

Figure 8.4 adds another couple of levels of inheritance to the class hierarchy.

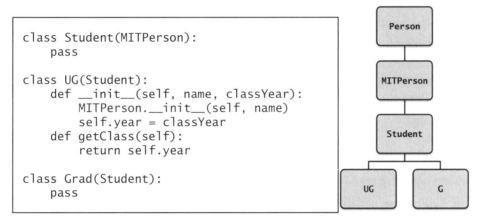

```
class Student(MITPerson):
    pass

class UG(Student):
    def __init__(self, name, classYear):
        MITPerson.__init__(self, name)
        self.year = classYear
    def getClass(self):
        return self.year

class Grad(Student):
    pass
```

Figure 8.4 Two kinds of students

Adding UG seems logical, because we want to associate a year of graduation (or perhaps anticipated graduation) with each undergraduate. But what is going on with the classes Student and Grad? By using the Python reserved word pass as the body, we indicate that the class has no attributes other than those inherited from its superclass. Why would one ever want to create a class with no new attributes?

By introducing the class Grad, we gain the ability to create two different kinds of students and use their types to distinguish one kind of object from another. For example, the code

```
p5 = Grad('Buzz Aldrin')
p6 = UG('Billy Beaver', 1984)
print p5, 'is a graduate student is', type(p5) == Grad
print p5, 'is an undergraduate student is', type(p5) == UG
```

will print

```
Buzz Aldrin is a graduate student is True
Buzz Aldrin is an undergraduate student is False
```

The utility of the intermediate type Student is a bit subtler. Consider going back to class MITPerson and adding the method

```
def isStudent(self):
    return isinstance(self, Student)
```

The function isinstance is built into Python. The first argument of isinstance can be any object, but the second argument must be an object of type type. The function returns True if and only if the first argument is an instance of the second argument. For example the value of isinstance([1,2], list) is True.

Returning to our example, the code

```
print p5, 'is a student is', p5.isStudent()
print p6, 'is a student is', p6.isStudent()
print p3, 'is a student is', p3.isStudent()
```

prints

```
Buzz Aldrin is a student is True
Billy Beaver is a student is True
Billy Bob Beaver is a student is False
```

Notice that `isinstance(p6, Student)` is quite different from
`type(p6) == Student`. The object to which p6 is bound is of type UG, not
student, but since UG is a subclass of Student, the object to which p6 is bound is
considered to be an instance of class Student (as well as an instance of
MITPerson and Person).

Since there are only two kinds of students, we could have implemented
isStudent as,

```
def isStudent(self):
    return type(self) == Grad or type(self) == UG
```

However, if a new type of student were introduced at some later point it would
be necessary to go back and edit the code implementing isStudent. By
introducing the intermediate class Student and using isinstance we avoid this
problem. For example, if we were to add

```
class TransferStudent(Student):

    def __init__(self, name, fromSchool):
        MITPerson.__init__(self, name)
        self.fromSchool = fromSchool

    def getOldSchool(self):
        return self.fromSchool
```

no change needs to be made to isStudent.

It is not unusual during the creation and later maintenance of a program to go
back and add new classes or new attributes to old classes. Good programmers
design their programs so as to minimize the amount of code that might need to
be changed when that is done.

8.2.2 The Substitution Principle

When subclassing is used to define a type hierarchy, the subclasses should be
thought of as extending the behavior of their superclasses. We do this by adding
new attributes or overriding attributes inherited from a superclass. For
example, TransferStudent extends Student by introducing a former school.

Sometimes, the subclass overrides methods from the superclass, but this must
be done with care. In particular, important behaviors of the supertype must be
supported by each of its subtypes. If client code works correctly using an
instance of the supertype, it should also work correctly when an instance of the
subtype is substituted for the instance of the supertype. For example, it should

be possible to write client code using the specification of Student and have it work correctly on a TransferStudent.[39]

Conversely, there is no reason to expect that code written to work for TransferStudent should work for arbitrary types of Student.

8.3 Encapsulation and Information Hiding

As long as we are dealing with students, it would be a shame not to make them suffer through taking classes and getting grades.

```python
class Grades(object):
    """A mapping from students to a list of grades"""
    def __init__(self):
        """Create empty grade book"""
        self.students = []
        self.grades = {}
        self.isSorted = True

    def addStudent(self, student):
        """Assumes: student is of type Student
           Add student to the grade book"""
        if student in self.students:
            raise ValueError('Duplicate student')
        self.students.append(student)
        self.grades[student.getIdNum()] = []
        self.isSorted = False

    def addGrade(self, student, grade):
        """Assumes: grade is a float
           Add grade to the list of grades for student"""
        try:
            self.grades[student.getIdNum()].append(grade)
        except:
            raise ValueError('Student not in mapping')

    def getGrades(self, student):
        """Return a list of grades for student"""
        try: #return copy of student's grades
            return self.grades[student.getIdNum()][:]
        except:
            raise ValueError('Student not in mapping')

    def getStudents(self):
        """Return a list of the students in the grade book"""
        if not self.isSorted:
            self.students.sort()
            self.isSorted = True
        return self.students[:] #return copy of list of students
```

Figure 8.5 Class Grades

---

[39] This **substitution principle** was first clearly enunciated by Barbara Liskov and Jeannette Wing in their 1994 paper, "A behavioral notion of subtyping."

Figure 8.5 contains a class that can be used to keep track of the grades of a
collection of students. Instances of class `Grades` are implemented using a list
and a dictionary. The list keeps track of the students in the class. The
dictionary maps a student's identification number to a list of grades.

Notice that `getGrades` returns a copy of the list of grades associated with a
student, and `getStudents` returns a copy of the list of students. The
computational cost of copying the lists could have been avoided by simply
returning the instance variables themselves. Doing so, however, is likely to lead
to problems. Consider the code

```
allStudents = course1.getStudents()
allStudents.extend(course2.getStudents())
```

If `getStudents` returned `self.students`, the second line of code would have the
(probably unexpected) side effect of changing the set of students in `course1`.

The instance variable `isSorted` is used to keep track of whether or not the list of
students has been sorted since the last time a student was added to it. This
allows the implementation of `getStudents` to avoid sorting an already sorted list.

Figure 8.6 contains a function that uses class `Grades` to produce a grade report
for some students taking 6.00, the MIT course for which this book was
developed.

```
def gradeReport(course):
    """Assumes course is of type Grades"""
    report = ''
    for s in course.getStudents():
        tot = 0.0
        numGrades = 0
        for g in course.getGrades(s):
            tot += g
            numGrades += 1
        try:
            average = tot/numGrades
            report = report + '\n'\
                     + str(s) + '\'s mean grade is ' + str(average)
        except ZeroDivisionError:
            report = report + '\n'\
                     + str(s) + ' has no grades'
    return report

ug1 = UG('Jane Doe', 2014)
ug2 = UG('John Doe', 2015)
ug3 = UG('David Henry', 2003)
g1 = Grad('Billy Buckner')
g2 = Grad('Bucky F. Dent')
sixHundred = Grades()
sixHundred.addStudent(ug1)
sixHundred.addStudent(ug2)
sixHundred.addStudent(g1)
sixHundred.addStudent(g2)
for s in sixHundred.getStudents():
    sixHundred.addGrade(s, 75)
sixHundred.addGrade(g1, 25)
sixHundred.addGrade(g2, 100)
sixHundred.addStudent(ug3)
print gradeReport(sixHundred)
```

Figure 8.6 Generating a grade report

When run, the code in the figure prints

```
Jane Doe's mean grade is 75.0
John Doe's mean grade is 75.0
David Henry has no grades
Billy Buckner's mean grade is 50.0
Bucky F. Dent's mean grade is 87.5
```

There are two important concepts at the heart of object-oriented programming. The first is the idea of **encapsulation**. By this we mean the bundling together of data attributes and the methods for operating on them. For example, if we write

```
Rafael = MITPerson()
```

we can use dot notation to access attributes such as Rafael's age and identification number.

The second important concept is **information hiding**. This is one of the keys to modularity. If those parts of the program that use a class (i.e., the clients of the class) rely only on the specifications of the methods in the class, a programmer implementing the class is free to change the implementation of the class (e.g., to improve efficiency) without worrying that the change will break code that uses the class.

Some programming languages (Java and C++, for example) provide mechanisms for enforcing information hiding. Programmers can make the data attributes of a class invisible to clients of the class, and thus require that the data be accessed only through the object's methods. So, for example, we could get the `idNum` associated with `Rafael` by executing `Rafael.getIdNum()` but not by writing `Rafael.idNum`.

Unfortunately, Python does not provide mechanisms for enforcing information hiding. There is no way for the implementer of a class to restrict access to the attributes of class instances. For example, a client of a `Person` can write the expression `Rafael.lastName` rather than `Rafael.getLastName()`.

Why is this unfortunate? Because the client code is relying upon something that is not part of the specification of `Person`, and is therefore subject to change. If the implementation of `Person` were changed, for example to extract the last name whenever it is requested rather than store it in an instance variable, then the client code would no longer work.

Not only does Python let programs read instance and class variables from outside the class definition, it also lets programs write these variables. So, for example, the code `Rafael.birthday = '8/21/50'` is perfectly legal. This would lead to a runtime type error, were `Rafael.getAge` invoked later in the computation. It is even possible to create instance variables from outside the class definition. For example, Python will not complain if the assignment statement `me.age = Rafael.getAge()` occurs outside the class definition.

While this weak static semantic checking is a flaw in Python, it is not a fatal flaw. A disciplined programmer can simply follow the sensible rule of not directly accessing data attributes from outside the class in which they are defined, as we do in this book.

8.3.1 Generators

A perceived risk of information hiding is that preventing client programs from directly accessing critical data structures leads to an unacceptable loss of efficiency. In the early days of data abstraction, many were concerned about the cost of introducing extraneous function/method calls. Modern compilation technology makes this concern moot. A more serious issue is that client programs will be forced to use inefficient algorithms.

Consider the implementation of `gradeReport` in Figure 8.6. The invocation of `course.getStudents` creates and returns a list of size n, where n is the number of students. This is probably not a problem for a grade book for a single class, but imagine keeping track of the grades of 1.7 million high school students taking the SAT's. Creating a new list of that size when the list already exists is a significant inefficiency. One solution is to abandon the abstraction and allow `gradeReport` to directly access the instance variable `course.students`, but that would violate information hiding. Fortunately, there is a better solution.

The code in Figure 8.7, replaces the getStudents function in class Grades with a function that uses a kind of statement we have not yet used: a **yield** statement.

```
def getStudents(self):
    """Return the students in the grade book one at a time"""
    if not self.isSorted:
        self.students.sort()
        self.isSorted = True
    for s in self.students:
        yield s
```

Figure 8.7 New version of getStudents

Any function definition containing a yield statement is treated in a special way. The presence of yield tells the Python system that the function is a **generator**. Generators are typically used in conjunction with for statements.[40]

At the start of the first iteration of a for loop, the interpreter starts executing the code in the body of the generator. It runs until the first time a yield statement is executed, at which point it returns the value of the expression in the yield statement. On the next iteration, the generator resumes execution immediately following the yield, with all local variables bound to the objects to which they were bound when the yield statement was executed, and again runs until a yield statement is executed. It continues to do this until it runs out of code to execute or executes a return statement, at which point the loop is exited.

The version of getStudents in Figure 8.7 allows programmers to use a for loop to iterate over the students in objects of type Grades in the same way they can use a for loop to iterate over elements of built-in types such as list. For example, the code

```
book = Grades()
book.addStudent(Grad('Julie'))
book.addStudent(Grad('Charlie'))
for s in book.getStudents():
    print s
```

prints

```
Julie
Charlie
```

Thus the loop in Figure 8.6 that starts with

```
for s in course.getStudents():
```

does not have to be altered to take advantage of the version of class Grades that contains the new implementation of getStudents. The same for loop can iterate over the values provided by getStudents regardless of whether getStudents returns a list of values or generates one value at a time. Generating one value at

---

[40] This explanation of generators is a bit simplistic. To fully understand generators, you need to understand the way built-in iterators are implemented in Python, which is not covered in this book.

a time will be more efficient, because a new list containing the students will not be created.

8.4 Mortgages, an Extended Example

A collapse in U.S. housing prices helped trigger a severe economic meltdown in the fall of 2008. One of the contributing factors was that many homeowners had taken on mortgages that ended up having unexpected consequences.[41]

In the beginning, mortgages were relatively simple beasts. One borrowed money from a bank and made a fixed-size payment each month for the life of the mortgage, which typically ranged from fifteen to thirty years. At the end of that period, the bank had been paid back the initial loan (the principal) plus interest, and the homeowner owned the house "free and clear."

Towards the end of the twentieth century, mortgages started getting a lot more complicated. People could get lower interest rates by paying "points" at the time they took on the mortgage. A point is a cash payment of 1% of the value of the loan. People could take mortgages that were "interest-only" for a period of time. That is to say, for some number of months at the start of the loan the borrower paid only the accrued interest and none of the principal. Other loans involved multiple rates. Typically the initial rate (called a "teaser rate") was low, and then it went up over time. Many of these loans were variable-rate—the rate to be paid after the initial period would vary depending upon some index intended to reflect the cost to the lender of borrowing on the wholesale credit market.[42]

In principle, giving consumers a variety of options is a good thing. However, unscrupulous loan purveyors were not always careful to fully explain the possible long-term implications of the various options, and some borrowers made choices that proved to have dire consequences.

Let's build a program that examines the costs of three kinds of loans:

- A fixed-rate mortgage with no points,

- A fixed-rate mortgage with points, and

- A mortgage with an initial teaser rate followed by a higher rate for the duration.

The point of this exercise is to provide some experience in the incremental development of a set of related classes, not to make you an expert on mortgages.

We will structure our code to include a `Mortgage` class, and subclasses corresponding to each of the three kinds of mortgages listed above.

---

[41] In this context, it is worth recalling the etymology of the word mortgage. *The American Heritage Dictionary of the English Language* traces the word back to the old French words for dead (*mort*) and pledge (*gage*). (This derivation also explains why the "t" in the middle of mortgage is silent.)

[42] The London Interbank Offered Rate (LIBOR) is probably the most commonly used index.

Figure 8.8 contains the **abstract class** Mortgage. This class contains methods that are shared by each of the subclasses, but it is not intended to be instantiated directly.

The function findPayment at the top of the figure computes the size of the fixed monthly payment needed to pay off the loan, including interest, by the end of its term. It does this using a well-known closed-form expression. This expression is not hard to derive, but it is a lot easier to just look it up and more likely to be correct than one derived on the spot.

When your code incorporates formulas you have looked up, make sure that:

- You have taken the formula from a reputable source. We looked at multiple reputable sources, all of which contained equivalent formulas.

- You fully understand the meaning of all the variables in the formula.

- You test your implementation against examples taken from reputable sources. After implementing this function, we tested it by comparing our results to the results supplied by a calculator available on the Web.

```
def findPayment(loan, r, m):
    """Assumes: loan and r are floats, m an int
       Returns the monthly payment for a mortgage of size
       loan at a monthly rate of r for m months"""
    return loan*((r*(1+r)**m)/((1+r)**m - 1))

class Mortgage(object):
    """Abstract class for building different kinds of mortgages"""
    def __init__(self, loan, annRate, months):
        """Create a new mortgage"""
        self.loan = loan
        self.rate = annRate/12.0
        self.months = months
        self.paid = [0.0]
        self.owed = [loan]
        self.payment = findPayment(loan, self.rate, months)
        self.legend = None #description of mortgage
    def makePayment(self):
        """Make a payment"""
        self.paid.append(self.payment)
        reduction = self.payment - self.owed[-1]*self.rate
        self.owed.append(self.owed[-1] - reduction)
    def getTotalPaid(self):
        """Return the total amount paid so far"""
        return sum(self.paid)
    def __str__(self):
        return self.legend
```

Figure 8.8 Mortgage base class

Looking at __init__, we see that all Mortgage instances will have instance variables corresponding to the initial loan amount, the monthly interest rate, the duration of the loan in months, a list of payments that have been made at the start of each month (the list starts with 0.0, since no payments have been made at the start of the first month), a list with the balance of the loan that is outstanding at the start of each month, the amount of money to be paid each month (initialized using the value returned by the function `findPayment`), and a description of the mortgage (which initially has a value of None). The `__init__` operation of each subclass of `Mortgage` is expected to start by calling `Mortgage.__init__`, and then to initialize `self.legend` to an appropriate description of that subclass.

The method `makePayment` is used to record mortgage payments. Part of each payment covers the amount of interest due on the outstanding loan balance, and the remainder of the payment is used to reduce the loan balance. That is why `makePayment` updates both `self.paid` and `self.owed`.

The method `getTotalPaid` uses the built-in Python function `sum`, which returns the sum of a sequence of numbers. If the sequence contains a non-number, an exception is raised.

Figure 8.9 contains classes implementing two types of mortgage. Each of these classes overrides `__init__` and inherits the other three methods from `Mortgage`.

```
class Fixed(Mortgage):
    def __init__(self, loan, r, months):
        Mortgage.__init__(self, loan, r, months)
        self.legend = 'Fixed, ' + str(r*100) + '%'

class FixedWithPts(Mortgage):
    def __init__(self, loan, r, months, pts):
        Mortgage.__init__(self, loan, r, months)
        self.pts = pts
        self.paid = [loan*(pts/100.0)]
        self.legend = 'Fixed, ' + str(r*100) + '%, '\
                        + str(pts) + ' points'
```

Figure 8.9 Fixed-rate mortgage classes

Figure 8.10 contains a third subclass of `Mortgage`. The class `TwoRate` treats the mortgage as the concatenation of two loans, each at a different interest rate. (Since `self.paid` is initialized with a `0.0`, it contains one more element than the number of payments that have been made. That's why `makePayment` compares `len(self.paid)` to `self.teaserMonths + 1`.).

```
class TwoRate(Mortgage):
    def __init__(self, loan, r, months, teaserRate, teaserMonths):
        Mortgage.__init__(self, loan, teaserRate, months)
        self.teaserMonths = teaserMonths
        self.teaserRate = teaserRate
        self.nextRate = r/12.0
        self.legend = str(teaserRate*100)\
                          + '% for ' + str(self.teaserMonths)\
                          + ' months, then ' + str(r*100) + '%'
    def makePayment(self):
        if len(self.paid) == self.teaserMonths + 1:
            self.rate = self.nextRate
            self.payment = findPayment(self.owed[-1], self.rate,
                                       self.months - self.teaserMonths)
        Mortgage.makePayment(self)
```

Figure 8.10 Mortgage with teaser rate

Figure 8.11 contains a function that computes and prints the total cost of each
kind of mortgage for a sample set of parameters. It begins by creating one
mortgage of each kind. It then makes a monthly payment on each for a given
number of years. Finally, it prints the total amount of the payments made for
each loan.

```
def compareMortgages(amt, years, fixedRate, pts, ptsRate,
                     varRate1, varRate2, varMonths):
    totMonths = years*12
    fixed1 = Fixed(amt, fixedRate, totMonths)
    fixed2 = FixedWithPts(amt, ptsRate, totMonths, pts)
    twoRate = TwoRate(amt, varRate2, totMonths, varRate1, varMonths)
    morts = [fixed1, fixed2, twoRate]
    for m in range(totMonths):
        for mort in morts:
            mort.makePayment()
    for m in morts:
        print m
        print ' Total payments = $' + str(int(m.getTotalPaid()))

compareMortgages(amt=200000, years=30, fixedRate=0.07,
                 pts = 3.25, ptsRate=0.05, varRate1=0.045,
                 varRate2=0.095, varMonths=48)
```

Figure 8.11 Evaluate mortgages

Notice that we used keyword rather than positional arguments in the invocation
of compareMortgages. We did this because compareMortgages has a large number
of formal parameters and using keyword arguments makes it easier to ensure
that we are supplying the intended actual values to each of the formals.

When the code in Figure 8.11 is run, it prints

```
Fixed, 7.0%
 Total payments = $479017
Fixed, 5.0%, 3.25 points
 Total payments = $393011
4.5% for 48 months, then 9.5%
 Total payments = $551444
```

At first glance, the results look pretty conclusive. The variable-rate loan is a bad idea (for the borrower, not the bank) and the fixed-rate loan with points costs the least. It's important to note, however, that total cost is not the only metric by which mortgages should be judged. For example, a borrower who expects to have a higher income in the future may be willing to pay more in the later years to lessen the burden of payments in the beginning.

This suggests that rather than looking at a single number, we should look at payments over time. This in turn suggests that our program should be producing plots designed to show how the mortgage behaves over time. We will do that in Section 11.2.

9 A SIMPLISTIC INTRODUCTION TO ALGORITHMIC COMPLEXITY

The most important thing to think about when designing and implementing a program is that it should produce results that can be relied upon. We want our bank balances to be calculated correctly. We want the fuel injectors in our automobiles to inject appropriate amounts of fuel. We would prefer that neither airplanes nor operating systems crash.

Sometimes performance is an important aspect of correctness. This is most obvious for programs that need to run in real time. A program that warns airplanes of potential obstructions needs to issue the warning before the obstructions are encountered. Performance can also affect the utility of many non-real-time programs. The number of transactions completed per minute is an important metric when evaluating the utility of database systems. Users care about the time required to start an application on their phone. Biologists care about how long their phylogenetic inference calculations take.

Writing efficient programs is not easy. The most straightforward solution is often not the most efficient. Computationally efficient algorithms often employ subtle tricks that can make them difficult to understand. Consequently, programmers often increase the **conceptual complexity** of a program in an effort to reduce its **computational complexity**. To do this in a sensible way, we need to understand how to go about estimating the computational complexity of a program. That is the topic of this chapter.

9.1 Thinking About Computational Complexity

How should one go about answering the question "How long will the following function take to run?"

```
def f(i):
    """Assumes i is an int and i >= 0"""
    answer = 1
    while i >= 1:
        answer *= i
        i -= 1
    return answer
```

We could run the program on some input and time it. But that wouldn't be particularly informative because the result would depend upon

1. the speed of the computer on which it is run,

2. the efficiency of the Python implementation on that machine, and

3. the value of the input.

We get around the first two issues by using a more abstract measure of time. Instead of measuring time in milliseconds, we measure time in terms of the number of basic steps executed by the program.

For simplicity, we will use a **random access machine** as our model of computation. In a random access machine, steps are executed sequentially, one at a time.[43] A **step** is an operation that takes a fixed amount of time, such as binding a variable to an object, making a comparison, executing an arithmetic operation, or accessing an object in memory.

Now that we have a more abstract way to think about the meaning of time, we turn to the question of dependence on the value of the input. We deal with that by moving away from expressing time complexity as a single number and instead relating it to the sizes of the inputs. This allows us to compare the efficiency of two algorithms by talking about how the running time of each grows with respect to the sizes of the inputs.

Of course, the actual running time of an algorithm depends not only upon the sizes of the inputs but also upon their values. Consider, for example, the linear search algorithm implemented by

```
def linearSearch(L, x):
    for e in L:
        if e == x:
            return True
    return False
```

Suppose that L is a million elements long and consider the call linearSearch(L, 3). If the first element in L is 3, linearSearch will return True almost immediately. On the other hand, if 3 is not in L, linearSearch will have to examine all one million elements before returning False.

In general, there are three broad cases to think about:

- The best-case running time is the running time of the algorithm when the inputs are as favorable as possible. I.e., the **best-case** running time is the minimum running time over all the possible inputs of a given size. For linearSearch, the best-case running time is independent of the size of L.

- Similarly, the **worst-case** running time is the maximum running time over all the possible inputs of a given size. For linearSearch, the worst-case running time is linear in the size of the list.

- By analogy with the definitions of the best-case and worst-case running time, the **average-case** (also called **expected-case**) running time is the average running time over all possible inputs of a given size. Alternatively, if one has some *a priori* information about the distribution of input values (e.g., that 90% of the time x is in L), one can take that into account.

People usually focus on the worst case. All engineers share a common article of faith, Murphy's Law: If something can go wrong, it will go wrong. The worst-case provides an **upper bound** on the running time. This is critical in situations where there is a time constraint on how long a computation can take. It is not

[43] A more accurate model for today's computers might be a parallel random access machine. However, that adds considerable complexity to the algorithmic analysis, and often doesn't make an important qualitative difference in the answer.

good enough to know that "most of the time" the air traffic control system warns of impending collisions before they occur.

Let's look at the worst-case running time of an iterative implementation of the factorial function

```
def fact(n):
    """Assumes n is a natural number
        Returns n!"""
    answer = 1
    while n > 1:
        answer *= n
        n -= 1
    return answer
```

The number of steps required to run this program is something like 2 (1 for the initial assignment statement and one for the `return`) + 5n (counting 1 step for the test in the `while`, 2 steps for the first assignment statement in the `while` loop and 2 steps for the second assignment statement in the loop). So, for example, if n is 1000, the function will execute roughly 5002 steps.

It should be immediately obvious that as n gets large, worrying about the difference between 5n and 5n+2 is kind of silly. For this reason, we typically ignore additive constants when reasoning about running time. Multiplicative constants are more problematical. Should we care whether the computation takes 1000 steps or 5000 steps? Multiplicative factors can be important. Whether a search engine takes a half second or 2.5 seconds to service a query can be the difference between whether people use that search engine or go to a competitor.

On the other hand, when one is comparing two different algorithms, it is often the case that even multiplicative constants are irrelevant. Recall that in Chapter 3 we looked at two algorithms, exhaustive enumeration and bisection search, for finding an approximation to the square root of a floating point number. Functions based on each of these algorithms are shown in Figure 9.1 and Figure 9.2.

```
def squareRootExhaustive(x, epsilon):
    """Assumes x and epsilon are positive floats & epsilon < 1
        Returns a y such that y*y is within epsilon of x"""
    step = epsilon**2
    ans = 0.0
    while abs(ans**2 - x) >= epsilon and ans*ans <= x:
        ans += step
    if ans*ans > x:
        raise ValueError
    return ans
```

Figure 9.1 Using exhaustive enumeration to approximate square root

```
def squareRootBi(x, epsilon):
    """Assumes x and epsilon are positive floats & epsilon < 1
       Returns a y such that y*y is within epsilon of x"""
    low = 0.0
    high = max(1.0, x)
    ans = (high + low)/2.0
    while abs(ans**2 - x) >= epsilon:
        if ans**2 < x:
            low = ans
        else:
            high = ans
        ans = (high + low)/2.0
    return ans
```

Figure 9.2 Using bisection search to approximate square root

We saw that exhaustive enumeration was so slow as to be impractical for many
combinations of x and epsilon. For example, evaluating
squareRootExhaustive(100, 0.0001) requires roughly one billion iterations of
the loop. In contrast, evaluating squareRootBi(100, 0.0001) takes roughly
twenty iterations of a slightly more complex while loop. When the difference in
the number of iterations is this large, it doesn't really matter how many
instructions are in the loop. I.e., the multiplicative constants are irrelevant.

9.2 Asymptotic Notation

We use something called **asymptotic notation** to provide a formal way to talk
about the relationship between the running time of an algorithm and the size of
its inputs. The underlying motivation is that almost any algorithm is sufficiently
efficient when run on small inputs. What we typically need to worry about is the
efficiency of the algorithm when run on very large inputs. As a proxy for "very
large," asymptotic notation describes the complexity of an algorithm as the size
of its inputs approaches infinity.

Consider, for example, the code

```
def f(x):
    """Assume x is an int > 0"""
    ans = 0
    #Loop that takes constant time
    for i in range(1000):
        ans += 1
    print 'Number of additions so far', ans
    #Loop that takes time x
    for i in range(x):
        ans += 1
    print 'Number of additions so far', ans
    #Nested loops take time x**2
    for i in range(x):
        for j in range(x):
            ans += 1
            ans += 1
    print 'Number of additions so far', ans
    return ans
```

If one assumes that each line of code takes one unit of time to execute, the running time of this function can be described as $1000 + x + 2x^2$. The constant 1000 corresponds to the number of times the first loop is executed. The term x corresponds to the number of times the second loop is executed. Finally, the term $2x^2$ corresponds to the time spent executing the two statements in the nested for loop. Consequently, the call f(10) will print

```
Number of additions so far 1000
Number of additions so far 1010
Number of additions so far 1210
```

For small values of x the constant term dominates. If x is 10, 1000 of the 1210 steps are accounted for by the first loop. On the other hand, if x is 1000, each of the first two loops accounts for only 0.05% of the steps. When x is 1,000,000, the first loop takes about 0.00000005% of the total time and the second loop about 0.00005%. A full 2,000,000,000,000 of the 2,000,001,001,000 steps are in the body of the inner for loop.

Clearly, we can get a meaningful notion of how long this code will take to run on very large inputs by considering only the inner loop, i.e., the quadratic component. Should we care about the fact that this loop takes $2x^2$ steps rather than x^2 steps? If your computer executes roughly 100 million steps per second, evaluating f will take about 5.5 hours. If we could reduce the complexity to x^2 steps, it would take about 2.25 hours. In either case, the moral is the same: we should probably look for a more efficient algorithm.

This kind of analysis leads us to use the following rules of thumb in describing the asymptotic complexity of an algorithm:

- If the running time is the sum of multiple terms, keep the one with the largest growth rate, and drop the others.

- If the remaining term is a product, drop any constants.

The most commonly used asymptotic notation is called "**Big O**" notation.[44] Big O notation is used to give an **upper bound** on the asymptotic growth (often called the **order of growth**) of a function. For example, the formula $f(x) \in O(x^2)$ means that the function f grows no faster than the quadratic polynomial x^2, in an asymptotic sense.

We, like many computer scientists, will often abuse Big O notation by making statements like, "the complexity of f(x) is $O(x^2)$." By this we mean that in the worst case f will take $O(x^2)$ steps to run. The difference between a function being "in $O(x^2)$" and "being $O(x^2)$" is subtle but important. Saying that $f(x) \in O(x^2)$ does not preclude the worst-case running time of f from being considerably less that $O(x^2)$.

---

[44] The phrase "Big O" was introduced in this context by the computer scientist Donald Knuth in the 1970s. He chose the Greek letter Omicron because number theorists had used that letter since the late 19th century to denote a related concept.

When we say that f(x) is $O(x^2)$, we are implying that x^2 is both an upper and a **lower bound** on the asymptotic worst-case running time. This is called a **tight bound**.[45]

9.3 Some Important Complexity Classes

Some of the most common instances of Big O are listed below. In each case, *n* is a measure of the size of the inputs to the function.

- O(1) denotes **constant** running time.

- O(log n) denotes **logarithmic** running time.

- O(n) denotes **linear** running time.

- O(n log n) denotes **log-linear** running time.

- $O(n^k)$ denotes **polynomial** running time. Notice that *k* is a constant.

- $O(c^n)$ denotes **exponential** running time. Here a constant is being raised to a power based on the size of the input.

9.3.1 Constant Complexity

This indicates that the asymptotic complexity is independent of the inputs. There are very few interesting programs in this class, but all programs have pieces (for example finding out the length of a Python list or multiplying two floating point numbers) that fit into this class. Constant running time does not imply that there are no loops or recursive calls in the code, but it does imply that the number of iterations or recursive calls is independent of the size of the inputs.

9.3.2 Logarithmic Complexity

Such functions have a complexity that grows as the log of at least one of the inputs. Binary search, for example, is logarithmic in the length of the list being searched. (We will look at binary search and analyze its complexity in the next chapter.) By the way, we don't care about the base of the log, since the difference between using one base and another is merely a constant multiplicative factor. For example, $O(\log_2(x)) = O(\log_2(10)*\log_{10}(x))$. There are lots of interesting functions with logarithmic complexity. Consider

---

[45] The more pedantic members of the computer science community use Big Theta, Θ, rather than Big O for this.

```
def intToStr(i):
    """Assumes i is a nonnegative int
       Returns a decimal string representation of i"""
    digits = '0123456789'
    if i == 0:
        return '0'
    result = ''
    while i > 0:
        result = digits[i%10] + result
        i = i//10
    return result
```

Since there are no function or method calls in this code, we know that we only have to look at the loops to determine the complexity class. There is only one loop, so the only thing that we need to do is characterize the number of iterations. That boils down to the number of times one can divide i by 10. So, the complexity of intToStr is O(log(i)).

What about the complexity of

```
def addDigits(n):
    """"Assumes n is a nonnegative int
       Returns the sum of the digits in n"""
    stringRep = intToStr(n)
    val = 0
    for c in stringRep:
        val += int(c)
    return val
```

The complexity of converting n to a string is O(log(n)) and intToStr returns a string of length O(log(n)). The for loop will be executed O(len(stringRep)) times, i.e., O(log(n)) times. Putting it all together, and assuming that a character representing a digit can be converted to an integer in constant time, the program will run in time proportional to O(log(n)) + O(log(n)), which makes it O(log(n)).

9.3.3 Linear Complexity

Many algorithms that deal with lists or other kinds of sequences are linear because they touch each element of the sequence a constant (greater than 0) number of times. Consider, for example,

```
def addDigits(s):
    """Assumes s is a str each character of which is a
           decimal digit.
       Returns an int that is the sum of the digits in s"""
    val = 0
    for c in s:
        val += int(c)
    return val
```

This function is linear in the length of s, i.e., O(len(s))—again assuming that a character representing a digit can be converted to an integer in constant time.

Of course, a program does not need to have a loop to have linear complexity.

Consider

```
def factorial(x):
    """Assumes that x is a positive int
        Returns x!"""
    if x == 1:
        return 1
    else:
        return x*factorial(x-1)
```

There are no loops in this code, so in order to analyze the complexity we need to figure out how many recursive calls get made. The series of calls is simply factorial(x), factorial(x-1), factorial(x-2), ... , factorial(1). The length of this series, and thus the complexity of the function, is O(x).

Thus far in this chapter we have looked only at the time complexity of our code. This is fine for algorithms that use a constant amount of space, but this implementation of factorial does not have that property. As we discussed in Chapter 4, each recursive call of factorial causes a new stack frame to be allocated, and that frame continues to occupy memory until the call returns. At the maximum depth of recursion, this code will have allocated x stack frames, so the space complexity is O(x).

The impact of space complexity is harder to appreciate than the impact of time complexity. Whether a program takes one minute or two minutes to complete is quite visible to its user, but whether it uses one megabyte or two megabytes of memory is largely invisible to users. This is why people typically give more attention to time complexity than to space complexity. The exception occurs when a program needs more space than is available in the main memory of the machine on which it is run.

9.3.4 Log-Linear Complexity

This is slightly more complicated than the complexity classes we have looked at thus far. It involves the product of two terms, each of which depends upon the size of the inputs. It is an important class, because many practical algorithms are log-linear. The most commonly used log-linear algorithm is probably merge sort, which is O(n log(n)), where n is the length of the list being sorted. We will look at that algorithm and analyze its complexity in the next chapter.

9.3.5 Polynomial Complexity

The most commonly used polynomial algorithms are **quadratic**, i.e., their complexity grows as the square of the size of their input. Consider, for example, the function in Figure 9.3, which implements a subset test.

```
def isSubset(L1, L2):
    """Assumes L1 and L2 are lists.
       Returns True if each element in L1 is also in L2
       and False otherwise."""
    for e1 in L1:
        matched = False
        for e2 in L2:
            if e1 == e2:
                matched = True
                break
        if not matched:
            return False
    return True
```

Figure 9.3 Implementation of subset test

Each time the inner loop is reached it is executed O(len(L2)) times. The function will execute the outer loop O(len(L1)) times, so the inner loop will be reached O(len(L1)) times. Therefore, the complexity of isSubset is O(len(L1)*len(L2)).

Now consider the function intersect in Figure 9.4.

```
def intersect(L1, L2):
    """Assumes: L1 and L2 are lists
       Returns a list that is the intersection of L1 and L2"""
    #Build a list containing common elements
    tmp = []
    for e1 in L1:
        for e2 in L2:
            if e1 == e2:
                tmp.append(e1)
    #Build a list without duplicates
    result = []
    for e in tmp:
        if e not in result:
            result.append(e)
    return result
```

Figure 9.4 Implementation of list intersection

The running time for the part building the list that might contain duplicates is clearly O(len(L1)*len(L2)). At first glance, it appears that the part of the code that builds the duplicate-free list is linear in the length of tmp, but it is not. The test e not in result potentially involves looking at each element in result, and is therefore O(len(result)); consequently the second part of the implementation is O(len(tmp)*len(result)). Since the lengths of result and tmp are bounded by the length of the smaller of L1 and L2, and since we ignore additive terms, the complexity of intersect is O(len(L1)*len(L2)).

9.3.6 Exponential Complexity

As we will see later in this book, many important problems are inherently exponential, i.e., solving them completely can require time that is exponential in the size of the input. This is unfortunate, since it rarely pays to write a program that has a reasonably high probability of taking exponential time to run.

Consider, for example, the code in Figure 9.5.

```
def getBinaryRep(n, numDigits):
    """Assumes n and numDigits are non-negative ints
       Returns a numDigits str that is a binary
       representation of n"""
    result = ''
    while n > 0:
        result = str(n%2) + result
        n = n//2
    if len(result) > numDigits:
        raise ValueError('not enough digits')
    for i in range(numDigits - len(result)):
        result = '0' + result
    return result

def genPowerset(L):
    """Assumes L is a list
       Returns a list of lists that contains all possible
       combinations of the elements of L.  E.g., if
       L is [1, 2] it will return a list with elements
       [], [1], [2], and [1,2]."""
    powerset = []
    for i in range(0, 2**len(L)):
        binStr = getBinaryRep(i, len(L))
        subset = []
        for j in range(len(L)):
            if binStr[j] == '1':
                subset.append(L[j])
        powerset.append(subset)
    return powerset
```

Figure 9.5 Generating the power set

The function genPowerset(L) returns a list a list of lists that contains all possible combinations of the elements of L. For example, if L is ['a', 'b'], the powerset of L will be a list containing the lists [], ['b'], ['a'], and ['a', 'b'].

The algorithm is a bit subtle. Consider a list of n elements. We can represent any combination of elements by a string of n 0's and 1's, where a 1 represents the presence of an element and a 0 its absence. The combination containing no items would be represented by a string of all 0's, the combination containing all of the items would be represented by a string of all 1's, the combination containing only the first and last elements would be represented by 100...001, etc. Therefore generating all sublists of a list L of length n can be done as follows:

1. Generate all n-bit binary numbers. These are the numbers from 0 to 2^n.

2. For each of these $2^n + 1$ binary numbers, b, generate a list by selecting those elements of L that have an index corresponding to a 1 in b. For example, if L is ['a', 'b'] and b is 01, generate the list ['b'].

Try running genPowerset on a list containing the first ten letters of the alphabet. It will finish quite quickly and produce a list with 1024 elements. Next, try running genPowerset on the first twenty letters of the alphabet. It will take more than a bit of time to run, and return a list with about a million elements. If you try running genPowerset on all twenty-six letters, you will probably get tired of waiting for it to complete, unless your computer runs out of memory trying to build a list with tens of millions of elements. Don't even think about trying to run `genPowerset` on a list containing all uppercase and lowercase letters. Step 1 of the algorithm generates $O(2^{\text{len}(L)})$ binary numbers, so the algorithm is exponential in `len(L)`.

Does this mean that we cannot use computation to tackle exponentially hard problems? Absolutely not. It means that we have to find algorithms that provide approximate solutions to these problems or that find perfect solutions on some instances of the problem. But that is a subject for later chapters.

9.3.7 Comparisons of Complexity Classes

The following plots are intended to convey an impression of the implications of an algorithm being in one or another of these complexity classes.

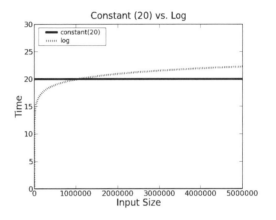

The plot on the right compares the growth of a constant-time algorithm to that of a logarithmic algorithm. Note that the size of the input has to reach about a million for the two of them to cross, even for the very small constant of twenty. When the size of the input is five million, the time required by a logarithmic algorithm is still quite small. The moral is that logarithmic algorithms are almost as good as constant-time ones.

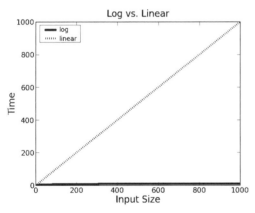

The plot on the left illustrates the dramatic difference between logarithmic algorithms and linear algorithms. Notice that the y-axis only goes as high as 1000. While we needed to look at large inputs to appreciate the difference between constant-time and logarithmic-time algorithms, the difference between logarithmic-time and linear-time algorithms is apparent even on small inputs. The dramatic difference in the relative performance of logarithmic and linear algorithms does not mean that linear algorithms are bad. In fact, most of the time a linear algorithm is acceptably efficient.

The plot below and on the left shows that there is a significant difference between O(n) and O(n log(n)). Given how slowly log(n) grows, this may seem a bit surprising, but keep in mind that it is a multiplicative factor. Also keep in mind that in most practical situations, O(n log(n)) is fast enough to be useful.

On the other hand, as the plot below and on the right suggests, there are many situations in which a quadratic rate of growth is prohibitive. The quadratic curve is rising so quickly that it is hard to see that the log-linear curve is even on the plot.

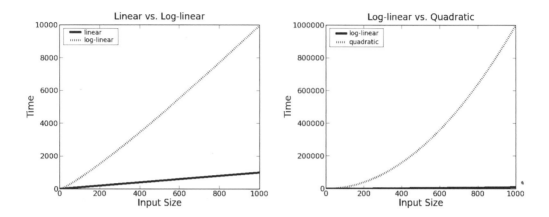

The final two plots are about exponential complexity.

In the plot on the left, the numbers to the left of the y-axis run from 0.0 to 1.2. However, the notation x1e301 on the top left means that each tick on the y-axis should be multiplied by 10^{301}. So, the plotted y-values range from 0 to roughly $1.1 \cdot 10^{301}$. It looks, however, almost as if there are no curves in the plot on the left. That's because an exponential function grows so quickly that relative to the y value of the highest point (which determines the scale of the y-axis), the y values of earlier points on the exponential curve (and all points on the quadratic curve) are almost indistinguishable from 0.

The plot on the right addresses this issue by using a logarithmic scale on the y-axis. One can readily see that exponential algorithms are impractical for all but the smallest of inputs.

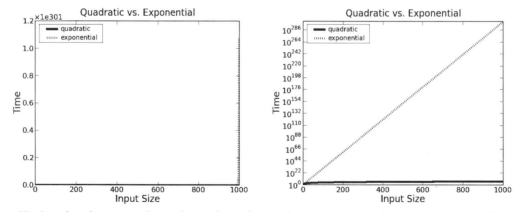

Notice, by the way, that when plotted on a logarithmic scale, an exponential curve appears as a straight line. We will have more to say about this in later chapters.

10 SOME SIMPLE ALGORITHMS AND DATA STRUCTURES

Though we expend a fair number of pages in this book talking about efficiency, the goal is not to make you expert in designing efficient programs. There are many long books (and even some good long books) devoted exclusively to that topic.[46] In Chapter 9, we introduced some of the basic concepts underlying complexity analysis. In this chapter we use those concepts to look at the complexity of a few classic algorithms. The goal of this chapter is to help you develop some general intuitions about how to approach questions of efficiency. By the time you get through this chapter you should understand why some programs complete in the blink of an eye, why some need to run overnight, and why some wouldn't complete in your lifetime.

The first algorithms we looked at in this book were based on brute-force exhaustive enumeration. We argued that modern computers are so fast that it is often the case that employing clever algorithms is a waste of time. Program something that is simple and obviously correct, and let it rip.

We then looked at some problems (e.g., finding an approximation to the roots of a polynomial) where the search space was too large to make brute force practical. This led us to consider more efficient algorithms such as bisection search and Newton-Raphson. The major point was that the key to efficiency is a good algorithm, not clever coding tricks.

In the sciences (physical, life, and social), programmers often start by quickly coding up a simple algorithm to test the plausibility of a hypothesis about a data set, and then run it on a small amount of data. If this yields encouraging results, the hard work of producing an implementation that can be run (perhaps over and over again) on large data sets begins. Such implementations need to be based on efficient algorithms.

Efficient algorithms are hard to invent. Successful professional computer scientists might invent maybe one algorithm during their whole career—if they are lucky. Most of us never invent a novel algorithm. What we do instead is learn to reduce the most complex aspects of the problems with which we are faced to previously solved problems. More specifically, we

- Develop an understanding of the inherent complexity of the problem with which we are faced,

- Think about how to break that problem up into subproblems, and

- Relate those subproblems to other problems for which efficient algorithms already exist.

---

[46] *Introduction to Algorithms*, by Cormen, Leiserson, Rivest, and Stein, is an excellent source for those of you not intimidated by a fair amount of mathematics.

This chapter contains a few examples intended to give you some intuition about algorithm design. Many other algorithms appear elsewhere in the book.

Keep in mind that the most efficient algorithm is not always the algorithm of choice. A program that does everything in the most efficient possible way is often needlessly difficult to understand. It is often a good strategy to start by solving the problem at hand in the most straightforward manner possible, instrument it to find any computational bottlenecks, and then look for ways to improve the computational complexity of those parts of the program contributing to the bottlenecks.

10.1 Search Algorithms

A **search algorithm** is a method for finding an item or group of items with specific properties within a collection of items. We refer to the collection of items as a **search space**. The search space might be something concrete, such as a set of electronic medical records, or something abstract, such as the set of all integers. A large number of problems that occur in practice can be formulated as search problems.

Many of the algorithms presented earlier in this book can be viewed as search algorithms. In Chapter 3, we formulated finding an approximation to the roots of a polynomial as a search problem, and looked at three algorithms—exhaustive enumeration, bisection search, and Newton-Raphson—for searching the space of possible answers.

In this section, we will examine two algorithms for searching a list. Each meets the specification

```
def search(L, e):
    """Assumes L is a list.
       Returns True if e is in L and False otherwise"""
```

The astute reader might wonder if this is not semantically equivalent to the Python expression e in L. The answer is yes, it is. And if one is unconcerned about the efficiency of discovering whether e is in L, one should simply write that expression.

10.1.1 Linear Search and Using Indirection to Access Elements

Python uses the following algorithm to determine if an element is in a list:

```
def search(L, e):
    for i in range(len(L)):
        if L[i] == e:
            return True
    return False
```

If the element e is not in the list the algorithm will perform O(len(L)) tests, i.e., the complexity is at best linear in the length of L. Why "at best" linear? It will be linear only if each operation inside the loop can be done in constant time. That raises the question of whether Python retrieves the ith element of a list in constant time. Since our model of computation assumes that fetching the contents of an address is a constant-time operation, the question becomes whether we can compute the address of the ith element of a list in constant time.

Let's start by considering the simple case where each element of the list is an integer. This implies that each element of the list is the same size, e.g., four units of memory (four eight-bit bytes[47]). In this case the address in memory of the ith element of the list is simply start + 4i, where start is the address of the start of the list. Therefore we can assume that Python could compute the address of the ith element of a list of integers in constant time.

Of course, we know that Python lists can contain objects of types other than int, and that the same list can contain objects of many different types and sizes. You might think that this would present a problem, but it does not.

In Python, a list is represented as a length (the number of objects in the list) and a sequence of fixed-size pointers[48] to objects. Figure 10.1 illustrates the use of these pointers. The shaded region represents a list containing four elements. The leftmost shaded box contains a pointer to an integer indicating the length of the list. Each of the other shaded boxes contains a pointer to an object in the list.

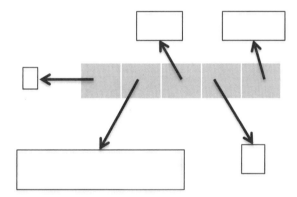

Figure 10.1 Implementing lists

If the length field is four units of memory, and each pointer (address) occupies four units of memory, the address of the ith element of the list is stored at the address start + 4 + 4i. Again, this address can be found in constant time, and then the value stored at that address can be used to access the ith element. This access too is a constant-time operation.

This example illustrates one of the most important implementation techniques used in computing: **indirection**.[49] Generally speaking, indirection involves accessing something by first accessing something else that contains a reference

---

[47] The number of bits used to store an integer, often called the word size, is typically dictated by the hardware of the computer.

[48] Of size 32 bits in some implementations and 64 bits in others.

[49] My dictionary defines "indirection" as "lack of straightforwardness and openness: deceitfulness." In fact, the word generally had a pejorative implication until about 1950, when computer scientists realized that it was the solution to many problems.

to the thing initially sought. This is what happens each time we use a variable to refer to the object to which that variable is bound. When we use a variable to access a list and then a reference stored in that list to access another object, we are going through two levels of indirection.[50]

10.1.2 Binary Search and Exploiting Assumptions

Getting back to the problem of implementing search(L, e), is O(len(L)) the best we can do? Yes, if we know nothing about the relationship of the values of the elements in the list and the order in which they are stored. In the worst case, we have to look at each element in L to determine whether L contains e.

But suppose we know something about the order in which elements are stored, e.g., suppose we know that we have a list of integers stored in ascending order. We could change the implementation so that the search stops when it reaches a number larger than the number for which it is searching:

```
def search(L, e):
    """Assumes L is a list, the elements of which are in
          ascending order.
       Returns True if e is in L and False otherwise"""
    for i in range(len(L)):
        if L[i] == e:
            return True
        if L[i] > e:
            return False
    return False
```

This would improve the average running time. However, it would not change the worst-case complexity of the algorithm, since in the worst case each element of L is examined.

We can, however, get a considerable improvement in the worst-case complexity by using an algorithm, **binary search**, that is similar to the bisection search algorithm used in Chapter 3 to find an approximation to the square root of a floating point number. There we relied upon the fact that there is an intrinsic total ordering on floating point numbers. Here we rely on the assumption that the list is ordered.

The idea is simple:

1. Pick an index, i, that divides the list L roughly in half.
2. Ask if L[i] == e.
3. If not, ask whether L[i] is larger or smaller than e.
4. Depending upon the answer, search either the left or right half of L for e.

---

[50] It has often been said that "any problem in computing can be solved by adding another level of indirection." Following three levels of indirection, we attribute this observation to David J. Wheeler. The paper "Authentication in Distributed Systems: Theory and Practice," by Butler Lampson *et al.*, contains the observation. It also contains a footnote saying that "Roger Needham attributes this observation to David Wheeler of Cambridge University."

Given the structure of this algorithm, it is not surprising that the most straightforward implementation of binary search uses recursion, as shown in Figure 10.2.

```python
def search(L, e):
    """Assumes L is a list, the elements of which are in
         ascending order.
       Returns True if e is in L and False otherwise"""

    def bSearch(L, e, low, high):
        #Decrements high - low
        if high == low:
            return L[low] == e
        mid = (low + high)//2
        if L[mid] == e:
            return True
        elif L[mid] > e:
            if low == mid: #nothing left to search
                return False
            else:
                return bSearch(L, e, low, mid - 1)
        else:
            return bSearch(L, e, mid + 1, high)

    if len(L) == 0:
        return False
    else:
        return bSearch(L, e, 0, len(L) - 1)
```

Figure 10.2 Recursive binary search

The outer function in Figure 10.2, search(L, e), has the same arguments as the function specified above, but a slightly different specification. The specification says that the implementation may assume that L is sorted in ascending order. The burden of making sure that this assumption is satisfied lies with the caller of search. If the assumption is not satisfied, the implementation has no obligation to behave well. It could work, but it could also crash or return an incorrect answer. Should search be modified to check that the assumption is satisfied? This might eliminate a source of errors, but it would defeat the purpose of using binary search, since checking the assumption would itself take O(len(L)) time.

Functions such as search are often called **wrapper functions**. The function provides a nice interface for client code, but is essentially a pass-through that does no serious computation. Instead, it calls the helper function bSearch with appropriate arguments. This raises the question of why not eliminate search and have clients call bSearch directly? The reason is that the parameters low and high have nothing to do with the abstraction of searching a list for an element. They are implementation details that should be hidden from those writing programs that call search.

Let us now analyze the complexity of bSearch. We showed in the last section that list access takes constant time. Therefore, we can see that excluding the recursive call, each instance of bSearch is O(1). Therefore, the complexity of bSearch depends only upon the number of recursive calls.

If this were a book about algorithms, we would now dive into a careful analysis using something called a recurrence relation. But since it isn't, we will take a much less formal approach that starts with the question "How do we know that the program terminates?" Recall that in Chapter 3 we asked the same question about a `while` loop. We answered the question by providing a decrementing function for the loop. We do the same thing here. In this context, the decrementing function has the properties:

1. It maps the values to which the formal parameters are bound to a nonnegative integer.

2. When its value is 0, the recursion terminates.

3. For each recursive call, the value of the decrementing function is less than the value of the decrementing function on entry to the instance of the function making the call.

The decrementing function for `bSearch` is `high-low`. The `if` statement in `search` ensures that the value of this decrementing function is at least 0 the first time `bSearch` is called (decrementing function property 1).

When `bSearch` is entered, if `high-low` is exactly 0, the function makes no recursive call—simply returning the value `L[low] == e` (satisfying decrementing function property 2).

The function `bSearch` contains two recursive calls. One call uses arguments that cover all of the elements to the left of `mid`, and the other call uses arguments that cover all of the elements to the right of `mid`. In either case, the value of `high-low` is cut in half (satisfying decrementing function property 3).

We now understand why the recursion terminates. The next question is how many times can the value of `high-low` be cut in half before `high-low == 0`? Recall that $\log_y(x)$ is the number of times that y has to be multiplied by itself to reach x. Conversely, if x is divided by y $\log_y(x)$ times, the result is 1. This implies that `high-low` can be cut in half at most $\log_2($`high-low`$)$ times before it reaches 0.

Finally, we can answer the question, what is the algorithmic complexity of binary search? Since when `search` calls `bSearch` the value of `high-low` is equal to `len(L)-1`, the complexity of `search` is $O(\log(len(L)))$.[51]

Finger exercise: Why does the code use `mid+1` rather than `mid` in the second recursive call?

---

[51] Recall that when looking at orders of growth the base of the logarithm is irrelevant.

10.2 Sorting Algorithms

We have just seen that if we happen to know that a list is sorted, we can exploit that information to greatly reduce the time needed to search a list. Does this mean that when asked to search a list one should first sort it and then perform the search?

Let O(sortComplexity(L)) be the complexity of sorting a list. Since we know that we can always search a list in O(len(L)) time, the question of whether we should first sort and then search boils down to the question, is (sortComplexity(L) + log(len(L))) < len(L)? The answer, sadly, is no. One cannot sort a list without looking at each element in the list at least once, so it is not possible to sort a list in sub-linear time.

Does this mean that binary search is an intellectual curiosity of no practical import? Happily, no. Suppose that one expects to search the same list many times. It might well make sense to pay the overhead of sorting the list once, and then **amortize** the cost of the sort over many searches. If we expect to search the list k times, the relevant question becomes, is (sortComplexity(L) + k*log(len(L))) less than k*len(L)? As k becomes large, the time required to sort the list becomes increasingly irrelevant.

How big k needs to be depends upon how long it takes to sort a list. If, for example, sorting were exponential in the size of the list, k would have to be quite large.

Fortunately, sorting can be done rather efficiently. For example, the standard implementation of sorting in most Python implementations runs in roughly O(n*log(n)) time, where n is the length of the list. In practice, you will rarely need to implement your own sort function. In most cases, the right thing to do is to use either Python's built-in `sort` method (`L.sort()` sorts the list L) or its built-in function `sorted` (`sorted(L)` returns a list with same elements as L, but does not mutate L). We present sorting algorithms here primarily to provide some practice in thinking about algorithm design and complexity analysis.

We begin with a simple but inefficient algorithm, **selection sort**. Selection sort, Figure 10.3, works by maintaining the **loop invariant** that, given a partitioning of the list into a prefix (`L[0:i]`) and a suffix (`L[i+1:len(L)]`), the prefix is sorted and no element in the prefix is larger than the smallest element in the suffix.

We use induction to reason about loop invariants.

- Base case: At the start of the first iteration, the prefix is empty, i.e., the suffix is the entire list. The invariant is (trivially) true.

- Induction step: At each step of the algorithm, we move one element from the suffix to the prefix. We do this by appending a minimum element of the suffix to the end of the prefix. Because the invariant held before we moved the element, we know that after we append the element the prefix is still sorted. We also know that since we removed the smallest element in the suffix, no element in the prefix is larger than the smallest element in the suffix.

- When the loop is exited, the prefix includes the entire list, and the suffix is empty. Therefore, the entire list is now sorted in ascending order.

```
def selSort(L):
    """Assumes that L is a list of elements that can be
        compared using >.
      Sorts L in ascending order"""
    suffixStart = 0
    while suffixStart != len(L):
        #look at each element in suffix
        for i in range(suffixStart, len(L)):
            if L[i] < L[suffixStart]:
                #swap position of elements
                L[suffixStart], L[i] = L[i], L[suffixStart]
        suffixStart += 1
```

Figure 10.3 Selection sort

It's hard to imagine a simpler or more obviously correct sorting algorithm. Unfortunately, it is rather inefficient.[52] The complexity of the inner loop is $O(len(L))$. The complexity of the outer loop is also $O(len(L))$. So, the complexity of the entire function is $O(len(L)^2)$. I.e., it is quadratic in the length of L.

10.2.1 Merge Sort

Fortunately, we can do a lot better than quadratic time using a **divide-and-conquer algorithm**. The basic idea is to combine solutions of simpler instances of the original problem. In general, a divide-and-conquer algorithm is characterized by

1. A threshold input size, below which the problem is not subdivided,

2. The size and number of sub-instances into which an instance is split, and

3. The algorithm used to combine sub-solutions.

The threshold is sometimes called the **recursive base**. For item 2 it is usual to consider the ratio of initial problem size to sub-instance size. In most of the examples we've seen so far, the ratio was 2.

---

[52] But not the most inefficient of sorting algorithms, as suggested by a successful candidate for the U.S. Presidency. See http://www.youtube.com/watch?v=k4RRi_ntQc8.

Merge sort is a prototypical divide-and-conquer algorithm. It was invented in 1945, by John von Neumann, and is still widely used. Like many divide-and-conquer algorithms it is most easily described recursively.

1. If the list is of length 0 or 1, it is already sorted.

2. If the list has more than one element, split the list into two lists, and use merge sort to sort each of them.

3. Merge the results.

The key observation made by von Neumann is that two sorted lists can be efficiently merged into a single sorted list. The idea is to look at the first element of each list, and move the smaller of the two to the end of the result list. When one of the lists is empty, all that remains is to copy the remaining items from the other list. Consider, for example, merging the two lists [1,5,12,18,19,20] and [2,3,4,17]:

Left in list 1	Left in list 2	Result
[1,5,12,18,19,20]	[2,3,4,17]	[]
[5,12,18,19,20]	[2,3,4,17]	[1]
[5,12,18,19,20]	[3,4,17]	[1,2]
[5,12,18,19,20]	[4,17]	[1,2,3]
[5,12,18,19,20]	[17]	[1,2,3,4]
[12,18,19,20]	[17]	[1,2,3,4,5]
[18,19,20]	[17]	[1,2,3,4,5,12]
[18,19,20]	[]	[1,2,3,4,5,12,17]
[]	[]	[1,2,3,4,5,12,17,18,19,20]

What is the complexity of the merge process? It involves two constant-time operations, comparing the values of elements and copying elements from one list to another. The number of comparisons is O(len(L)), where L is the longer of the two lists. The number of copy operations is O(len(L1) + len(L2)), because each element gets copied exactly once. Therefore, merging two sorted lists is linear in the length of the lists.

Figure 10.4 contains an implementation of the merge sort algorithm. Notice that we have made the comparison operator a parameter of the mergeSort function. The parameter's default value is the lt operator defined in the standard Python module named operator. This module defines a set of functions corresponding to the built-in operators of Python (for example < for numbers). In Section 10.2.2, we will exploit this flexibility.

```
def merge(left, right, compare):
    """Assumes left and right are sorted lists and
          compare defines an ordering on the elements.
       Returns a new sorted (by compare) list containing the
          same elements as (left + right) would contain."""

    result = []
    i,j = 0, 0
    while i < len(left) and j < len(right):
        if compare(left[i], right[j]):
            result.append(left[i])
            i += 1
        else:
            result.append(right[j])
            j += 1
    while (i < len(left)):
        result.append(left[i])
        i += 1
    while (j < len(right)):
        result.append(right[j])
        j += 1
    return result

import operator

def mergeSort(L, compare = operator.lt):
    """Assumes L is a list, compare defines an ordering
          on elements of L
       Returns a new sorted list containing the same elements as L"""
    if len(L) < 2:
        return L[:]
    else:
        middle = len(L)//2
        left = mergeSort(L[:middle], compare)
        right = mergeSort(L[middle:], compare)
        return merge(left, right, compare)
```

Figure 10.4 Merge sort

Let's analyze the complexity of mergeSort. We already know that the time complexity of merge is O(len(L)). At each level of recursion the total number of elements to be merged is len(L). Therefore, the time complexity of mergeSort is O(len(L)) multiplied by the number of levels of recursion. Since mergeSort divides the list in half each time, we know that the number of levels of recursion is O(log(len(L)). Therefore, the time complexity of mergeSort is O(n*log(n)), where n is len(L).

This is a lot better than selection sort's $O(len(L)^2)$. For example, if L has 10,000 elements, $len(L)^2$ is a hundred million but $len(L)*log_2(len(L))$ is about 130,000.

This improvement in time complexity comes with a price. Selection sort is an example of an **in-place** sorting algorithm. Because it works by swapping the place of elements within the list, it uses only a constant amount of extra storage (one element in our implementation). In contrast, the merge sort algorithm involves making copies of the list. This means that its space complexity is O(len(L)). This can be an issue for large lists.[53]

10.2.2 Exploiting Functions as Parameters

Suppose we want to sort a list of names written as firstName lastName, e.g., the list ['Chris Terman', 'Tom Brady', 'Eric Grimson', 'Gisele Bundchen']. Figure 10.5 defines two ordering functions, and then uses these to sort a list in two different ways. Each function imports the standard Python module string, and uses the split function from that module. The two arguments to split are strings. The second argument specifies a separator (a blank space in the code in Figure 10.5) that is used to split the first argument into a sequence of substrings. The second argument is optional. If that argument is omitted the first string is split using arbitrary strings of whitespace characters (space, tab, newline, return, and formfeed).

```
def lastNameFirstName(name1, name2):
    import string
    name1 = string.split(name1, ' ')
    name2 = string.split(name2, ' ')
    if name1[1] != name2[1]:
        return name1[1] < name2[1]
    else: #last names the same, sort by first name
        return name1[0] < name2[0]

def firstNameLastName(name1, name2):
    import string
    name1 = string.split(name1, ' ')
    name2 = string.split(name2, ' ')
    if name1[0] != name2[0]:
        return name1[0] < name2[0]
    else: #first names the same, sort by last name
        return name1[1] < name2[1]

L = ['Chris Terman', 'Tom Brady', 'Eric Grimson', 'Gisele Bundchen']
newL = mergeSort(L, lastNameFirstName)
print 'Sorted by last name =', newL
newL = mergeSort(L, firstNameLastName)
print 'Sorted by first name =', newL
```

Figure 10.5 Sorting a list of names

---

[53] **Quicksort**, invented by C.A.R. Hoare in 1960, is conceptually similar to merge sort, but considerably more complex. It has the advantage of needing only log(n) additional space. Unlike merge sort, its running time depends upon the way the elements in the list to be sorted are ordered relative to each other. Though its worst-case running time is $O(n^2)$, its expected running time is only O(n*log(n)).

10.2.3 Sorting in Python

The sorting algorithm used in most Python implementations is called **timsort**.[54] The key idea is to take advantage of the fact that in a lot of data sets the data is already partially sorted. Timsort's worst-case performance is the same as merge sort's, but on average it performs considerably better.

As mentioned earlier, the Python method `list.sort` takes a list as its first argument and modifies that list. In contrast, the Python function `sorted` takes an iterable object (e.g., a list or a dictionary) as its first argument and returns a new sorted list. For example, the code

```
L = [3,5,2]
D = {'a':12, 'c':5, 'b':'dog'}
print sorted(L)
print L
L.sort()
print L
print sorted(D)
D.sort()
```

will print

```
[2, 3, 5]
[3, 5, 2]
[2, 3, 5]
['a', 'b', 'c']
Traceback (most recent call last):
  File "/current/mit/Teaching/600/book/10-
AlgorithmsChapter/algorithms.py", line 168, in <module>
    D.sort()
AttributeError: 'dict' object has no attribute 'sort'
```

Notice that when the `sorted` function is applied to a dictionary, it returns a sorted list of the keys of the dictionary. In contrast, when the `sort` method is applied to a dictionary, it causes an exception to be raised since there is no method `dict.sort`.

Both the `list.sort` method and the `sorted` function can have two additional parameters. The key parameter plays the same role as `compare` in our implementation of merge sort: it is used to supply the comparison function to be used. The `reverse` parameter specifies whether the list is to be sorted in ascending or descending order. For example, the code

```
L = [[1,2,3], (3,2,1,0), 'abc']
print sorted(L, key = len, reverse = True)
```

sorts the elements of L in reverse order of length and prints

```
[(3, 2, 1, 0), [1, 2, 3], 'abc']
```

---

[54] Timsort was invented by Tim Peters in 2002 because he was unhappy with the previous algorithm used in Python.

Both the `list.sort` method and the `sorted` function provide **stable sorts**. This means that if two elements are equal with respect to the comparison used in the sort, their relative ordering in the original list (or other iterable object) is preserved in the final list.

10.3 Hash Tables

If we put merge sort together with binary search, we have a nice way to search lists. We use merge sort to preprocess the list in $O(n*log(n))$ time, and then we use binary search to test whether elements are in the list in $O(log(n))$ time. If we search the list k times, the overall time complexity is $O(n*log(n) + k*log(n))$.

This is good, but we can still ask, is logarithmic the best that we can do for search when we are willing to do some preprocessing?

When we introduced the type `dict` in Chapter 5, we said that dictionaries use a technique called hashing to do the lookup in time that is nearly independent of the size of the dictionary. The basic idea behind a **hash table** is simple. We convert the key to an integer, and then use that integer to index into a list, which can be done in constant time. In principle, values of any immutable type can be easily converted to an integer. After all, we know that the internal representation of each object is a sequence of bits, and any sequence of bits can be viewed as representing an integer. For example, the internal representation of `'abc'` is the string of bits 0110000101100010011000011, which can be viewed as a representation of the decimal integer 6,382,179. Of course, if we want to use the internal representation of strings as indices into a list, the list is going to have to be pretty darn long.

What about situations where the keys are already integers? Imagine, for the moment, that we are implementing a dictionary all of whose keys are U.S. Social Security numbers.[55] If we represented the dictionary by a list with 10^9 elements and used Social Security numbers to index into the list, we could do lookups in constant time. Of course, if the dictionary contained entries for only ten thousand (10^4) people, this would waste quite a lot of space.

Which gets us to the subject of hash functions. A **hash function** maps a large space of inputs (e.g., all natural numbers) to a smaller space of outputs (e.g., the natural numbers between 0 and 5000). Hash functions can be used to convert a large space of keys to a smaller space of integer indices.

Since the space of possible outputs is smaller than the space of possible inputs, a hash function is a **many-to-one mapping**, i.e., multiple different inputs may be mapped to the same output. When two inputs are mapped to the same output, it is called a **collision**—a topic which we will to return shortly. A good hash function produces a **uniform distribution**, i.e., every output in the range is equally probable, which minimizes the probability of collisions.

---

[55] A United States Social Security number is a nine-digit integer.

Designing good hash functions is surprisingly challenging. The problem is that one wants the outputs to be uniformly distributed given the expected distribution of inputs. Suppose, for example, that one hashed surnames by performing some calculation on the first three letters. In the Netherlands, where roughly 5% of surnames begin with "van" and another 5% with "de," the distribution would be far from uniform.

Figure 10.6 uses a simple hash function (recall that i%j returns the remainder when the integer i is divided by the integer j) to implement a dictionary with integers as keys.

The basic idea is to represent an instance of class intDict by a list of **hash buckets**, where each bucket is a list of key/value pairs. By making each bucket a list, we handle collisions by storing all of the values that hash to the same bucket in the list.

The hash table works as follows: The instance variable buckets is initialized to a list of numBuckets empty lists. To store or look up an entry with key dictKey, we use the hash function % to convert dictKey into an integer, and use that integer to index into buckets to find the hash bucket associated with dictKey. We then search that bucket (which is a list) linearly to see if there is an entry with the key dictKey. If we are doing a lookup and there is an entry with the key, we simply return the value stored with that key. If there is no entry with that key, we return None. If a value is to be stored, then we either replace the value in the existing entry, if one was found, or append a new entry to the bucket if none was found.

There are many other ways to handle collisions, some considerably more efficient than using lists. But this is probably the simplest mechanism, and it works fine if the hash table is big enough and the hash function provides a good enough approximation to a uniform distribution.

Notice that the __str__ method produces a representation of a dictionary that is unrelated to the order in which elements were added to it, but is instead ordered by the values to which the keys happen to hash. This explains why we can't predict the order of the keys in an object of type dict.

```
class intDict(object):
    """A dictionary with integer keys"""

    def __init__(self, numBuckets):
        """Create an empty dictionary"""
        self.buckets = []
        self.numBuckets = numBuckets
        for i in range(numBuckets):
            self.buckets.append([])

    def addEntry(self, dictKey, dictVal):
        """Assumes dictKey an int.  Adds an entry."""
        hashBucket = self.buckets[dictKey%self.numBuckets]
        for i in range(len(hashBucket)):
            if hashBucket[i][0] == dictKey:
                hashBucket[i] = (dictKey, dictVal)
                return
        hashBucket.append((dictKey, dictVal))

    def getValue(self, dictKey):
        """Assumes dictKey an int.  Returns entry associated
           with the key dictKey"""
        hashBucket = self.buckets[dictKey%self.numBuckets]
        for e in hashBucket:
            if e[0] == dictKey:
                return e[1]
        return None

    def __str__(self):
        result = '{'
        for b in self.buckets:
            for e in b:
                result = result + str(e[0]) + ':' + str(e[1]) + ','
        return result[:-1] + '}' #result[:-1] omits the last comma
```

Figure 10.6 Implementing dictionaries using hashing

The following code first constructs an intDict with twenty entries. The values of the entries are the integers 0 to 19. The keys are chosen at random from integers in the range 0 to 10^5 - 1. (We discuss the random module in Chapter 12.) The code then goes on to print the intDict using the __str__ method defined in the class. Finally it prints the individual hash buckets by iterating over D.buckets. (This is a terrible violation of information hiding, but pedagogically useful.)

```
import random #a standard library module

D = intDict(29)
for i in range(20):
    #choose a random int between 0 and 10**5
    key = random.randint(0, 10**5)
    D.addEntry(key, i)
print 'The value of the intDict is:'
print D
print '\n', 'The buckets are:'
for hashBucket in D.buckets: #violates abstraction barrier
    print '   ', hashBucket
```

When we ran this code it printed[56]

```
The value of the intDict is:
{93467:5,78736:19,90718:4,529:16,12130:1,7173:7,68075:10,15851:0,
47027:14,45288:8,5819:17,83076:6,55236:13,19481:9,11854:12,29604:11,
45902:15,14408:18,24965:3,89377:2}

The buckets are:
   [(93467, 5)]
   [(78736, 19)]
   []
   []
   []
   []
   [(90718, 4)]
   [(529, 16)]
   [(12130, 1)]
   []
   [(7173, 7)]
   []
   [(68075, 10)]
   []
   []
   []
   []
   [(15851, 0)]
   [(47027, 14)]
   [(45288, 8), (5819, 17)]
   [(83076, 6), (55236, 13)]
   []
   [(19481, 9), (11854, 12)]
   []
   [(29604, 11), (45902, 15), (14408, 18)]
   [(24965, 3)]
   []
   []
   [(89377, 2)]
```

When we violate the abstraction barrier and peek at the representation of the
intDict, we see that many of the hash buckets are empty. Others contain one,
two, or three tuples—depending upon the number of collisions that occurred.

What is the complexity of getValue? If there were no collisions it would be O(1),
because each hash bucket would be of length 0 or 1. But, of course, there might
be collisions. If everything hashed to the same bucket, it would be O(n) where n
is the number of entries in the dictionary, because the code would perform a
linear search on that hash bucket. By making the hash table large enough, we
can reduce the number of collisions sufficiently to allow us to treat the
complexity as O(1). That is, we can trade space for time. But what is the
tradeoff? To answer this question, one needs to know a tiny bit of probability, so
we defer the answer to Chapter 12.

---

[56] Since the integers were chosen at random, you will probably get different results if you
run it.

11 PLOTTING AND MORE ABOUT CLASSES

Often text is the best way to communicate information, but sometimes there is a lot of truth to the Chinese proverb, 圖片的意義可以表達近萬字 ("A picture's meaning can express ten thousand words"). Yet most programs rely on textual output to communicate with their users. Why? Because in many programming languages presenting visual data is too hard. Fortunately, it is simple to do in Python.

11.1 Plotting Using PyLab

PyLab is a Python standard library module that provides many of the facilities of MATLAB, "a high-level technical computing language and interactive environment for algorithm development, data visualization, data analysis, and numeric computation."[57] Later in the book, we will look at some of the more advanced features of PyLab, but in this chapter we focus on some of its facilities for plotting data. A complete user's guide for PyLab is at the Web site matplotlib.sourceforge.net/users/index.html. There are also a number of Web sites that provide excellent tutorials. We will not try to provide a user's guide or a complete tutorial here. Instead, in this chapter we will merely provide a few example plots and explain the code that generated them. Other examples appear in later chapters.

Let's start with a simple example that uses `pylab.plot` to produce two plots. Executing

```
import pylab

pylab.figure(1) #create figure 1
pylab.plot([1,2,3,4], [1,7,3,5]) #draw on figure 1
pylab.show() #show figure on screen
```

will cause a window to appear on your computer monitor. Its exact appearance may depend on the operating system on your machine, but it will look similar to the following:

[57] http://www.mathworks.com/products/matlab/description1.html?s_cid=ML_b1008_desintro

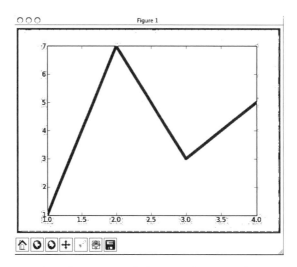

The bar at the top contains the name of the window, in this case "Figure 1."

The middle section of the window contains the plot generated by the invocation of `pylab.plot`. The two parameters of `pylab.plot` must be sequences of the same length. The first specifies the x-coordinates of the points to be plotted, and the second specifies the y-coordinates. Together, they provide a sequence of four <x, y> coordinate pairs, `[(1,1), (2,7), (3,3), (4,5)]`. These are plotted in order. As each point is plotted, a line is drawn connecting it to the previous point.

The final line of code, `pylab.show()`, causes the window to appear on the computer screen.[58] If that line were not present, the figure would still have been produced, but it would not have been displayed. This is not as silly as it at first sounds, since one might well choose to write a figure directly to a file, as we will do later, rather than display it on the screen.

The bar at the bottom of the window contains a number of push buttons. The rightmost button is used to write the plot to a file.[59] The next button to the left is used to adjust the appearance of the plot in the window. The next four buttons are used for panning and zooming. And the button on the left is used to restore the figure to its original appearance after you are done playing with pan and zoom.

It is possible to produce multiple figures and to write them to files. These files can have any name you like, but they will all have the file extension `.png`. The file extension `.png` indicates that the file is in the Portable Networks Graphics format. This is a public domain standard for representing images.

---

[58] In some operating systems, `pylab.show()` causes the process running Python to be suspended until the figure is closed (by clicking on the round red button at the upper left-hand corner of the window). This is unfortunate. The usual workaround is to ensure that `pylab.show()` is the last line of code to be executed.

[59] For those of you too young to know, the icon represents a "floppy disk." Floppy disks were first introduced by IBM in 1971. They were 8 inches in diameter and held all of 80,000 bytes. Unlike later floppy disks, they actually were floppy. The original IBM PC had a single 160Kbyte 5.5-inch floppy disk drive. For most of the 1970s and 1980s, floppy disks were the primary storage device for personal computers. The transition to rigid enclosures (as represented in the icon that launched this digression) started in the mid-1980s (with the Macintosh), which didn't stop people from continuing to call them floppy disks.

The code

```
pylab.figure(1) #create figure 1
pylab.plot([1,2,3,4], [1,2,3,4]) #draw on figure 1
pylab.figure(2) #create figure 2
pylab.plot([1,4,2,3], [5,6,7,8]) #draw on figure 2
pylab.savefig('Figure-Addie') #save figure 2
pylab.figure(1) #go back to working on figure 1
pylab.plot([5,6,10,3]) #draw again on figure 1
pylab.savefig('Figure-Jane') #save figure 1
```

produces and saves to files named `Figure-Jane.png` and `Figure-Addie.png` the two plots below.

Observe that the last call to `pylab.plot` is passed only one argument. This argument supplies the y values. The corresponding x values default to `range(len([5, 6, 10, 3]))`, which is why they range from 0 to 3 in this case.

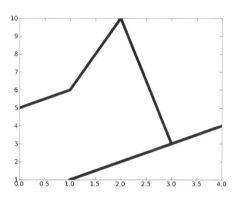
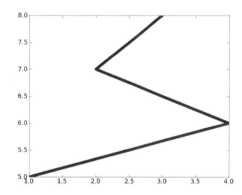

Contents of Figure-Jane.png   **Contents of Figure-Addie.png**

PyLab has a notion of "current figure." Executing `pylab.figure(x)` sets the current figure to the figure numbered x. Subsequently executed calls of plotting functions implicitly refer to that figure until another invocation of `pylab.figure` occurs. This explains why the figure written to the file `Figure-Addie.png` was the second figure created.

Let's look at another example. The code

```
principal = 10000 #initial investment
interestRate = 0.05
years = 20
values = []
for i in range(years + 1):
    values.append(principal)
    principal += principal*interestRate
pylab.plot(values)
```

produces the plot on the left below.

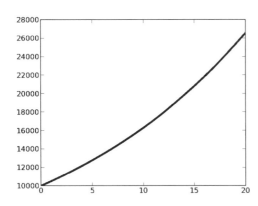
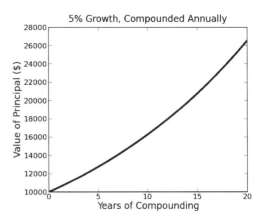

If we look at the code, we can deduce that this is a plot showing the growth of an initial investment of $10,000 at an annually compounded interest rate of 5%. However, this cannot be easily inferred by looking only at the plot itself. That's a bad thing. All plots should have informative titles, and all axes should be labeled.

If we add to the end of our the code the lines

```
pylab.title('5% Growth, Compounded Annually')
pylab.xlabel('Years of Compounding')
pylab.ylabel('Value of Principal ($)')
```

we get the plot above and on the right.

For every plotted curve, there is an optional argument that is a format string indicating the color and line type of the plot.[60] The letters and symbols of the format string are derived from those used in MATLAB, and are composed of a color indicator followed by a line-style indicator. The default format string is `'b-'`, which produces a solid blue line. To plot the above with red circles, one would replace the call `pylab.plot(values)` by `pylab.plot(values, 'ro')`, which

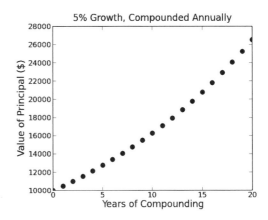

produces the plot on the right. For a complete list of color and line-style indicators, see

http://matplotlib.sourceforge.net/api/pyplot_api.html#matplotlib.pyplot.plot.

---

[60] In order to keep the price down, we chose to publish this book in black and white. That posed a dilemma: should we discuss how to use color in plots or not? We concluded that color is too important to ignore. If you want to see what the plots look like in color, run the code.

It's also possible to change the type size and line width used in plots. This can be done using keyword arguments in individual calls to functions, e.g., the code

```
principal = 10000 #initial investment
interestRate = 0.05
years = 20
values = []
for i in range(years + 1):
    values.append(principal)
    principal += principal*interestRate
pylab.plot(values, linewidth = 30)
pylab.title('5% Growth, Compounded Annually',
            fontsize = 'xx-large')
pylab.xlabel('Years of Compounding', fontsize = 'x-small')
pylab.ylabel('Value of Principal ($)')
```

produces the intentionally bizarre-looking plot

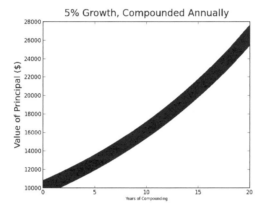

It is also possible to change the default values, which are known as "rc settings." (The name "rc" is derived from the `.rc` file extension used for runtime configuration files in Unix.) These values are stored in a dictionary-like variable that can be accessed via the name `pylab.rcParams`. So, for example, you can set the default line width to 6 points[61] by executing the code `pylab.rcParams['lines.linewidth'] = 6`.

---

[61] The point is a measure used in typography. It is equal to 1/72 of an inch, which is 0.3527mm.

The default values used in most of the examples in this book were set with the code

```
#set line width
pylab.rcParams['lines.linewidth'] = 4
#set font size for titles
pylab.rcParams['axes.titlesize'] = 20
#set font size for labels on axes
pylab.rcParams['axes.labelsize'] = 20
#set size of numbers on x-axis
pylab.rcParams['xtick.labelsize'] = 16
#set size of numbers on y-axis
pylab.rcParams['ytick.labelsize'] = 16
#set size of ticks on x-axis
pylab.rcParams['xtick.major.size'] = 7
#set size of ticks on y-axis
pylab.rcParams['ytick.major.size'] = 7
#set size of markers
pylab.rcParams['lines.markersize'] = 10
```

If you are viewing plots on a color display, you will have little reason to customize these settings. We customized the settings we used so that it would be easier to read the plots when we shrank them and converted them to black and white. For a complete discussion of how to customize settings, see http://matplotlib.sourceforge.net/users/customizing.html.

11.2 Plotting Mortgages, an Extended Example

In Chapter 8, we worked our way through a hierarchy of mortgages as way of illustrating the use of subclassing. We concluded that chapter by observing that "our program should be producing plots designed to show how the mortgage behaves over time." Figure 11.1 enhances class Mortgage by adding methods that make it convenient to produce such plots. (The function findPayment, which is used in Mortgage, is defined in Figure 8.8.)

The methods plotPayments and plotBalance are simple one-liners, but they do use a form of pylab.plot that we have not yet seen. When a figure contains multiple plots, it is useful to produce a key that identifies what each plot is intended to represent. In Figure 11.1, each invocation of pylab.plot uses the label keyword argument to associate a string with the plot produced by that invocation. (This and other keyword arguments must follow any format strings.) A key can then be added to the figure by calling the function pylab.legend, as shown in Figure 11.3.

The nontrivial methods in class Mortgage are plotTotPd and plotNet. The method plotTotPd simply plots the cumulative total of the payments made. The method plotNet plots an approximation to the total cost of the mortgage over time by plotting the cash expended minus the equity acquired by paying off part of the loan.[62]

---

[62] It is an approximation because it does not perform a net present value calculation to take into account the time value of cash.

```
class Mortgage(object):
    """Abstract class for building different kinds of mortgages"""

    def __init__(self, loan, annRate, months):
        """Create a new mortgage"""
        self.loan = loan
        self.rate = annRate/12.0
        self.months = months
        self.paid = [0.0]
        self.owed = [loan]
        self.payment = findPayment(loan, self.rate, months)
        self.legend = None #description of mortgage

    def makePayment(self):
        """Make a payment"""
        self.paid.append(self.payment)
        reduction = self.payment - self.owed[-1]*self.rate
        self.owed.append(self.owed[-1] - reduction)

    def getTotalPaid(self):
        """Return the total amount paid so far"""
        return sum(self.paid)

    def __str__(self):
        return self.legend

    def plotPayments(self, style):
        pylab.plot(self.paid[1:], style, label = self.legend)

    def plotBalance(self, style):
        pylab.plot(self.owed, style, label = self.legend)

    def plotTotPd(self, style):
        """Plot the cumulative total of the payments made"""
        totPd = [self.paid[0]]
        for i in range(1, len(self.paid)):
            totPd.append(totPd[-1] + self.paid[i])
        pylab.plot(totPd, style, label = self.legend)

    def plotNet(self, style):
        """Plot an approximation to the total cost of the mortgage
           over time by plotting the cash expended minus the equity
           acquired by paying off part of the loan"""
        totPd = [self.paid[0]]
        for i in range(1, len(self.paid)):
            totPd.append(totPd[-1] + self.paid[i])
        #Equity acquired through payments is amount of original loan
        #  paid to date, which is amount of loan minus what is still owed
        equityAcquired = pylab.array([self.loan]*len(self.owed))
        equityAcquired = equityAcquired - pylab.array(self.owed)
        net = pylab.array(totPd) - equityAcquired
        pylab.plot(net, style, label = self.legend)
```

Figure 11.1 Class Mortgage with plotting methods

The expression pylab.array(self.owed) in plotNet performs a type conversion. Thus far, we have been calling the plotting functions of PyLab with arguments of type list. Under the covers, PyLab has been converting these lists to a different

type, **array**, which PyLab inherits from NumPy.[63]   The invocation pylab.array
makes this explicit. There are a number of convenient ways to manipulate arrays
that are not readily available for lists. In particular, expressions can be formed
using arrays and arithmetic operators. Consider, for example, the code

```
a1 = pylab.array([1, 2, 4])
print 'a1 =', a1
a2 = a1*2
print 'a2 =', a2
print 'a1 + 3 =', a1 + 3
print '3 - a1 =', 3 - a1
print 'a1 - a2 =', a1 - a2
print 'a1*a2 =', a1*a2
```

The expression a1*2 multiplies each element of a1 by the constant 2. The
expression a1+3 adds the integer 3 to each element of a1. The expression a1-a2
subtracts each element of a2 from the corresponding element of a1 (if the arrays
had been of different length, an error would have occurred). The expression
a1*a2 multiplies each element of a1 by the corresponding element of a2. When the
above code is run it prints

```
a1 = [1 2 4]
a2 = [2 4 8]
a1 + 3 = [4 5 7]
3 - a1 = [ 2  1 -1]
a1 - a2 = [-1 -2 -4]
a1*a2 = [ 2  8 32]
```

There are a number of ways to create arrays in PyLab, but the most common way
is to first create a list, and then convert it.

Figure 11.2 repeats the three subclasses of Mortgage from Chapter 8. Each has a
distinct __init__ that overrides the __init__ in Mortgage. The subclass TwoRate
also overrides the makePayment method of Mortgage.

---

[63] NumPy is a Python module that provides tools for scientific computing. In addition to
providing multi-dimensional arrays it provides a variety of linear algebra tools.

```
class Fixed(Mortgage):
    def __init__(self, loan, r, months):
        Mortgage.__init__(self, loan, r, months)
        self.legend = 'Fixed, ' + str(r*100) + '%'

class FixedWithPts(Mortgage):
    def __init__(self, loan, r, months, pts):
        Mortgage.__init__(self, loan, r, months)
        self.pts = pts
        self.paid = [loan*(pts/100.0)]
        self.legend = 'Fixed, ' + str(r*100) + '%, '\
                    + str(pts) + ' points'

class TwoRate(Mortgage):
    def __init__(self, loan, r, months, teaserRate, teaserMonths):
        Mortgage.__init__(self, loan, teaserRate, months)
        self.teaserMonths = teaserMonths
        self.teaserRate = teaserRate
        self.nextRate = r/12.0
        self.legend = str(teaserRate*100)\
                    + '% for ' + str(self.teaserMonths)\
                    + ' months, then ' + str(r*100) + '%'

    def makePayment(self):
        if len(self.paid) == self.teaserMonths + 1:
            self.rate = self.nextRate
            self.payment = findPayment(self.owed[-1], self.rate,
                                        self.months - self.teaserMonths)
        Mortgage.makePayment(self)
```

Figure 11.2 Subclasses of `Mortgage`

Figure 11.3 contain functions that can be used to generate plots intended to provide insight about the different kinds of mortgages.

The function `plotMortgages` generates appropriate titles and axis labels for each plot, and then uses the methods in `MortgagePlots` to produce the actual plots. It uses calls to `pylab.figure` to ensure that the appropriate plots appear in a given figure. It uses the index i to select elements from the lists `morts` and `styles` in a way that ensures that different kinds of mortgages are represented in a consistent way across figures. For example, since the third element in `morts` is a variable-rate mortgage and the third element in `styles` is `'b:'`, the variable-rate mortgage is always plotted using a blue dotted line.

The function `compareMortgages` generates a list of different mortgages, and simulates making a series of payments on each, as it did in Chapter 8. It then calls `plotMortgages` to produce the plots.

```
def plotMortgages(morts, amt):
    styles = ['b-', 'b-.', 'b:']
    #Give names to figure numbers
    payments = 0
    cost = 1
    balance = 2
    netCost = 3
    pylab.figure(payments)
    pylab.title('Monthly Payments of Different $' + str(amt)
                + ' Mortgages')
    pylab.xlabel('Months')
    pylab.ylabel('Monthly Payments')
    pylab.figure(cost)
    pylab.title('Cash Outlay of Different $' + str(amt) + ' Mortgages')
    pylab.xlabel('Months')
    pylab.ylabel('Total Payments')
    pylab.figure(balance)
    pylab.title('Balance Remaining of $' + str(amt) + ' Mortgages')
    pylab.xlabel('Months')
    pylab.ylabel('Remaining Loan Balance of $')
    pylab.figure(netCost)
    pylab.title('Net Cost of $' + str(amt) + ' Mortgages')
    pylab.xlabel('Months')
    pylab.ylabel('Payments - Equity $')
    for i in range(len(morts)):
        pylab.figure(payments)
        morts[i].plotPayments(styles[i])
        pylab.figure(cost)
        morts[i].plotTotPd(styles[i])
        pylab.figure(balance)
        morts[i].plotBalance(styles[i])
        pylab.figure(netCost)
        morts[i].plotNet(styles[i])
    pylab.figure(payments)
    pylab.legend(loc = 'upper center')
    pylab.figure(cost)
    pylab.legend(loc = 'best')
    pylab.figure(balance)
    pylab.legend(loc = 'best')

def compareMortgages(amt, years, fixedRate, pts, ptsRate,
                     varRate1, varRate2, varMonths):
    totMonths = years*12
    fixed1 = Fixed(amt, fixedRate, totMonths)
    fixed2 = FixedWithPts(amt, ptsRate, totMonths, pts)
    twoRate = TwoRate(amt, varRate2, totMonths, varRate1, varMonths)
    morts = [fixed1, fixed2, twoRate]
    for m in range(totMonths):
        for mort in morts:
            mort.makePayment()
    plotMortgages(morts, amt)
```

Figure 11.3 Generate Mortgage Plots

The call

```
compareMortgages(amt=200000, years=30, fixedRate=0.07,
                 pts = 3.25, ptsRate=0.05,
                 varRate1=0.045, varRate2=0.095, varMonths=48)
```

produces plots that shed some light on the mortgages discussed in Chapter 8.

The first plot, which was produced by invocations of `plotPayments`, simply plots each payment of each mortgage against time. The box containing the key appears where it does because of the value supplied to the keyword argument `loc` used in the call to `pylab.legend`. When `loc` is bound to `'best'` the location is chosen automatically. This plot makes it clear how the monthly payments vary (or don't) over time,

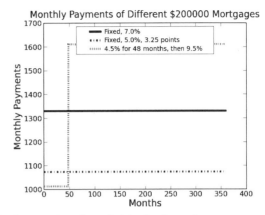

but doesn't shed much light on the relative costs of each kind of mortgage.

The next plot was produced by invocations of `plotTotPd`. It sheds some light on the cost of each kind of mortgage by plotting the cumulative costs that have been incurred at the start of each month. The entire plot is on the left, and an enlargement of the left part of the plot is on the right.

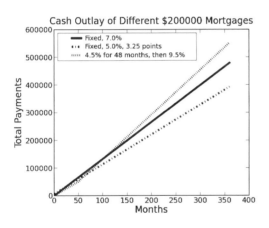
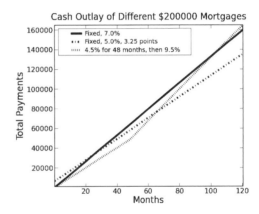

The next two plots show the remaining debt (on the left) and the total net cost of having the mortgage (on the right).

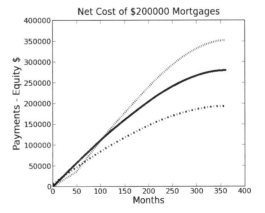

12 STOCHASTIC PROGRAMS, PROBABILITY, AND STATISTICS

There is something very comforting about Newtonian mechanics. You push down on one end of a lever, and the other end goes up. You throw a ball up in the air; it travels a parabolic path, and comes down. $\vec{F} = m\vec{a}$. In short, everything happens for a reason. The physical world is a completely predictable place—all future states of a physical system can be derived from knowledge about its current state.

For centuries, this was the prevailing scientific wisdom; then along came quantum mechanics and the Copenhagen Doctrine. The doctrine's proponents, led by Bohr and Heisenberg, argued that at its most fundamental level the behavior of the physical world cannot be predicted. One can make probabilistic statements of the form "x is highly likely to occur," but not statements of the form "x is certain to occur." Other distinguished physicists, most notably Einstein and Schrödinger, vehemently disagreed.

This debate roiled the worlds of physics, philosophy, and even religion. The heart of the debate was the validity of **causal nondeterminism**, i.e., the belief that not every event is caused by previous events. Einstein and Schrödinger found this view philosophically unacceptable, as exemplified by Einstein's often-repeated comment, "God does not play dice." What they could accept was **predictive nondeterminism**, i.e., the concept that our inability to make accurate measurements about the physical world makes it impossible to make precise predictions about future states. This distinction was nicely summed up by Einstein, who said, "The essentially statistical character of contemporary theory is solely to be ascribed to the fact that this theory operates with an incomplete description of physical systems."

The question of causal nondeterminism is still unsettled. However, whether the reason we cannot predict events is because they are truly unpredictable or is because we don't have enough information to predict them is of no practical importance. While the Bohr/Einstein debate was about how to understand the lowest levels of the physical world, the same issues arise at the macroscopic level. Perhaps the outcomes of horse races, spins of roulette wheels, and stock market investments are causally deterministic. However, there is ample evidence that it is perilous to treat them as predictably deterministic.[64]

This book is about using computation to solve problems. Thus far, we have focused our attention on problems that can be solved by a predictably deterministic computation. Such computations are highly useful, but clearly not sufficient to tackle some kinds of problems. Many aspects of the world in

---

[64] Of course this doesn't stop people from believing that they are, and losing a lot of money based on that belief.

which we live can be accurately modeled only as **stochastic**[65] **processes**. A process is stochastic if its next state depends upon both previous states and some random element.

12.1 Stochastic Programs

A program is **deterministic** if whenever it is run on the same input, it produces the same output. Notice that this is not the same as saying that the output is completely defined by the specification of the problem. Consider, for example, the specification of `squareRoot`:

```
def squareRoot(x, epsilon):
    """Assumes x and epsilon are of type float; x >= 0 and epsilon > 0
        Returns float y such that x-epsilon <= y*y <= x+epsilon"""
```

This specification admits many possible return values for the function call `squareRoot(2, 0.001)`. However, the successive approximation algorithm we looked at in Chapter 3 will always return the same value. The specification doesn't require that the implementation be deterministic, but it does allow deterministic implementations.

Not all interesting specifications can be met by deterministic implementations. Consider, for example, implementing a program to play a dice game, say backgammon or craps. Somewhere in the program there may be a function that simulates a fair roll[66] of a single six-sided die. Suppose it had a specification something like

```
def rollDie():
    """Returns an int between 1 and 6"""
```

This would be problematic, since it allows the implementation to return the same number each time it is called, which would make for a pretty boring game. It would be better to specify that `rollDie` "returns a randomly chosen int between 1 and 6."

Most programming languages, including Python, include simple ways to write programs that use randomness. The code in Figure 12.1 uses one of several useful functions found in the imported Python standard library module `random`. The function `random.choice` takes a non-empty sequence as its argument and returns a randomly chosen member of that sequence. Almost all of the functions in `random` are built using the function `random.random`, which generates a random floating point number between `0.0` and `1.0`.[67]

---

[65] The word stems from the Greek word *stokhastikos*, which means something like "capable of divining." A stochastic program, as we shall see, is aimed at getting a good result, but the exact results are not guaranteed.

[66] A roll is fair if each of the six possible outcomes is equally likely.

[67] In point of fact, the function is not truly random. It is what mathematicians call **pseudorandom**. For almost all practical purposes outside of cryptography, this distinction is not relevant and we shall ignore it.

```
import random

def rollDie():
    """Returns a random int between 1 and 6"""
    return random.choice([1,2,3,4,5,6])

def rollN(n):
    result = ''
    for i in range(n):
        result = result + str(rollDie())
    print result
```

Figure 12.1 Roll die

Now, imagine running rollN(10). Would you be more surprised to see it print 1111111111 or 5442462412? Or, to put it another way, which of these two sequences is more random? It's a trick question. Each of these sequences is equally likely, because the value of each roll is independent of the values of earlier rolls. In a stochastic process two events are **independent** if the outcome of one event has no influence on the outcome of the other.

This is a bit easier to see if we simplify the situation by thinking about a two-sided die (also known as a coin) with the values 0 and 1. This allows us to think of the output of a call of rollN as a binary number (see Chapter 3). When we use a binary die, there are 2^n possible sequences that testN might return. Each of these is equally likely; therefore each has a probability of occurring of $(1/2)^n$.

Let's go back to our six-sided die. How many different sequences are there of length 10? 6^{10}. So, the probability of rolling ten consecutive 1's is $1/6^{10}$. Less than one out of sixty million. Pretty low, but no lower than the probability of any other particular sequence, e.g., 5442462412, of ten rolls.

In general, when we talk about the probability of a result having some property (e.g., all 1's) we are asking what fraction of all possible results has that property. This is why probabilities range from 0 to 1. Suppose we want to know the probability of getting any sequence other than all 1's when rolling the die? It is simply $1 - (1/6^{10})$, because the probability of something happening and the probability of the same thing not happening must add up to 1.

Suppose we want to know the probability of rolling the die ten times without getting a single 1. One way to answer this question is to transform it into the question of how many of the 6^{10} possible sequences don't contain a 1.

This can be computed as follows:

- The probability of not rolling a 1 on any single roll is 5/6.

- The probability of not rolling a 1 on either the first or the second roll is (5/6)*(5/6), or $(5/6)^2$.

- So, the probability of not rolling a 1 ten times in a row is $(5/6)^{10}$, slightly more than 0.16.

We will return to the subject of probability in a bit more detail later.

12.2 Inferential Statistics and Simulation

The tiny program in Figure 12.1 is a **simulation model**. Rather than asking some person to roll a die multiple times, we wrote a program to simulate that activity.

We often use simulations to estimate the value of an unknown quantity by making use of the principles of **inferential statistics**. In brief (since this is not a book about statistics), the guiding principle of inferential statistics is that a random sample tends to exhibit the same properties as the population from which it is drawn.

Suppose Harvey Dent (also known as Two-Face) flipped a coin, and it came up heads. You would not infer from this that the next flip would also come up heads. Suppose he flipped it twice, and it came up heads both time. You might reason that the probability of this happening for a fair coin (i.e., a coin where heads and tails are equally likely) was 0.25, so there was still no reason to assume the next flip would be heads. Suppose, however, 100 out of 100 flips came up heads. $1/2^{100}$ is a pretty small number, so you might feel safe in inferring that the coin has a head on both sides.

Your belief in whether the coin is fair is based on the intuition that the behavior of a sample of 100 flips is similar to the behavior of the population of all flips of your coin. This belief seems pretty sound when all 100 flips are heads. Suppose, that 55 flips came up heads and 45 tails. Would you feel comfortable in predicting that the next 100 flips would have the same ratio of heads to tails? For that matter, how comfortable would you feel about even predicting that there would be more heads than tails in the next 100 flips? Take a few minutes to think about this, and then try the experiment using the code in Figure 12.2.

The function `flip` in Figure 12.2 simulates flipping a fair coin `numFlips` times, and returns the fraction of flips that came up heads. For each flip, `random.random()` returns a random floating point number between `0.0` and `1.0`. Numbers less than or greater than `0.5` are treated as heads or tails respectively. The value `0.5`, is arbitrarily assigned the value tails. Given the vast number of floating point values between `0.0` and `1.0`, it is highly unlikely that this will affect the result.

```
def flip(numFlips):
    heads = 0.0
    for i in range(numFlips):
        if random.random() < 0.5:
            heads += 1
    return heads/numFlips

def flipSim(numFlipsPerTrial, numTrials):
    fracHeads = []
    for i in range(numTrials):
        fracHeads.append(flip(numFlipsPerTrial))
    mean = sum(fracHeads)/len(fracHeads)
    return mean
```

Figure 12.2 Flipping a coin

Try executing the function flipSim(100, 1) a couple of times. Here's what we saw the first two times we tried it:

```
>>> flipSim(100, 1)
0.44
>>> flipSim(100, 1)
0.57999999999999996
```

It seems that it would be inappropriate to assume much (other than that the coin has both heads and tails) from any one trial of 100 flips. That's why we typically structure our simulations to include multiple trials and compare the results. Let's try flipSim(100, 100):

```
>>> flipSim(100, 100)
0.4993
>>> flipSim(100, 100)
0.4953
```

Intuitively, we can feel better about these results. How about flipSim(100, 100000):

```
>>> flipSim(100, 1000000)
0.49999221
>>> flipSim(100, 100000)
0.50003922
```

This looks really good (especially since we know that the answer should be 0.5, but that's cheating). Now it seems we can safely conclude something about the next flip, i.e., that heads and tails are about equally likely. But why do we think that we can conclude that?

What we are depending upon is the **law of large numbers** (also known as **Bernoulli's theorem**[68]). This law states that in repeated independent experiments (e.g., flipping a fair coin 100 times and counting the fraction of heads) with the same expected value (0.5 in this case), the average value of the

---

[68] Though the law of large numbers had been discussed in the 16th century by Cardano, the first proof was published by Jacob Bernoulli in the early 18th century. It is unrelated to the theorem about fluid dynamics called Bernoulli's theorem, which was proved by Jacob's nephew Daniel.

experiments approaches the expected value as the number of experiments goes to infinity.

It is worth noting that the law of large numbers does not imply, as too many seem to think, that if deviations from expected behavior occur, these deviations are likely to be evened out by opposite deviations in the future. This misapplication of the law of large numbers is known as the **gambler's fallacy**. [69]

Note that "large" is a relative concept. For example, if we were to flip a fair coin on the order of $10^{1,000,000}$ times, we should expect to encounter several sequences of at least a million consecutive heads. If we looked only at the subset of flips containing these heads, we would inevitably jump to the wrong conclusion about the fairness of the coin. In fact, if every subsequence of a large sequence of events appears to be random, it is highly likely that the sequence itself is not truly random. If your iTunes shuffle mode doesn't play the same song first once in a while, you can assume that the shuffle is not really random.

Finally, notice that in the case of coin flips the law of large numbers does not imply that the absolute difference between the number of heads and the number of tails decreases as the number of flips increases. In fact, we can expect that number to increase. What decreases is the ratio of the absolute difference to the number of flips.

Figure 12.3 contains a function, flipPlot, that produces some plots intended to show the law of large numbers at work. The line random.seed(0) near the bottom ensures that the pseudo-random number generator used by random.random will generate the same sequence of pseudorandom numbers each time this code is executed. This is convenient for debugging.

---

[69] "On August 18, 1913, at the casino in Monte Carlo, black came up a record twenty-six times in succession [in roulette]. ... [There] was a near-panicky rush to bet on red, beginning about the time black had come up a phenomenal fifteen times. In application of the maturity [of the chances] doctrine, players doubled and tripled their stakes, this doctrine leading them to believe after black came up the twentieth time that there was not a chance in a million of another repeat. In the end the unusual run enriched the Casino by some millions of francs." Huff and Geis, *How to Take a Chance*, pp. 28-29.

```
def flipPlot(minExp, maxExp):
    """Assumes minExp and maxExp positive integers; minExp < maxExp
       Plots results of 2**minExp to 2**maxExp coin flips"""
    ratios = []
    diffs = []
    xAxis = []
    for exp in range(minExp, maxExp + 1):
        xAxis.append(2**exp)
    for numFlips in xAxis:
        numHeads = 0
        for n in range(numFlips):
            if random.random() < 0.5:
                numHeads += 1
        numTails = numFlips - numHeads
        ratios.append(numHeads/float(numTails))
        diffs.append(abs(numHeads - numTails))
    pylab.title('Difference Between Heads and Tails')
    pylab.xlabel('Number of Flips')
    pylab.ylabel('Abs(#Heads - #Tails)')
    pylab.plot(xAxis, diffs)
    pylab.figure()
    pylab.title('Heads/Tails Ratios')
    pylab.xlabel('Number of Flips')
    pylab.ylabel('#Heads/#Tails')
    pylab.plot(xAxis, ratios)

random.seed(0)
flipPlot(4, 20)
```

Figure 12.3 Plotting the results of coin flips

The call `flipPlot(4, 20)` produces the two plots:

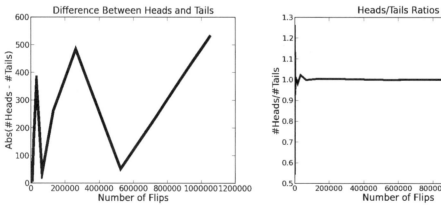 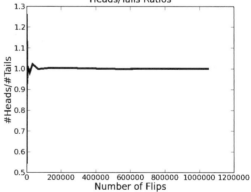

The plot on the left seems to suggest that the absolute difference between the number of heads and the number of tails fluctuates in the beginning, crashes downwards, and then moves rapidly upwards. However, we need to keep in mind that we have only two data points to the right of x = 300,000. That `pylab.plot` connected these points with lines may mislead us into seeing trends when all we have are isolated points. This is not an uncommon phenomenon, so you should always ask how many points a plot actually contains before jumping to any conclusion about what it means.

It's hard to see much of anything in the plot on the right, which is mostly a flat line. This too is deceptive. Even though there are sixteen data points, most of them are crowded into a small amount of real estate on the left side of the plot, so that the detail is impossible to see. This occurs because values on the x-axis range from 16 to 1,0485,76, and unless instructed otherwise PyLab will space these points evenly along the axis. This is called **linear scaling**.

Fortunately, these visualization problems are easy to address in PyLab. As we saw in Chapter 11, we can easily instruct our program to plot unconnected points, e.g., by writing pylab.plot(xAxis, diffs, 'bo').

We can also instruct PyLab to use a **logarithmic scale** on either or both of the x and y axes by calling the functions pylab.semilogx and pylab.semilogy. These functions are always applied to the current figure.

Both plots use a logarithmic scale on the x-axis. Since the x-values generated by flipPlot are 2^{minExp}, $2^{minExp+1}$, .., 2^{maxExp}, using a logarithmic x-axis causes the points to be evenly spaced along the x-axis—providing maximum separation between points. The left-hand plot below also uses a logarithmic scale on the y-axis. The y values on this plot range from nearly 0 to nearly 1000. If the y-axis were linearly scaled, it would be difficult to see the relatively small differences in y values on the left side of the plot. On the other hand, on the plot on the right the y values are fairly tightly grouped, so we use a linear y-axis.

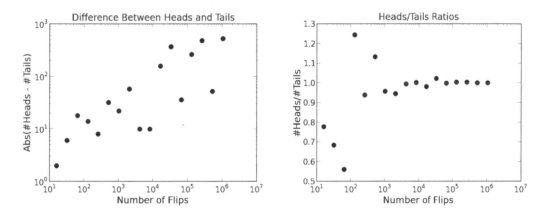

Finger exercise: Modify the code in Figure 12.3 so that it produces plots like those shown above.

These plots are easier to interpret than the earlier plots. The plot on the right suggests pretty strongly that the ratio of heads to tails converges to 1.0 as the number of flips gets large. The meaning of the plot on the left is a bit less clear. It appears that the absolute difference grows with the number of flips, but it is not completely convincing.

It is never possible to achieve perfect accuracy through sampling without sampling the entire population. No matter how many samples we examine, we can never be sure that the sample set is typical until we examine every element of the population (and since we are usually dealing with infinite populations, e.g., all possible sequences of coin flips, this is usually impossible). Of course, this is not to say that an estimate cannot be precisely correct. We might flip a coin twice, get one heads and one tails, and conclude that the true probability of each is 0.5. We would have reached the right conclusion, but our reasoning would have been faulty.

How many samples do we need to look at before we can have justified confidence in our answer? This depends on the **variance** in the underlying distribution. Roughly speaking, variance is a measure of how much spread there is in the possible different outcomes.

We can formalize this notion relatively simply by using the concept of **standard deviation**. Informally, the standard deviation tells us what fraction of the values are close to the mean. If many values are relatively close to the mean, the standard deviation is relatively small. If many values are relatively far from the mean, the standard deviation is relatively large. If all values are the same, the standard deviation is zero.

More formally, the standard deviation, σ (sigma), of a collection of values, X, is defined as $\sigma(X) = \sqrt[2]{\frac{1}{|X|}\sum_{x \in X}(x - \mu)^2}$, where $|X|$ is the size of the collection and μ (mu) its mean. Figure 12.4 contains a Python implementation of standard deviation.[70] We apply the type conversion float, because if each of the elements of X is an int, the type of the sum will be an int.

```
def stdDev(X):
    """Assumes that X is a list of numbers.
       Returns the standard deviation of X"""
    mean = float(sum(X))/len(X)
    tot = 0.0
    for x in X:
        tot += (x - mean)**2
    return (tot/len(X))**0.5 #Square root of mean difference
```

Figure 12.4 Standard deviation

We can use the notion of standard deviation to think about the relationship between the number of samples we have looked at and how much confidence we should have in the answer we have computed. Figure 12.5 contains a modified version of flipPlot. It runs multiple trials of each number of coin flips, and plots the means for abs(heads - tails) and the heads/tails ratio. It also plots the standard deviation of each.

---

[70] You'll probably never need to implement this yourself. Statistical libraries implement this and many other standard statistical functions. However, we present the code here on the off chance that some readers prefer looking at code to looking at equations.

The implementation of `flipPlot1` uses two helper functions. The function `makePlot` contains the code used to produce the plots. The function `runTrial` simulates one trial of `numFlips` coins.

```
def makePlot(xVals, yVals, title, xLabel, yLabel, style,
             logX = False, logY = False):
    """Plots xVals vs. yVals with supplied titles and labels."""
    pylab.figure()
    pylab.title(title)
    pylab.xlabel(xLabel)
    pylab.ylabel(yLabel)
    pylab.plot(xVals, yVals, style)
    if logX:
        pylab.semilogx()
    if logY:
        pylab.semilogy()

def runTrial(numFlips):
    numHeads = 0
    for n in range(numFlips):
        if random.random() < 0.5:
            numHeads += 1
    numTails = numFlips - numHeads
    return (numHeads, numTails)

def flipPlot1(minExp, maxExp, numTrials):
    """Assumes minExp and maxExp positive ints; minExp < maxExp
          numTrials a positive integer
       Plots summaries of results of numTrials trials of
          2**minExp to 2**maxExp coin flips"""
    ratiosMeans, diffsMeans, ratiosSDs, diffsSDs = [], [], [], []
    xAxis = []
    for exp in range(minExp, maxExp + 1):
        xAxis.append(2**exp)
    for numFlips in xAxis:
        ratios = []
        diffs = []
        for t in range(numTrials):
            numHeads, numTails = runTrial(numFlips)
            ratios.append(numHeads/float(numTails))
            diffs.append(abs(numHeads - numTails))
        ratiosMeans.append(sum(ratios)/float(numTrials))
        diffsMeans.append(sum(diffs)/float(numTrials))
        ratiosSDs.append(stdDev(ratios))
        diffsSDs.append(stdDev(diffs))
    numTrialsString = ' (' + str(numTrials) + ' Trials)'
    title = 'Mean Heads/Tails Ratios' + numTrialsString
    makePlot(xAxis, ratiosMeans, title,
             'Number of flips', 'Mean Heads/Tails', 'bo', logX = True)
    title = 'SD Heads/Tails Ratios' + numTrialsString
    makePlot(xAxis, ratiosSDs, title,
             'Number of Flips', 'Standard Deviation', 'bo',
             logX = True, logY = True)
```

Figure 12.5 Coin-flipping simulation

Let's try `flipPlot1(4, 20, 20)`. It generates the plots

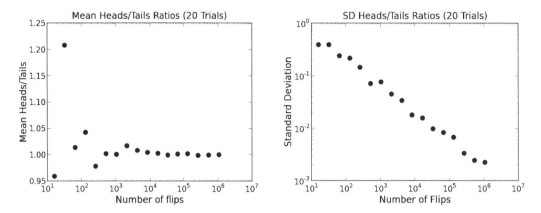

This is encouraging. The ratio heads/tails is converging towards 1 and the log of the standard deviation is falling linearly with the log of the number of flips per trial. By the time we get to about 10^6 coin flips per trial, the standard deviation (about 10^{-3}) is roughly three decimal orders of magnitude smaller than the mean (about 1), indicating that the variance across the trials was small. We can, therefore, have considerable confidence that the expected heads/tails ratio is quite close to 1.0. As we flip more coins, not only do we have a more precise answer, but more important, we also have reason to be more confident that it is close to the right answer.

What about the absolute difference between the number of heads and the number of tails? We can take a look at that by adding to the end of `flipPlot1` the code in Figure 12.6.

```
title = 'Mean abs(#Heads - #Tails)' + numTrialsString
makePlot(xAxis, diffsMeans, title,
     'Number of Flips', 'Mean abs(#Heads - #Tails)', 'bo',
     logX = True, logY = True)
title = 'SD abs(#Heads - #Tails)' + numTrialsString
makePlot(xAxis, diffsSDs, title,
     'Number of Flips', 'Standard Deviation', 'bo',
     logX = True, logY = True)
```

Figure 12.6 Absolute differences

This produces the additional plots

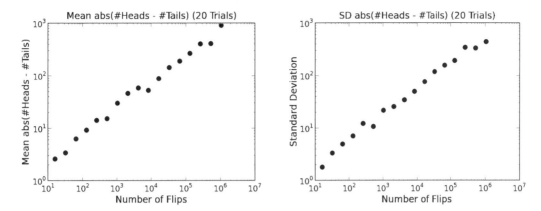

As expected, the absolute difference between the numbers of heads and tails grows with the number of flips. Furthermore, since we are averaging the results over twenty trials, the plot is considerably smoother than when we plotted the results of a single trial. But what's up with the last plot? The standard deviation is growing with the number of flips. Does this mean that as the number of flips increases we should have less rather than more confidence in the estimate of the expected value of the difference between heads and tails?

No, it does not. The standard deviation should always be viewed in the context of the mean. If the mean were a billion and the standard deviation 100, we would view the dispersion of the data as small. But if the mean were 100 and the standard deviation 100, we would view the dispersion as quite large.

The **coefficient of variation** is the standard deviation divided by the mean. When comparing data sets with highly variable means (as here), the coefficient of variation is often more informative than the standard deviation. As you can see from its implementation in Figure 12.7, the coefficient of variation is not defined when the mean is 0.

```
def CV(X):
    mean = sum(X)/float(len(X))
    try:
        return stdDev(X)/mean
    except ZeroDivisionError:
        return float('nan')
```

Figure 12.7 Coefficient of variation

Figure 12.8 contains a version of `flipPlot1` that plots coefficients of variation.

```
def flipPlot1(minExp, maxExp, numTrials):
    """Assumes minExp and maxExp positive ints; minExp < maxExp
        numTrials a positive integer
       Plots summaries of results of numTrials trials of
       2**minExp to 2**maxExp coin flips"""
    ratiosMeans, diffsMeans, ratiosSDs, diffsSDs = [], [], [], []
    ratiosCVs, diffsCVs = [], []
    xAxis = []
    for exp in range(minExp, maxExp + 1):
        xAxis.append(2**exp)
    for numFlips in xAxis:
        ratios = []
        diffs = []
        for t in range(numTrials):
            numHeads, numTails = runTrial(numFlips)
            ratios.append(numHeads/float(numTails))
            diffs.append(abs(numHeads - numTails))
        ratiosMeans.append(sum(ratios)/float(numTrials))
        diffsMeans.append(sum(diffs)/float(numTrials))
        ratiosSDs.append(stdDev(ratios))
        diffsSDs.append(stdDev(diffs))
        ratiosCVs.append(CV(ratios))
        diffsCVs.append(CV(diffs))
    numTrialsString = ' (' + str(numTrials) + ' Trials)'
    title = 'Mean Heads/Tails Ratios' + numTrialsString
    makePlot(xAxis, ratiosMeans, title,
             'Number of flips', 'Mean Heads/Tails', 'bo', logX = True)
    title = 'SD Heads/Tails Ratios' + numTrialsString
    makePlot(xAxis, ratiosSDs, title,
             'Number of Flips', 'Standard Deviation', 'bo',
             logX = True, logY = True)
    title = 'Mean abs(#Heads - #Tails)' + numTrialsString
    makePlot(xAxis, diffsMeans, title,
        'Number of Flips', 'Mean abs(#Heads - #Tails)', 'bo',
        logX = True, logY = True)
    title = 'SD abs(#Heads - #Tails)' + numTrialsString
    makePlot(xAxis, diffsSDs, title,
        'Number of Flips', 'Standard Deviation', 'bo',
        logX = True, logY = True)
    title = 'Coeff. of Var. abs(#Heads - #Tails)' + numTrialsString
    makePlot(xAxis, diffsCVs, title, 'Number of Flips',
             'Coeff. of Var.', 'bo', logX = True)
    title = 'Coeff. of Var. Heads/Tails Ratio' + numTrialsString
    makePlot(xAxis, ratiosCVs, title, 'Number of Flips',
             'Coeff. of Var.', 'bo', logX = True, logY = True)
```

Figure 12.8 Final version of `flipPlot1`

It produces the additional plots

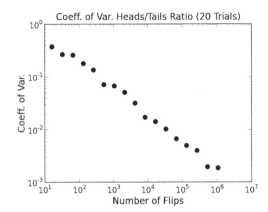

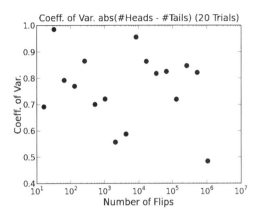

In this case we see that the plot of coefficient of variation for the heads/tails ratio is not much different from the plot of the standard deviation. This is not surprising, since the only difference between the two is the division by the mean, and since the mean is close to 1 that makes little difference.

On the other hand, the plot of the coefficient of variation for the absolute difference between heads and tails is a different story. It would take a brave person to argue that it is trending in any direction. It seems to be fluctuating widely. This suggests that dispersion in the values of abs(heads - tails) is independent of the number of flips. It's not growing, as the standard deviation might have misled us to believe, but it's not shrinking either. Perhaps a trend would appear if we tried 1000 trials instead of 20. Let's see.

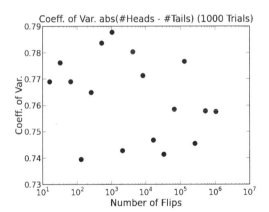

It looks as if once the number of flips reaches somewhere around 1000, the coefficient of variation settles in somewhere in the neighborhood of 0.75. In general, distributions with a coefficient of variation of less than 1 are considered low-variance.

Beware that if the mean is near zero, small changes in the mean lead to large (but not necessarily meaningful) changes in the coefficient of variation, and when the mean is zero, the coefficient of variation is undefined. Also, as we shall see shortly, the standard deviation can be used to construct a confidence interval, but the coefficient of variation cannot.

12.3 Distributions

A **histogram** is a plot designed to show the distribution of values in a set of
data. The values are first sorted, and then divided into a fixed number of equal-
width bins. A plot is then drawn that shows the number of elements in each
bin. Consider, for example, the code

```
vals = [1, 200] #guarantee that values will range from 1 to 200
for i in range(1000):
    num1 = random.choice(range(1, 100))
    num2 = random.choice(range(1, 100))
    vals.append(num1+num2)
pylab.hist(vals, bins = 10)
```

The function call `pylab.hist(vals, bins = 10)` produces the histogram, with

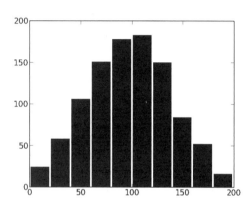

ten bins, on the left. PyLab has
automatically chosen the width of each
bin. Looking at the code, we know that
the smallest number in `vals` will be 1
and the largest number 200. Therefore,
the possible values on the x-axis range
from 1 to 200. Each bin represents an
equal fraction of the values on the x-
axis, so the first bin will contain the
elements 1-20, the next bin the elements
21-40, etc. Since the mean values
chosen for `num1` and `num2` will be in the

vicinity of 50, it is not surprising that there are more elements in the middle bins
than in the bins near the edges.

By now you must be getting awfully bored with flipping coins. Nevertheless, we
are going to ask you to look at yet one more coin-flipping simulation. The
simulation in Figure 12.9 illustrates more of PyLab's plotting capabilities and
gives us an opportunity to get a visual notion of what standard deviation means.

The simulation uses the function `pylab.xlim` to control the extent of the x-axis.
The function call `pylab.xlim()` returns a tuple composed of the minimal and
maximal values of the x-axis of the current figure. The function call
`pylab.xlim(xmin, xmax)` sets the minimal and maximal values of the x-axis of
the current figure. The function `pylab.ylim` works the same way.

```
def flip(numFlips):
    heads = 0.0
    for i in range(numFlips):
        if random.random() < 0.5:
            heads += 1
    return heads/numFlips

def flipSim(numFlipsPerTrial, numTrials):
    fracHeads = []
    for i in range(numTrials):
        fracHeads.append(flip(numFlipsPerTrial))
    mean = sum(fracHeads)/len(fracHeads)
    sd = stdDev(fracHeads)
    return (fracHeads, mean, sd)

def labelPlot(numFlips, numTrials, mean, sd):
    pylab.title(str(numTrials) + ' trials of '
                + str(numFlips) + ' flips each')
    pylab.xlabel('Fraction of Heads')
    pylab.ylabel('Number of Trials')
    xmin, xmax = pylab.xlim()
    ymin, ymax = pylab.ylim()
    pylab.text(xmin + (xmax-xmin)*0.02, (ymax-ymin)/2,
               'Mean = ' + str(round(mean, 4))
               + '\nSD = ' + str(round(sd, 4)), size='x-large')

def makePlots(numFlips1, numFlips2, numTrials):
    val1, mean1, sd1 = flipSim(numFlips1, numTrials)
    pylab.hist(val1, bins = 20)
    xmin,xmax = pylab.xlim()
    ymin,ymax = pylab.ylim()
    labelPlot(numFlips1, numTrials, mean1, sd1)
    pylab.figure()
    val2, mean2, sd2 = flipSim(numFlips2, numTrials)
    pylab.hist(val2, bins = 20)
    pylab.xlim(xmin, xmax)
    labelPlot(numFlips2, numTrials, mean2, sd2)

random.seed(0)
makePlots(100,1000,100000)
```

Figure 12.9 Plot histograms demonstrating normal distributions

When the code in Figure 12.9 is run, it produces the plots

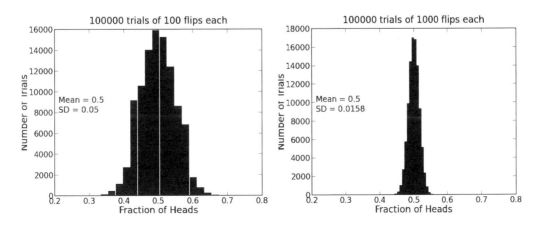

Notice that while the means in both plots are about the same, the standard deviations are quite different. The spread of outcomes is much tighter when we flip the coin 1000 times per trial than when we flip the coin 100 times per trial. To make this clear, we have used `pylab.xlim` to force the bounds of the x-axis in the second plot to match those in the first plot, rather than letting PyLab choose the bounds. We have also used `pylab.xlim` and `pylab.ylim` to choose a set of coordinates for displaying a text box with the mean and standard deviation.

12.3.1 Normal Distributions and Confidence Levels

The distribution of results in each of these plots is close to what is called a **normal distribution.** Technically speaking, a normal distribution is defined by the formula

$$f(x) = \frac{1}{\sigma\sqrt{2\pi}} * e^{-\frac{(x-\mu)^2}{2\sigma^2}}$$

where μ is the mean, σ the standard deviation, and e Euler's number (roughly 2.718). If you don't feel like studying this equation, that's fine. Just remember that normal distributions peak at the mean, fall off symmetrically above and below the mean, and asymptotically approach 0. They have the nice mathematical property of being completely specified by two parameters: the mean and the standard deviation (the only two parameters in the equation). Knowing these is equivalent to knowing the entire distribution. The shape of the normal distribution resembles (in the eyes of some) that of a bell, so it sometimes is referred to as a **bell curve**.

As we can see by zooming in on the center of the plot for 1000 flips/trial, the distribution is not perfectly symmetrical, and therefore not quite normal. However, as we increase the number of trials, the distribution will converge towards normal.

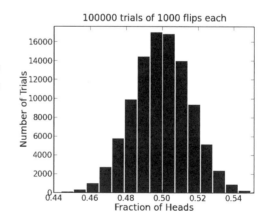

Normal distributions are frequently used in constructing probabilistic models for three reasons: 1) they have nice mathematical properties, 2) many naturally occurring distributions are indeed close to normal, and 3) they can be used to produce **confidence intervals**.

Instead of estimating an unknown parameter by a single value (e.g., the mean of a set of trials), a confidence interval provides a range that is likely to contain the unknown value and a degree of confidence that the unknown value lies within that range. For example, a political poll might indicate that a candidate is likely to get 52% of the vote ±4% (i.e., the confidence interval is of size 8) with a **confidence level** of 95%. What this means is that the pollster believes that 95% of the time the candidate will receive between 48% and 56% of the vote. Together the confidence interval and the confidence level indicate the reliability of the estimate. Almost always, increasing the confidence level will widen the confidence interval.

The calculation of a confidence interval generally requires assumptions about the nature of the space being sampled. It assumes that the distribution of errors of estimation is normal and has a mean of zero. The **empirical rule for normal distributions** provides a handy way to estimate confidence intervals and levels given the mean and standard deviation:

- 68% of the data will fall within 1 standard deviation of the mean,

- 95% of the data will fall within 2 standard deviations of the mean, and

- almost all (99.7%) of the data will fall within 3 standard deviations of the mean. [71]

Suppose that we run 100 trials of 100 coin flips each. Suppose further that the mean fraction of heads is 0.4999 and the standard deviation 0.0497. If we assume that the distribution of the means of the trials was normal, we can conclude that if we conducted more trials of 100 flips each,

- 95% of the time the fraction of heads will be 0.4999 ±0.0994 and

- >99% of the time the fraction of heads will be 0.4999 ±0.1491.

It is often useful to visualize confidence intervals using **error bars**. The code in Figure 12.10 calls the version of flipSim in Figure 12.9 and then uses

```
pylab.errorbar(xVals, means, yerr = 2*pylab.array(sds))
```

to produce the plot on the right. The first two arguments give the x and y values to be plotted. The third argument says that the values in sds should be used to create vertical error bars. The call

```
showErrorBars(3, 10, 100)
```

produces the plot on the right. Unsurprisingly, the error bars shrink as the number of flips per trial grows.

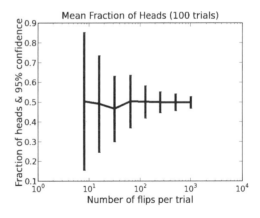

[71] These values are approximations. For example, 95% of the data will fall within 1.96 standard deviations of the mean; 2 standard deviations is a convenient approximation.

```
def showErrorBars(minExp, maxExp, numTrials):
    """Assumes minExp and maxExp positive ints; minExp < maxExp
        numTrials a positive integer
      Plots mean fraction of heads with error bars"""
    means, sds = [], []
    xVals = []
    for exp in range(minExp, maxExp + 1):
        xVals.append(2**exp)
        fracHeads, mean, sd = flipSim(2**exp, numTrials)
        means.append(mean)
        sds.append(sd)
    pylab.errorbar(xVals, means,
                   yerr=2*pylab.array(sds))
    pylab.semilogx()
    pylab.title('Mean Fraction of Heads (' + str(numTrials) + ' trials)')
    pylab.xlabel('Number of flips per trial')
    pylab.ylabel('Fraction of heads & 95% confidence')
```

Figure 12.10 Produce plot with error bars

Of course, finding a mathematically nice model is of no use if it provides a bad model of the actual data. Fortunately, many random variables have an approximately normal distribution. For example, physical properties of plants and animals (e.g., height, weight, body temperature) typically have approximately normal distributions. Importantly, many experimental setups have normally distributed measurement errors. This assumption was used in the early 1800s by the German mathematician and physicist Karl Gauss, who assumed a normal distribution of measurement errors in his analysis of astronomical data (which led to the normal distribution becoming known as the **Gaussian distribution** in much of the scientific community).

Normal distributions can be easily generated by calling random.gauss(mu, sigma), which returns a randomly chosen floating point number from a normal distribution with mean mu and standard deviation sigma.

It is important, however, to remember that not all distributions are normal.

12.3.2 Uniform Distributions

Consider rolling a single die. Each of the six outcomes is equally probable. If one were to roll a single die a million times and create a histogram showing how often each number came up, each column would be almost the same height. If one were to plot the probability of each possible lottery number being chosen, it would be a flat line (at 1 divided by the range of the lottery numbers). Such distributions are called **uniform**. One can fully characterize a uniform distribution with a single parameter, its range (i.e., minimum and maximum values). While uniform distributions are quite common in games of chance, they rarely occur in nature, nor are they usually useful for modeling complex man-made systems.

Uniform distributions can easily be generated by calling random.uniform(min, max) which returns a randomly chosen floating point number between min and max.

12.3.3 Exponential and Geometric Distributions

Exponential distributions, unlike uniform distributions, occur quite commonly. They are often used to model inter-arrival times, e.g., of cars entering a highway or requests for a Web page. They are especially important because they have the **memoryless property**.

Consider, for example, the concentration of a drug in the human body. Assume that at each time step each molecule has a probability P of being cleared (i.e., of no longer being in the body). The system is memoryless in the sense that at each time step the probability of a molecule being cleared is independent of what happened at previous times. At time $t = 0$, the probability of an individual molecule still being in the body is 1. At time $t = 1$, the probability of that molecule still being in the body is $1 - P$. At time $t = 2$, the probability of that molecule still being in the body is $(1 - P)^2$. More generally, at time t the probability of an individual molecule having survived is $(1 - P)^t$.

Suppose that at time t_0 there are M_0 molecules of the drug. In general, at time t, the number of molecules will be M_0 multiplied by the probability that an individual module has survived to time t. The function implemented in Figure 12.11 plots the expected number of remaining molecules versus time.

```
def clear(n, p, steps):
    """Assumes n & steps positive ints, p a float
        n: the initial number of molecules
        p: the probability of a molecule being cleared
        steps: the length of the simulation"""
    numRemaining = [n]
    for t in range(steps):
        numRemaining.append(n*((1-p)**t))
    pylab.plot(numRemaining)
    pylab.xlabel('Time')
    pylab.ylabel('Molecules Remaining')
    pylab.title('Clearance of Drug')
```

Figure 12.11 Exponential clearance of molecules

The call `clear(1000, 0.01, 1000)` produces the plot on the left.

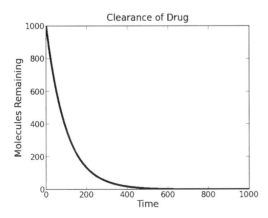
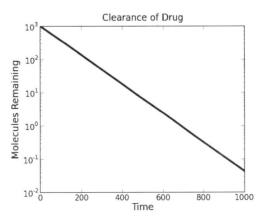

This is an example of **exponential decay**. In practice, exponential decay is often talked about in terms of **half-life**, i.e., the expected time required for the initial value to decay by 50%. One can also talk about the half-life of a single item. For example, the half-life of a single radioactive atom is the time at which the probability of that atom having decayed is 0.5. Notice that as time increases the number of remaining molecules approaches zero. But it will never quite get there. This should not be interpreted as suggesting that a fraction of a molecule remains. Rather it should be interpreted as saying that since the system is probabilistic, one can never guarantee that all of the molecules have been cleared.

What happens if we make the y-axis logarithmic (by using pylab.semilogy)? We get the plot above and on the right. The values on the y-axis are changing exponentially quickly relative to the values on the x-axis. If we make the y-axis itself change exponentially quickly, we get a straight line. The slope of that line is the rate of decay.

Exponential growth is the inverse of exponential decay. It too is quite commonly seen in nature. Compound interest, the growth of algae in a swimming pool, and the chain reaction in an atomic bomb are all examples of exponential growth.

Exponential distributions can easily be generated by calling random.expovariate.

The **geometric distribution** is the discrete analog of the exponential distribution.[72] It is usually thought of as describing the number of independent attempts required to achieve a first success (or a first failure). Imagine, for example, that you have a crummy car that starts only half of the time you turn the key. A geometric distribution could be used to characterize the expected number of times you would have to attempt to start the car before being successful. This is illustrated by the histogram on the right, which was produced by the code in Figure 12.12. The histogram implies that most of the time you'll get the car going within a few attempts. On the other hand, the long tail suggests that on occasion you may run the risk of draining your battery before the car gets going.

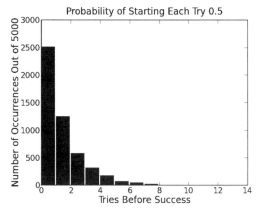

---

[72] The name "geometric distribution" arises from its similarity to a "geometric progression." A geometric progression is any sequence of numbers in which each number other than the first is derived by multiplying the previous number by a constant nonzero number. Euclid's *Elements* proves a number of interesting theorems about geometric progressions.

```
def successfulStarts(eventProb, numTrials):
    """Assumes eventProb is a float representing a probability
          of a single attempt being successful. numTrials a positive int
       Returns a list of the number of attempts needed before a
          success for each trial."""
    triesBeforeSuccess = []
    for t in range(numTrials):
        consecFailures = 0
        while random.random() > eventProb:
            consecFailures += 1
        triesBeforeSuccess.append(consecFailures)
    return triesBeforeSuccess

random.seed(0)
probOfSuccess = 0.5
numTrials = 5000
distribution = successfulStarts(probOfSuccess, numTrials)
pylab.hist(distribution, bins = 14)
pylab.xlabel('Tries Before Success')
pylab.ylabel('Number of Occurrences Out of ' + str(numTrials))
pylab.title('Probability of Starting Each Try ' + str(probOfSuccess))
```

Figure 12.12 A geometric distribution

12.3.4 Benford's Distribution

Benford's law defines a really strange distribution. Let S be a large set of decimal integers. How frequently would you expect each digit to appear as the first digit? Most of us would probably guess one ninth of the time. And when people are making up sets of numbers (e.g., faking experimental data or perpetrating financial fraud) this is typically true. It is not, however, typically true of many naturally occurring data sets. Instead, they follow a distribution predicted by Benford's law.

A set of decimal numbers is said to satisfy **Benford's law**[73] if the probability of the first digit being d is consistent with $P(d) = \log_{10}(1 + 1/d)$.

For example, this law predicts that the probability of the first digit being 1 is about 30%! Shockingly, many actual data sets seem to observe this law. It is possible to show that the Fibonacci sequence, for example, satisfies it perfectly. That's kind of plausible, since the sequence is generated by a formula. It's less easy to understand why such diverse data sets as iPhone pass codes, the number of Twitter followers per user, the population of countries, or the distance of stars from the earth closely approximate Benford's law.[74]

---

[73] The law is named after the physicist Frank Benford, who published a paper in 1938 showing that the law held on over 20,000 observations drawn from twenty different domains. However, it was first postulated in 1881 by the astronomer Simon Newcomb.

[74] http://testingbenfordslaw.com/

12.4 How Often Does the Better Team Win?

Thus far we have looked at using statistical methods to help understand possible outcomes of games in which skill is not intended to play a role. It is also common to apply these methods to situations in which there is, presumably, some skill involved. Setting odds on a football match, choosing a political candidate with a chance of winning, investing in the stock market, and so on.

Almost every October two teams from American Major League Baseball meet in something called the World Series. They play each other repeatedly until one of the teams has won four games, and that team is called (not entirely appropriately) "the world champion."

Setting aside the question of whether there is reason to believe that one of the participants in the World Series is indeed the best team in the world, how likely is it that a contest that can be at most seven games long will determine which of the two participants is better?

Clearly, each year one team will emerge victorious. So the question is whether we should attribute that victory to skill or to luck. To address that question we can use something called a **p-value**. P-values are used to determine whether or not a result is **statistically significant**.

To compute a p-value one needs two things:

*   A **null hypothesis**. This hypothesis describes the result that one would get if the results were determined entirely by chance. In this case, the null hypothesis would be that the teams are equally talented, so if the two teams were to play an infinite number of seven-game series, each would win half the time.

*   An observation. Data gathered either by observing what happens or by running a simulation that one believes provides an accurate model of what would happen.

The p-value gives us the likelihood that the observation is consistent with the null hypothesis. The smaller the p-value, the more likely it is that we should reject the hypothesis that the observation is due entirely to chance. Usually, we insist that p be no larger than 0.05 before we consider a result to be statistically significant. I.e., we insist that there is no more than a 5% chance that the null hypothesis holds.

Getting back to the World Series, should we consider the results of those seven-game series to be statistically significant? That is, should we conclude that the better team did indeed win?

Figure 12.13 contains code that can provide us with some insight into that question. The function simSeries has one argument, numSeries, a positive integer describing the number of seven-game series to be simulated. It plots the probability of the better team winning the series against the probability of that team winning a single game. It varies the probability of the better team winning a single game from 0.5 to 1.0, and produces a plot.

```
def playSeries(numGames, teamProb):
    """Assumes numGames an odd integer,
         teamProb a float between 0 and 1
       Returns True if better team wins series"""
    numWon = 0
    for game in range(numGames):
        if random.random() <= teamProb:
            numWon += 1
    return (numWon > numGames//2)

def simSeries(numSeries):
    prob = 0.5
    fracWon = []
    probs = []
    while prob <= 1.0:
        seriesWon = 0.0
        for i in range(numSeries):
            if playSeries(7, prob):
                seriesWon += 1
        fracWon.append(seriesWon/numSeries)
        probs.append(prob)
        prob += 0.01
    pylab.plot(probs, fracWon, linewidth = 5)
    pylab.xlabel('Probability of Winning a Game')
    pylab.ylabel('Probability of Winning a Series')
    pylab.axhline(0.95)
    pylab.ylim(0.5, 1.1)
    pylab.title(str(numSeries) + ' Seven-Game Series')

simSeries(400)
```

Figure 12.13 World Series simulation

When `simSeries` is used to simulate 400 seven-game series, it produces the plot on the right. Notice that for the better team to win 95% of the time (0.95 on the y-axis), it needs to be more than three times better than its opponent. That is to say, the better team needs to win, on average, more than three out of four games (0.75 on the x-axis). For comparison, in 2009, the two teams in the World Series had regular season winning percentages of 63.6% (New York Yankees) and 57.4% (Philadelphia Phillies). This suggests that New York should

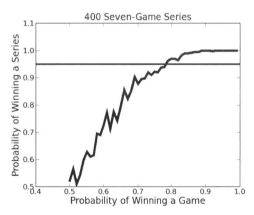

win about 52.5% of the games between the two teams. Our plot tells us that even if they were to play each other in 400 seven-game series, the Yankees would win less than 60% of the time.

Suppose we assume that these winning percentages are accurate reflections of the relative strengths of these two teams. How many games long should the

World Series be in order for us to get results that would allow us to reject the null hypothesis, i.e., the hypothesis that the teams are evenly matched?

The code in Figure 12.14 simulates 200 instances of series of varying lengths, and plots an approximation of the probability of the better team winning.

```
def findSeriesLength(teamProb):
    numSeries = 200
    maxLen = 2500
    step = 10

    def fracWon(teamProb, numSeries, seriesLen):
        won = 0.0
        for series in range(numSeries):
            if playSeries(seriesLen, teamProb):
                won += 1
        return won/numSeries

    winFrac = []
    xVals = []
    for seriesLen in range(1, maxLen, step):
        xVals.append(seriesLen)
        winFrac.append(fracWon(teamProb, numSeries, seriesLen))
    pylab.plot(xVals, winFrac, linewidth = 5)
    pylab.xlabel('Length of Series')
    pylab.ylabel('Probability of Winning Series')
    pylab.title(str(round(teamProb, 4)) +
                ' Probability of Better Team Winning a Game')
    pylab.axhline(0.95) #draw horizontal line at y = 0.95

YanksProb = 0.636
PhilsProb = 0.574
findSeriesLength(YanksProb/(YanksProb + PhilsProb))
```

Figure 12.14 How long should the World Series be?

The output of `findSeriesLength` suggests that under these circumstances the World Series would have to be approximately 1000 games long before we could reject the null hypothesis and confidently say that the better team had almost certainly won. Scheduling a series of this length might present some practical problems.

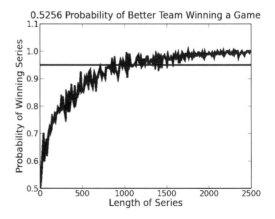

12.5 Hashing and Collisions

In Section 10.3 we pointed out that by using a larger hash table one could reduce the incidence of collisions, and thus reduce the expected time to retrieve a value. We now have the intellectual tools needed to examine that tradeoff more precisely.

First, let's get a precise formulation of the problem.

1. Assume:

 a. The range of the hash function is 1 to n,

 b. The number of insertions is K, and

 c. The hash function produces a perfectly uniform distribution of the keys used in insertions, i.e., for all keys, key, and for integers, i, in the range 1 to n, the probability that hash(key) is i is 1/n.

2. What is the probability that at least one collision occurs?

The question is exactly equivalent to asking "given K randomly generated integers in the range 1 to n, what is the probability that at least two of them are equal." If K ≥ n, the probability is clearly 1. But what about when K < n?

As is often the case, it is easiest to start by answering the inverse question, "given K randomly generated integers in the range 1 to n, what is the probability that none of them are equal?"

When we insert the first element, the probability of not having a collision is clearly 1. How about the second insertion? Since there are n-1 hash results left that are not equal to the result of the first hash, n-1 out of n choices will not yield a collision. So, the probability of not getting a collision on the second insertion is $\frac{n-1}{n}$, and the probability of not getting a collision on either of the first two insertions is $1 * \frac{n-1}{n}$. We can multiply these probabilities because for each insertion the value produced by the hash function is independent of anything that has preceded it.

The probability of not having a collision after three insertions is $1 * \frac{n-1}{n} * \frac{n-2}{n}$. And after K insertions it is $1 * \frac{n-1}{n} * \frac{n-2}{n} * ... * \frac{n-(K-1)}{n}$.

To get the probability of having at least one collision, we subtract this value from 1, i.e., the probability is

$$1 - (\frac{n-1}{n} * \frac{n-2}{n} * ... * \frac{n-(K-1)}{n})$$

Given the size of the hash table and the number of expected insertions, we can use this formula to calculate the probability of at least one collision. If K were reasonably large, say 10,000, it would be a bit tedious to compute the probability with pencil and paper. That leaves two choices, mathematics and programming. Mathematicians have used some fairly advanced techniques to find a way to approximate the value of this series. But unless K is very large, it is easier to run some code to compute the exact value of the series:

```
def collisionProb(n, k):
    prob = 1.0
    for i in range(1, k):
        prob = prob * ((n - i)/float(n))
    return 1 - prob
```

If we try `collisionProb(1000, 50)` we get a probability of about 0.71 of there being at least one collision. If we consider 200 insertions, the probability of a collision is nearly one. Does that seem a bit high to you? Let's write a simulation, Figure 12.15, to estimate the probability of at least one collision, and see if we get similar results.

```
def simInsertions(numIndices, numInsertions):
    """Assumes numIndices and numInsertions are positive ints.
       Returns 1 if there is a collision; 0 otherwise"""
    choices = range(numIndices) #list of possible indices
    used = []
    for i in range(numInsertions):
        hashVal = random.choice(choices)
        if hashVal in used: #there is a collision
            return 1
        else:
            used.append(hashVal)
    return 0

def findProb(numIndices, numInsertions, numTrials):
    collisions = 0.0
    for t in range(numTrials):
        collisions += simInsertions(numIndices, numInsertions)
    return collisions/numTrials
```

Figure 12.15 Simulating a hash table

If we run the code

```
print 'Actual probability of a collision =', collisionProb(1000, 50)
print 'Est. probability of a collision =', findProb(1000, 50, 10000)
print 'Actual probability of a collision =', collisionProb(1000, 200)
print 'Est. probability of a collision =', findProb(1000, 200, 10000)
```

it prints

```
Actual probability of a collision = 0.71226865688
Est. probability of a collision = 0.7119
Actual probability of a collision = 0.999999999478
Est. probability of a collision = 1.0
```

The simulation results are comfortingly similar to what we derived analytically.

Should the high probability of a collision make us think that hash tables have to be enormous to be useful? No. The probability of there being at least one collision tells us little about the expected lookup time. The expected time to look up a value depends upon the average length of the lists implementing the buckets that hold the values that collided. This is simply the number of insertions divided by the number of buckets.

13 RANDOM WALKS AND MORE ABOUT DATA VISUALIZATION

In 1827, the Scottish botanist Robert Brown observed that pollen particles suspended in water seemed to float around at random. He had no plausible explanation for what came to be known as Brownian motion, and made no attempt to model it mathematically.[75] A clear mathematical model of the phenomenon was first presented in 1900 in Louis Bachelier's doctoral thesis, *The Theory of Speculation*. However, since this thesis dealt with the then disreputable problem of understanding financial markets, it was largely ignored by respectable academics. Five years later, a young Albert Einstein brought this kind of stochastic thinking to the world of physics with a mathematical model almost the same as Bachelier's and a description of how it could be used to confirm the existence of atoms.[76] For some reason, people seemed to think that understanding physics was more important than making money, and the world started paying attention. Times were certainly different.

Brownian motion is an example of a **random walk**. Random walks are widely used to model physical processes (e.g., diffusion), biological processes (e.g., the kinetics of displacement of RNA from heteroduplexes by DNA), and social processes (e.g., movements of the stock market).

In this chapter we look at random walks for three reasons:

1. Random walks are intrinsically interesting.

2. It provides us with a good example of how to use abstract data types and inheritance to structure programs in general and simulations in particular.

3. It provides an opportunity to introduce a few more features of Python and to demonstrate some additional techniques for producing plots.

13.1 The Drunkard's Walk

Let's look at a random walk that actually involves walking. A drunken farmer is standing in the middle of a field, and every second the farmer takes one step in a random direction. What is her (or his) expected distance from the origin in 1000

---

[75] Nor was he the first to observe it. As early as 60 BC, the Roman Titus Lucretius, in his poem "On the Nature of Things," described a similar phenomenon, and even implied that it was caused by the random movement of atoms.

[76] "On the movement of small particles suspended in a stationary liquid demanded by the molecular-kinetic theory of heat," *Annalen der Physik*, May 1905. Einstein would come to describe 1905 as his "*annus mirabilis*." That year, in addition to his paper on Brownian motion, he published papers on the production and transformation of light (pivotal to the development of quantum theory), on the electrodynamics of moving bodies (special relativity), and on the equivalence of matter and energy ($E = mc^2$). Not a bad year for a newly minted PhD.

seconds? If she takes many steps, is she likely to move ever further from the origin, or is she more likely to wander back to the origin over and over, and end up not far from where she started? Let's write a simulation to find out.

Before starting to design a program, it is always a good idea to try to develop some intuition about the situation the program is intended to model. Let's start by sketching a simple model of the situation using Cartesian coordinates. Assume that the farmer is standing in a field where the grass has, mysteriously, been cut to resemble a piece of graph paper. Assume further that each step the farmer takes is of length one and is parallel to either the x-axis or y-axis.

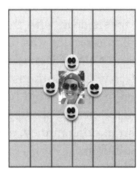 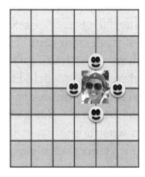

The picture on the left depicts a farmer[77] standing in the middle of the field. The smiley faces indicate all the places the farmer might be after one step. Notice that after one step she is always exactly one unit away from where she started. Let's assume that she wanders eastward from her initial location on her first step. How far away might she be from her initial location after her second step? Looking at the smiley faces in the picture on the right, we see that with a probability of 0.25 she will be 0 units away, with a probability of 0.25 she will be 2 units away, and with a probability of 0.5 she will be $\sqrt{2}$ units away[78]. So, on average she will be further away after two steps than after one step. What about the third step? If the second step is to the top or bottom smiley face, the third step will bring the farmer closer to origin half the time and further half the time. If the second step is to the left smiley face (the origin), the third step will be away from the origin. If the second step is to the right smiley face, the third step will be closer to the origin a quarter of the time, and further away three quarters of the time.

It seems like the more steps the drunk takes, the greater the expected distance from the origin. We could continue this exhaustive enumeration of possibilities and perhaps develop a pretty good intuition about how this distance grows with respect to the number of steps. However, it is getting pretty tedious, so it seems like a better idea to write a program to do it for us.

Let's begin the design process by thinking about some data abstractions that are likely to be useful in building this simulation and perhaps simulations of other kinds of random walks. As usual we should try to invent types that correspond

---

[77] To be honest, the person pictured here is a professional actor impersonating a farmer.

[78] Why $\sqrt{2}$? We are using the Pythagorean theorem.

to the kinds of things that appear in the situation we are attempting to model. Three obvious types are `Location`, `Field`, and `Drunk`. As we look at the classes providing these types, it is worthwhile to think about what each might imply about the kinds of simulation models they will allow us to build.

Let's start with `Location`.

```python
class Location(object):

    def __init__(self, x, y):
        """x and y are floats"""
        self.x = x
        self.y = y

    def move(self, deltaX, deltaY):
        """deltaX and deltaY are floats"""
        return Location(self.x + deltaX, self.y + deltaY)

    def getX(self):
        return self.x

    def getY(self):
        return self.y

    def distFrom(self, other):
        ox = other.x
        oy = other.y
        xDist = self.x - ox
        yDist = self.y - oy
        return (xDist**2 + yDist**2)**0.5

    def __str__(self):
        return '<' + str(self.x) + ', ' + str(self.y) + '>'
```

Figure 13.1 `Location` **class**

This is a simple class, but it does embody two important decisions. It tells us that the simulation will involve at most two dimensions. E.g., the simulation will not model changes in altitude. This is consistent with the pictures above. Also, since the values of `deltaX` and `deltaY` are floats rather than integers, there is no built-in assumption in this class about the set of directions in which a drunk might move. This is a generalization of the informal model in which each step was of length one and was parallel to the x-axis or y-axis.

Class `Field` is also quite simple, but it too embodies notable decisions. It simply maintains a mapping of drunks to locations. It places no constraints on locations, so presumably a `Field` is of unbounded size. It allows multiple drunks to be added into a `Field` at random locations. It says nothing about the patterns in which drunks move, nor does it prohibit multiple drunks from occupying the same location or moving through spaces occupied by other drunks.

```
class Field(object):

    def __init__(self):
        self.drunks = {}

    def addDrunk(self, drunk, loc):
        if drunk in self.drunks:
            raise ValueError('Duplicate drunk')
        else:
            self.drunks[drunk] = loc

    def moveDrunk(self, drunk):
        if drunk not in self.drunks:
            raise ValueError('Drunk not in field')
        xDist, yDist = drunk.takeStep()
        currentLocation = self.drunks[drunk]
        #use move method of Location to get new location
        self.drunks[drunk] = currentLocation.move(xDist, yDist)

    def getLoc(self, drunk):
        if drunk not in self.drunks:
            raise ValueError('Drunk not in field')
        return self.drunks[drunk]
```

Figure 13.2 Field class

The classes Drunk and UsualDrunk define the ways in which a drunk might wander through the field. In particular the value of stepChoices in UsualDrunk restores the restriction that each step is of length one and is parallel to either the x-axis or y-axis. It also captures the assumption that each kind of step is equally likely and not influenced by previous steps. A bit later we will look at subclasses of Drunk with different kinds of behaviors.

```
class Drunk(object):
    def __init__(self, name = None):
        """Assumes name is a str"""
        self.name = name

    def __str__(self):
        if self != None:
            return self.name
        return 'Anonymous'

class UsualDrunk(Drunk):
    def takeStep(self):
        stepChoices = [(0.0,1.0), (0.0,-1.0), (1.0, 0.0), (-1.0, 0.0)]
        return random.choice(stepChoices)
```

Figure 13.3 Drunk base class

The next step is to use these classes to build a simulation that answers the original question. Figure 13.4 contains three functions used in this simulation. The function walk simulates one walk of numSteps steps. The function simWalks calls walk to simulate numTrials walks of numSteps steps each. The function drunkTest calls simWalks to simulate walks of varying lengths.

The parameter dClass of simWalks is of type class, and is used in the first line of code to create a Drunk of the appropriate subclass. Later, when drunk.takeStep is invoked from Field.moveDrunk, the method from the appropriate subclass is automatically selected.

The function drunkTest also has a parameter, dClass, of type class. It is used twice, once in the call to simWalks and once in the first print statement. In the print statement, the built-in class attribute __name__ is used to get a string with the name of the class. The function drunkTest calculates the coefficient of variation of the distance from the origin using the CV function defined in Figure 12.7.

```
def walk(f, d, numSteps):
    """Assumes: f a Field, d a Drunk in f, and numSteps an int >= 0.
       Moves d numSteps times, and returns the difference between
       the final location and the location at the start of the walk."""
    start = f.getLoc(d)
    for s in range(numSteps):
        f.moveDrunk(d)
    return start.distFrom(f.getLoc(d))

def simWalks(numSteps, numTrials, dClass):
    """Assumes numSteps an int >= 0, numTrials an int > 0,
         dClass a subclass of Drunk
       Simulates numTrials walks of numSteps steps each.
       Returns a list of the final distances for each trial"""
    Homer = dClass()
    origin = Location(0.0, 0.0)
    distances = []
    for t in range(numTrials):
        f = Field()
        f.addDrunk(Homer, origin)
        distances.append(walk(f, Homer, numTrials))
    return distances

def drunkTest(walkLengths, numTrials, dClass):
    """Assumes walkLengths a sequence of ints >= 0
         numTrials an int > 0, dClass a subclass of Drunk
       For each number of steps in walkLengths, runs simWalks with
         numTrials walks and prints results"""
    for numSteps in walkLengths:
        distances = simWalks(numSteps, numTrials, dClass)
        print dClass.__name__, 'random walk of', numSteps, 'steps'
        print ' Mean =', sum(distances)/len(distances),\
              'CV =', CV(distances)
        print ' Max =', max(distances), 'Min =', min(distances)
```

Figure 13.4 The drunkard's walk (with a bug)

When we executed drunkTest((10, 100, 1000, 10000), 100, UsualDrunk), it printed

```
UsualDrunk random walk of 10 steps
  Mean = 9.10300189235 CV = 0.493919383186
  Max = 23.4093998214 Min = 1.41421356237
UsualDrunk random walk of 100 steps
  Mean = 9.72504983765 CV = 0.583886747239
  Max = 21.5406592285 Min = 0.0
UsualDrunk random walk of 1000 steps
  Mean = 9.42444322989 CV = 0.492682758402
  Max = 21.0237960416 Min = 0.0
UsualDrunk random walk of 10000 steps
  Mean = 9.27206514705 CV = 0.540211143752
  Max = 24.6981780705 Min = 0.0
```

This is surprising, given the intuition we developed earlier that the mean distance should grow with the number of steps. It could mean that our intuition is wrong, or it could mean that our simulation is buggy, or both.

The first thing to do at this point is to run the simulation on values for which we already think we know the answer, and make sure that what the simulation produces matches the expected result. Let's try walks of zero steps (for which the mean, minimum and maximum distances from the origin should all be 0) and one step (for which the mean, minimum and maximum distances from the origin should all be 1).

When we ran drunkTest((0,1), 100, UsualDrunk), we got the highly suspect result

```
UsualDrunk random walk of 0 steps
  Mean = 9.10300189235 CV = 0.493919383186
  Max = 23.4093998214 Min = 1.41421356237
UsualDrunk random walk of 1 steps
  Mean = 9.72504983765 CV = 0.583886747239
  Max = 21.5406592285 Min = 0.0
```

How on earth can the mean distance of a walk of zero steps be over 9?

We must have at least one bug in our simulation. After some investigation, the problem is clear. In simWalks, the call walk(f, homer, numTrials) should have been walk(f, homer, numSteps). The moral here is an important one: Always bring some skepticism to bear when looking at the results of a simulation. Ask if the results are plausible, and "smoke test"[79] the simulation on parameters for which you have a strong intuition about what the results should be.

---

[79] In the 19th century, it became standard practice for plumbers to test closed systems of pipes for leaks by filling the system with smoke. Later, electronic engineers adopted the term to cover the very first test of a piece of electronics—turning on the power and looking for smoke. Still later, software developers starting using the term for a quick test to see if a program did anything useful.

When the corrected version of the simulation is run on our two simple cases, it yields exactly the expected answers:

```
UsualDrunk random walk of 0 steps
  Mean = 0.0 CV = nan⁸⁰
  Max = 0.0 Min = 0.0
UsualDrunk random walk of 1 steps
  Mean = 1.0 CV = 0.0
  Max = 1.0 Min = 1.0
```

When run on longer walks it printed

```
UsualDrunk random walk of 10 steps
  Mean = 2.97977767074 CV = 0.497873216438
  Max = 6.0 Min = 0.0
UsualDrunk random walk of 100 steps
  Mean = 9.34012695549 CV = 0.481221153556
  Max = 23.4093998214 Min = 1.41421356237
UsualDrunk random walk of 1000 steps
  Mean = 28.6328252832 CV = 0.510288443239
  Max = 70.2139587262 Min = 3.16227766017
UsualDrunk random walk of 10000 steps
  Mean = 85.9223793386 CV = 0.516182207636
  Max = 256.007812381 Min = 17.7200451467
```

As anticipated, the average distance from the origin grows with the number of steps.

Now let's look at a plot of the mean distances from the origin. To give a sense of how fast the distance is growing, we have placed on the plot a line showing the square root of the number of steps (and increased the number of steps to 1,000,000).[81]

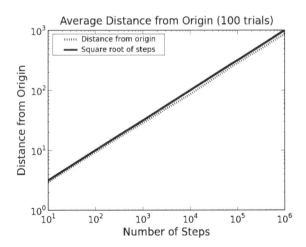

Does this plot provide any information about the expected final location of a drunk? It does tell us that on average the drunk will be somewhere on a circle with its center at the origin and with a radius equal to the expected distance from the origin. However, it tells us very little about where we might actually find the drunk at the end of any particular walk. We return to this topic later in this chapter.

---

[80] Since the mean was zero, the coefficient of variation is undefined. Hence our implementation of CV returned the special "not a number" floating point value.

[81] The plot showing the square root of the number of steps versus the distance from the origin is a straight line because we used a logarithmic scale on both axes.

13.2 Biased Random Walks

Now that we have a working simulation, we can start modifying it to investigate other kinds of random walks. Suppose, for example, that we want to consider the behavior of a drunken farmer in the northern hemisphere who hates the cold, and even in his drunken stupor is able to move twice as fast when his random movements take him in a southward direction. Or maybe a phototropic drunk who always moves towards the sun (east in the morning and west in the afternoon). These are all examples of **biased random walks**. The walk is still stochastic, but there is a bias in the outcome.

Figure 13.5 defines two additional subclasses of Drunk. In each case the specialization involves choosing an appropriate value for stepChoices. The function simAll iterates over a sequence of subclasses of Drunk to generate information about how each kind behaves.

```
class ColdDrunk(Drunk):
    def takeStep(self):
        stepChoices = [(0.0,1.0), (0.0,-2.0), (1.0, 0.0), (-1.0, 0.0)]
        return random.choice(stepChoices)

class EWDrunk(Drunk):
    def takeStep(self):
        stepChoices = [(1.0, 0.0), (-1.0, 0.0)]
        return random.choice(stepChoices)

def simAll(drunkKinds, walkLengths, numTrials):
    for dClass in drunkKinds:
        drunkTest(walkLengths, numTrials, dClass)
```

Figure 13.5 Subclasses of Drunk base class

When we ran simAll((UsualDrunk, ColdDrunk, EWDrunk), (100, 1000), 10) it printed

```
UsualDrunk random walk of 100 steps
 Mean = 8.37073251526 CV = 0.482770539323
 Max = 14.7648230602 Min = 1.41421356237
UsualDrunk random walk of 1000 steps
 Mean = 21.0385788624 CV = 0.5489414497
 Max = 36.6878726557 Min = 3.16227766017
ColdDrunk random walk of 100 steps
 Mean = 23.9034750714 CV = 0.401318542296
 Max = 37.1214223865 Min = 5.83095189485
ColdDrunk random walk of 1000 steps
 Mean = 238.833279891 CV = 0.125076661085
 Max = 288.140590684 Min = 182.024723595
EWDrunk random walk of 100 steps
 Mean = 8.6 CV = 0.58879018145
 Max = 18.0 Min = 0.0
EWDrunk random walk of 1000 steps
 Mean = 27.0 CV = 0.726719143346
 Max = 74.0 Min = 2.0
```

This is quite a bit of output to digest. It does appear that our heat-seeking drunk moves away from the origin faster than the other two kinds of drunk. However, it is not easy to digest all of the information in this output.

It is once again time to move away from textual output and start using plots.

Since we are showing a number of different kinds of drunks on the same plot, we will associate a distinct style with each type of drunk so that it is easy to differentiate among them. The style will have three aspects:

- The color of the line and points,
- The shape of the marker used to indicate a point, and
- The style of a line, e.g., solid or dotted.

The class `styleIterator`, in Figure 13.6, rotates through a sequence of styles defined by the argument to `styleIterator.__init__`.

```
class styleIterator(object):
    def __init__(self, styles):
        self.index = 0
        self.styles = styles

    def nextStyle(self):
        result = self.styles[self.index]
        if self.index == len(self.styles) - 1:
            self.index = 0
        else:
            self.index += 1
        return result
```

Figure 13.6 Iterating over styles

The code in Figure 13.7 is similar in structure to that in Figure 13.4. The `print` statements in `simDrunk` and `simAll` contribute nothing to the result of the simulation. They are there because this simulation can take a rather long time to complete, and printing an occasional message indicating that progress is being made can be quite reassuring to a user who might be wondering if the program is actually making progress. (Recall that `stdDev` was defined in Figure 12.4.)

```
def simDrunk(numTrials, dClass, walkLengths):
    meanDistances = []
    cvDistances = []
    for numSteps in walkLengths:
        print 'Starting simulation of', numSteps, 'steps'
        trials = simWalks(numSteps, numTrials, dClass)
        mean = sum(trials)/float(len(trials))
        meanDistances.append(mean)
        cvDistances.append(stdDev(trials)/mean)
    return (meanDistances, cvDistances)

def simAll(drunkKinds, walkLengths, numTrials):
    styleChoice = styleIterator(('b-', 'r:', 'm-.'))
    for dClass in drunkKinds:
        curStyle = styleChoice.nextStyle()
        print 'Starting simulation of', dClass.__name__
        means, cvs = simDrunk(numTrials, dClass, walkLengths)
        cvMean = sum(cvs)/float(len(cvs))
        pylab.plot(walkLengths, means, curStyle,
                   label = dClass.__name__ +
                       '(CV = ' + str(round(cvMean, 4)) + ')')
    pylab.title('Mean Distance from Origin ('
                + str(numTrials) + ' trials)')
    pylab.xlabel('Number of Steps')
    pylab.ylabel('Distance from Origin')
    pylab.legend(loc = 'best')
    pylab.semilogx()
    pylab.semilogy()

simAll((UsualDrunk, ColdDrunk, EWDrunk), (10,100,1000,10000,100000), 100)
```

Figure 13.7 Plotting the walks of different drunks

The code in Figure 13.7 produces the plot on the right. The usual drunk and the phototropic drunk (EWDrunk) seem to be moving away from the origin at approximately the same pace, but the heat-seeking drunk (ColdDrunk) seems to be moving away orders of magnitude faster. This is interesting given that on average he is only moving 25% faster (he takes, on average, five steps for every four taken by the others). Also, the coefficients of variation show quite a spread, but the plot doesn't shed any light on why.

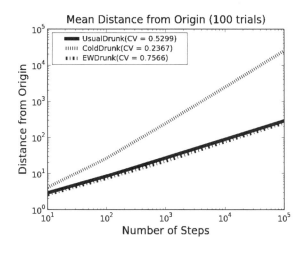

Let's construct a different plot, that may help us get more insight into the behavior of these three classes. Instead of plotting the change in distance over time for an increasing number of steps, the code in Figure 13.8 plots the distribution of final locations for a single number of steps.

```
def getFinalLocs(numSteps, numTrials, dClass):
    locs = []
    d = dClass()
    origin = Location(0, 0)
    for t in range(numTrials):
        f = Field()
        f.addDrunk(d, origin)
        for s in range(numSteps):
            f.moveDrunk(d)
        locs.append(f.getLoc(d))
    return locs

def plotLocs(drunkKinds, numSteps, numTrials):
    styleChoice = styleIterator(('b+', 'r^', 'mo'))
    for dClass in drunkKinds:
        locs = getFinalLocs(numSteps, numTrials, dClass)
        xVals, yVals = [], []
        for l in locs:
            xVals.append(l.getX())
            yVals.append(l.getY())
        meanX = sum(xVals)/float(len(xVals))
        meanY = sum(yVals)/float(len(yVals))
        curStyle = styleChoice.nextStyle()
        pylab.plot(xVals, yVals, curStyle,
                   label = dClass.__name__ + ' Mean loc. = <'
                   + str(meanX) + ', ' + str(meanY) + '>')
    pylab.title('Location at End of Walks ('
                + str(numSteps) + ' steps)')
    pylab.xlabel('Steps East/West of Origin')
    pylab.ylabel('Steps North/South of Origin')
    pylab.legend(loc = 'lower left', numpoints = 1)

plotLocs((UsualDrunk, ColdDrunk, EWDrunk), 100, 200)
```

Figure 13.8 Plotting final locations

The first thing `plotLocs` does is initialize `styleChoice` with three different styles
of markers. It then uses `pylab.plot` to place a marker at a location

corresponding to the end of each
trial. The call to `pylab.plot` sets
the color and shape of the marker
to be plotted using the values
returned by the iterator
`styleIterator`. The call
`plotLocs((UsualDrunk, ColdDrunk,
EWDrunk), 100, 200)` produces the
plot on the right. The first thing to
say is that our drunks seem to be
behaving as advertised. The
`EWDrunk` ends up on the x-axis, the
`ColdDrunk` seem to make progress
southwards, and the `UsualDrunk`
seem to have wandered aimlessly.

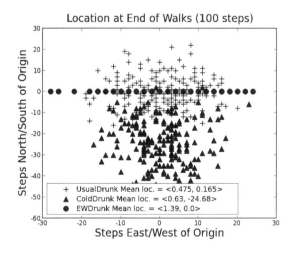

But why do there appear to be far fewer circle markers than triangle or +
markers? Because many of the EWDrunk's walks ended up at the same place.

This is not surprising, given the
small number of possible endpoints
(200) for the EWDrunk. Also the circle
markers seem to be fairly uniformly
spaced across the x-axis, which is
consistent with the relatively high
coefficient of variation that we
noticed earlier.

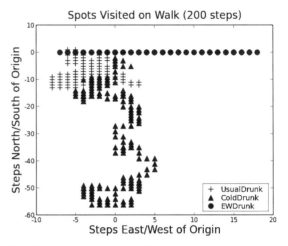

It is still not obvious, at least to us,
why the ColdDrunk manages, on
average, to get so much further
from the origin than the other kinds
of drunks. Perhaps it's time to look
not at the average endpoint of many walks, but at the path followed by a single
walk. The code in Figure 13.9 produces the plot on the right.

```
def traceWalk(drunkKinds, numSteps):
    styleChoice = styleIterator(('b+', 'r^', 'mo'))
    f = Field()
    for dClass in drunkKinds:
        d = dClass()
        f.addDrunk(d, Location(0, 0))
        locs = []
        for s in range(numSteps):
            f.moveDrunk(d)
            locs.append(f.getLoc(d))
        xVals = []
        yVals = []
        for l in locs:
            xVals.append(l.getX())
            yVals.append(l.getY())
        curStyle = styleChoice.nextStyle()
        pylab.plot(xVals, yVals, curStyle,
                   label = dClass.__name__)
    pylab.title('Spots Visited on Walk ('
                + str(numSteps) + ' steps)')
    pylab.xlabel('Steps East/West of Origin')
    pylab.ylabel('Steps North/South of Origin')
    pylab.legend(loc = 'best')

traceWalk((UsualDrunk, ColdDrunk, EWDrunk), 200)
```

Figure 13.9 Tracing walks

Since the walk is 200 steps long and the EWDrunk's walk visits fewer than 30
different locations, it's clear that he is spending a lot of time retracing his steps.
The same kind of observation holds for the UsualDrunk. In contrast, while the
ColdDrunk is not exactly making a beeline for Florida, he is managing to spend
relatively less time visiting places he has already been.

None of these simulations is interesting in its own right. (In the next chapter, we will look at more intrinsically interesting simulations.) But there are some points worth taking away:

- Initially we divided our simulation code into four separate chunks. Three of them were classes (`Location`, `Field`, and `Drunk`) corresponding to abstract data types that appeared in the informal description of the problem. The fourth chunk was a group of functions that used these classes to perform a simple simulation.

- We then elaborated `Drunk` into a hierarchy of classes so that we could observe different kinds of biased random walks. The code for `Location` and `Field` remained untouched, but the simulation code was changed to iterate through the different subclasses of `Drunk`. In doing this, we took advantage of the fact that a class is itself an object, and therefore can be passed as an argument.

- Finally, we made a series of incremental changes to the simulation that did not involve any changes to the classes representing the abstract types. These changes mostly involved introducing plots designed to provide insight into the different walks. This is very typical of the way in which simulations are developed. One gets the basic simulation working first, and then starts adding features.

13.3 Treacherous Fields

Did you ever play the board game known as *Chutes and Ladders* in the U.S. and *Snakes and Ladders* in the UK? This children's game originated in India (perhaps in the 2nd century BC), where it was called *Moksha-patamu*. Landing on a square representing virtue (e.g., generosity) sent a player up a ladder to a higher tier of life. Landing on a square representing evil (e.g., lust), sent a player back to a lower tier of life.

We can easily add this kind of feature to our random walks by creating a `Field` with wormholes,[82] as shown in Figure 13.10, and replacing the second line of code in the function `traceWalk` by the line of code
`f = oddField(1000, 100, 200)`.

---

[82] This kind of wormhole is a hypothetical concept invented by theoretical physicists. It provides shortcuts through the time/space continuum.

```
class oddField(Field):
    def __init__(self, numHoles, xRange, yRange):
        Field.__init__(self)
        self.wormholes = {}
        for w in range(numHoles):
            x = random.randint(-xRange, xRange)
            y = random.randint(-yRange, yRange)
            newX = random.randint(-xRange, xRange)
            newY = random.randint(-yRange, yRange)
            newLoc = Location(newX, newY)
            self.wormholes[(x, y)] = newLoc

    def moveDrunk(self, drunk):
        Field.moveDrunk(self, drunk)
        x = self.drunks[drunk].getX()
        y = self.drunks[drunk].getY()
        if (x, y) in self.wormholes:
            self.drunks[drunk] = self.wormholes[(x, y)]
```

Figure 13.10 Fields with strange properties

When we ran `traceWalk((UsualDrunk, ColdDrunk, EWDrunk), 500)`, we got the rather odd-looking plot

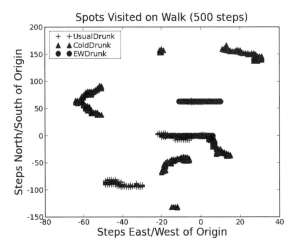

Clearly changing the properties of the field has had a dramatic effect. However, that is not the point of this example. The main points are:

*   Because of the way we structured our code, it was easy to accommodate a significant change to the situation being modeled. Just as we could add different kinds of drunks without touching `Field`, we can add a new kind of `Field` without touching `Drunk` or any of its subclasses. (Had we been sufficiently prescient to make the field a parameter of `traceWalk`, we wouldn't have had to change `traceWalk` either.)

*   While it would have been feasible to analytically derive different kinds of information about the expected behavior of the simple random walk and even the biased random walks, it would have been challenging to do so once the wormholes were introduced. Yet it was exceedingly simple to change the simulation to model the new situation. Simulation models often enjoy this advantage relative to analytic models.

14 MONTE CARLO SIMULATION

In the previous two chapters we looked at different ways of using randomness in computations. Many of the examples we presented fall into the class of computation known as **Monte Carlo simulation**.

Stanislaw Ulam and Nicholas Metropolis coined the term Monte Carlo simulation in 1949 in homage to the games of chance played in the casino in the Principality of Monaco. Ulam, who is best known for designing the hydrogen bomb with Edward Teller, described the invention of the model as follows:

> *The first thoughts and attempts I made to practice [the Monte Carlo Method] were suggested by a question which occurred to me in 1946 as I was convalescing from an illness and playing solitaires. The question was what are the chances that a Canfield solitaire laid out with 52 cards will come out successfully? After spending a lot of time trying to estimate them by pure combinatorial calculations, I wondered whether a more practical method than "abstract thinking" might not be to lay it out say one hundred times and simply observe and count the number of successful plays. This was already possible to envisage with the beginning of the new era of fast computers,[83] and I immediately thought of problems of neutron diffusion and other questions of mathematical physics, and more generally how to change processes described by certain differential equations into an equivalent form interpretable as a succession of random operations. Later ... [in 1946, I] described the idea to John von Neumann, and we began to plan actual calculations.[84]*

The technique was effectively used during the Manhattan Project to predict what would happen during a nuclear fission reaction, but did not really take off until the 1950s when computers became both more common and more powerful.

Ulam was not the first mathematician to think about using the tools of probability to understand a game of chance. The history of probability is intimately connected to the history of gambling. It is the existence of uncertainty that makes gambling possible. And the existence of gambling provoked the development of much of the mathematics needed to reason about uncertainty. Contributions to the foundations of probability theory by Cardano, Pascal, Fermat, Bernoulli, de Moivre, and Laplace were all motivated by a desire to better understand (and perhaps profit from) games of chance.

---

[83] "Fast" is a relative term. Ulam was probably referring to the ENIAC, which could perform about 10^3 additions a second (and weighed more than 25 tons). Today's computers perform about 10^9 additions a second (and weigh maybe 10^{-3} tons).

[84] Eckhardt, Roger (1987). "Stan Ulam, John von Neumann, and the Monte Carlo method," *Los Alamos Science*, Special Issue (15), 131-137.

14.1 Pascal's Problem

Most of the early work on probability theory revolved around games using dice.[85] Reputedly, Pascal's interest in the field that came to be known as probability theory began when a friend asked him whether or not it would be profitable to bet that within twenty-four rolls of a pair of dice he would roll a double six. This was considered a hard problem in the mid-17th century. Pascal and Fermat, two pretty smart guys, exchanged a number of letters about how to resolve the issue, but it now seems like an easy question to answer:

- On the first roll the probability of rolling a six on each die is 1/6, so the probability of rolling a six with both dice is 1/36.

- Therefore, the probability of not rolling a double six on the first roll is 1 - 1/36 = 35/36.

- Therefore the probability of not rolling a double six twenty-four consecutive times is $(35/36)^{24}$, nearly 0.51, and therefore the probability of rolling a double six is $1 - (35/36)^{24}$, about 0.49. In the long run it would not be profitable to bet on rolling a double six within twenty-four rolls. [86]

Just to be safe, let's write a little program to simulate Pascal's friend's game and confirm that we get the same answer as Pascal.

```
def rollDie():
    return random.choice([1,2,3,4,5,6])

def checkPascal(numTrials):
    """Assumes numTrials an int > 0
       Prints an estimate of the probability of winning"""
    numWins = 0.0
    for i in range(numTrials):
        for j in range(24):
            d1 = rollDie()
            d2 = rollDie()
            if d1 == 6 and d2 == 6:
                numWins += 1
                break
    print 'Probability of winning =', numWins/numTrials
```

Figure 14.1 Checking Pascal's analysis

---

[85] Archeological excavations suggest that dice are the human race's oldest gambling implement. The oldest known "modern" six-sided die dates to about 600 BC, but Egyptian tombs dating to two millennia before the birth of Christ contain artifacts resembling dice. Typically, these early dice were made from animal bones; in gambling circles people still use the phrase "rolling the bones."

[86] As with our earlier analyses, this is true only under the assumption that each die is fair, i.e., the outcome of a roll is truly random and each of the six outcomes is equally probable. This is not always to be taken for granted. Excavations of Pompeii discovered "loaded" dice in which small lead weights had been inserted to bias the outcome of a roll. More recently, an online vendor's site said, "Are you unusually unlucky when it comes to rolling dice? Investing in a pair of dice that's more, uh, reliable might be just what you need."

When run the first time, the call `checkPascal(1000000)` printed

    Probability of winning = 0.491204

This is indeed quite close to $1 - (35/36)^{24}$; typing `1 - (35.0/36.0)**24` into the Python shell produces `0.49140387613090342`.

14.2 Pass or Don't Pass?

Not all questions about games of chance are so easily answered. In the game craps, the shooter (the person who rolls the dice) chooses between making a "pass line" or a "don't pass line" bet.

- Pass Line: Shooter wins if the first roll (called coming out) is a "natural" (7 or 11) and loses if it is "craps" (2, 3, or 12). If some other number is rolled, that number becomes the "point" and the shooter keeps rolling. If the shooter rolls the point before rolling a 7, the shooter wins. Otherwise the shooter loses.

- Don't Pass Line: Shooter loses if the first roll is 7 or 11, wins if it is 2 or 3, and ties (a "push" in gambling jargon) if it is 12. If some other number is rolled, that number becomes the point and shooter keeps rolling. If the shooter rolls a 7 before rolling the point, the shooter wins. Otherwise the shooter loses.

Is one of these a better bet than the other? Is either a good bet? It is possible to analytically derive the answer to these questions, but it seems easier (at least to us) to write a program that simulates a craps game, and see what happens.

Figure 14.2 contains the heart of such a simulation. The values of the instance variables of an instance of class `CrapsGame` records the performance of the pass and don't pass lines since the start of the game. The observer methods `passResults` and `dpResults` return these values. The method `playHand` simulates one "hand"[87] of a game. The bulk of the code in `playHand` is merely an algorithmic description of the rules stated above. Notice that there is a loop in the `else` clause corresponding to what happens after a point is established. It is exited using a `break` statement when either a seven or the point is rolled.

---

[87] A hand starts when the shooter is "coming out," the term used in craps for a roll before a point is established. A hand ends when the shooter has won or lost his or her initial bet.

```
class CrapsGame(object):
    def __init__(self):
        self.passWins, self.passLosses = (0,0)
        self.dpWins, self.dpLosses, self.dpPushes = (0,0,0)

    def playHand(self):
        throw = rollDie() + rollDie()
        if throw == 7 or throw == 11:
            self.passWins += 1
            self.dpLosses += 1
        elif throw == 2 or throw == 3 or throw == 12:
            self.passLosses += 1
            if throw == 12:
                self.dpPushes += 1
            else:
                self.dpWins += 1
        else:
            point = throw
            while True:
                throw = rollDie() + rollDie()
                if throw == point:
                    self.passWins += 1
                    self.dpLosses += 1
                    break
                elif throw == 7:
                    self.passLosses += 1
                    self.dpWins += 1
                    break

    def passResults(self):
        return (self.passWins, self.passLosses)

    def dpResults(self):
        return (self.dpWins, self.dpLosses, self.dpPushes)
```

Figure 14.2 `CrapsGame` **class**

Figure 14.3 contains a function that uses class `CrapsGame`. Its structure is typical of many simulation programs:

1. It runs multiple games (think of each game as analogous to a trial in our earlier simulations) and accumulates the results. Each game includes multiple hands, so there is a nested loop.

2. It then produces and stores statistics for each game.

3. Finally it produces and outputs summary statistics. In this case, it prints the expected return on investment (ROI) or each kind of betting line and the standard deviation of that ROI.

Return on investment is defined by the equation

$$ROI = \frac{gain\ from\ investment - cost\ of\ investment}{cost\ of\ investment}$$

Since the pass and don't pass lines pay even money (if you bet $1 and win, you gain is $1), the ROI is

$$ROI = \frac{number\ of\ wins - number\ of\ losses}{number\ of\ bets}$$

For example, if you made 100 pass line bets and won half of them, your ROI would be

$$\frac{50-50}{100}=0$$

If you bet the don't pass line 100 times and had 25 wins and 5 pushes the ROI would be

$$\frac{25-70}{100}=\frac{-45}{100}=-4.5$$

Note that in crapsSim we use xrange rather than range in the for loops in anticipation of running large simulations. Recall that in Python 2.7 range(n) creates a sequence with n elements whereas xrange(n) generates the values only as they are needed by the for loop.

```
def crapsSim(handsPerGame, numGames):
    """Assumes handsPerGame and numGames are ints > 0
       Play numGames games of handsPerGame hands, and print results"""
    games = []

    #Play numGames games
    for t in xrange(numGames):
        c = CrapsGame()
        for i in xrange(handsPerGame):
            c.playHand()
        games.append(c)

    #Produce statistics for each game
    pROIPerGame, dpROIPerGame = [], []
    for g in games:
        wins, losses = g.passResults()
        pROIPerGame.append((wins - losses)/float(handsPerGame))
        wins, losses, pushes = g.dpResults()
        dpROIPerGame.append((wins - losses)/float(handsPerGame))

    #Produce and print summary statistics
    meanROI = str(round((100.0*sum(pROIPerGame)/numGames), 4)) + '%'
    sigma = str(round(100.0*stdDev(pROIPerGame), 4)) + '%'
    print 'Pass:', 'Mean ROI =', meanROI, 'Std. Dev. =', sigma
    meanROI = str(round((100.0*sum(dpROIPerGame)/numGames), 4)) + '%'
    sigma = str(round(100.0*stdDev(dpROIPerGame), 4)) + '%'
    print 'Don\'t pass:','Mean ROI =', meanROI, 'Std Dev =', sigma
```

Figure 14.3 Simulating a craps game

Let's run our craps simulation and see what happens:[88]

```
>>> crapsSim(20, 10)
Pass: Mean ROI = -7.0% Std. Dev. = 23.6854%
Don't pass: Mean ROI = 4.0% Std Dev = 23.5372%
```

[88] Keep in mind that since these programs incorporate randomness, you should not expect to get identical results if you run the code yourself. More importantly, do not make any bets until you have read the entire section.

It looks as if it would be a good idea to avoid the pass line—where the expected return on investment is a 7% loss. But the don't pass line looks like a pretty good bet. Or does it?

Looking at the standard deviations, it seems that perhaps the don't pass line is not such a good bet after all. Recall that under the assumption that the distribution is normal, the 95% confidence interval is encompassed by two standard deviations on either side of the mean. For the don't pass line, the 95% confidence interval is [4.0 – 2*23.5372, 4.0 + 2*23.5372]—roughly [-43%, +51%]. That certainly doesn't suggest that betting the don't pass line is a sure thing.

Time to put the law of large numbers to work.

```
>>> crapsSim(10000000, 10)
Pass: Mean ROI = -1.4216% Std. Dev. = 0.0322%
Don't pass: Mean ROI = -1.3579% Std Dev = 0.0334%
```

We can now be pretty safe in assuming that neither of these is a good bet. It looks as if the don't pass line may be slightly less bad. However, because the 95% confidence interval [-1.486, -1.3572] for the pass line overlaps with that for the don't pass line [-1.4247, -1.2911], we cannot say with 95% confidence that the don't pass line is a better bet.

Suppose that instead of increasing the number of hands per game, we increased the number of games, e.g., by making the call crapsSim(20, 1000000). As shown below, the mean of the estimated ROIs are close to the actual ROIs. However, the standard deviations are still be high—indicating that the outcome of a single game of 20 hands is highly uncertain.

```
>>>crapsSim(20, 10000000)
Pass: Mean ROI = -1.4133% Std. Dev. = 22.3571%
Don't pass: Mean ROI = -1.3649% Std Dev = 22.0446%
```

One of the nice things about simulations is that they make it easy to perform "what if" experiments. For example, what if a player could sneak in a pair of cheater's dice that favored 5 over 2 (5 and 2 are on the opposite sides of a die)? To test this out, all we have to do is replace the implementation of rollDie by something like

```
def rollDie():
    return random.choice([1,1,2,3,3,4,4,5,5,5,6,6])
```

This relatively small change in the die makes a dramatic difference in the odds,

```
>>> crapsSim(1000000, 10)
Pass: Mean ROI = 6.7066% Std. Dev. = 0.0208%
Don't pass: Mean ROI = -9.4824% Std Dev = 0.02%
```

No wonder casinos go to a lot of trouble to make sure that players don't introduce their own dice into the game!

14.3 Using Table Lookup to Improve Performance

You might not want to try running `crapsSim(100000000, 10)` at home. It takes a long time to complete on most computers. That raises the question of whether there is a simple way to speed up the simulation.

The complexity of `crapsSim` is O(playHand)*handsPerGame*numGames. The running time of `playHand` depends upon the number of times the loop in it is executed. In principle, the loop could be executed an unbounded number of times since there is no bound on how long it could take to roll either a seven or the point. In practice, of course, we have every reason to believe it will always terminate.

Notice, however, that the result of a call to `playHand` does not depend on how many times the loop is executed, but only on which exit condition is reached. For each possible point, one can easily calculate the probability of rolling that point before rolling a seven. For example, using a pair of dice one can roll a 4 in three different ways: <1, 3>, <3, 1>, and <2, 2>; and one can roll a 7 in six different ways: <1, 6>, <6, 1>, <2, 5>, <5, 2>, <3, 4>, and <4, 3>. Therefore, exiting the loop by rolling a 7 is twice as likely as exiting the loop by rolling a 4.

Figure 14.4 contains an implementation of `playHand` that exploits this thinking. We have pre-computed the probability of making the point before rolling a 7 for each possible value of the point, and stored those values in a dictionary. Suppose, for example, that the point is 8. The shooter continues to roll until he either rolls the point or rolls craps. There are five ways of rolling an 8 (<6,2>, <2,6>, <5,3>, <3,5>, and <4,4>) and six ways of rolling a 7. So, the value for the dictionary key 8 is the value of the expression 5/11.0. Having this table allows us to replace the inner loop, which contained an unbounded number of rolls, with a test against one call to `random.random`. The asymptotic complexity of this version of `playHand` is O(1).

The idea of replacing computation by **table lookup** has broad applicability and is frequently used when speed is an issue. Table lookup is an example of the general idea of **trading time for space**. We saw another example of this technique in our analysis of hashing: the larger the table, the fewer the collisions, and the faster the average lookup. In this case, the table is small, so the space cost is negligible.

```
def playHand(self):
    #An alternative, faster, implementation of playHand
    pointsDict = {4:1/3.0, 5:2/5.0, 6:5/11.0, 8:5/11.0,
                  9:2/5.0, 10:1/3.0}
    throw = rollDie() + rollDie()
    if throw == 7 or throw == 11:
        self.passWins += 1
        self.dpLosses += 1
    elif throw == 2 or throw == 3 or throw == 12:
        self.passLosses += 1
        if throw == 12:
            self.dpPushes += 1
        else:
            self.dpWins += 1
    else:
        if random.random() <= pointsDict[throw]: # point before 7
            self.passWins += 1
            self.dpLosses += 1
        else:                                     # 7 before point
            self.passLosses += 1
            self.dpWins += 1
```

Figure 14.4 Using table lookup to improve performance

14.4 Finding π

It is easy to see how Monte Carlo simulation is useful for tackling problems in which nondeterminism plays a role. Interestingly, however, Monte Carlo simulation (and randomized algorithms in general) can be used to solve problems that are not inherently stochastic, i.e., for which there is no uncertainty about outcomes.

Consider π.

For thousands of years, people have known that there is a constant, called π (pi) since the 18th century, such that the circumference of a circle is equal to π*diameter and the area of the circle equal to π*radius². What they did not know was the value of this constant.

One of the earliest estimates, 4*(8/9)² = 3.16, can found in the Egyptian *Rhind Papyrus*, circa 1650 BC. More than a thousand years later, the *Old Testament* implied a different value for π when giving the specifications of one of King Solomon's construction projects,

> *And he made a molten sea, ten cubits from the one brim to the other: it was round all about, and his height was five cubits: and a line of thirty cubits did compass it round about.*[89]

Solving for π, 10π = 30, so π = 3. Perhaps the *Bible* is simply wrong, or perhaps the molten sea wasn't perfectly circular, or perhaps the circumference was

---

[89]King James Bible, 1 Kings 7.23.

measured from the outside of the wall and the diameter from the inside, or perhaps it's just poetic license. We leave it to the reader to decide.

Archimedes of Syracuse (287-212 BC) derived upper and lower bounds on the value of π by using a high-degree polygon to approximate a circular shape. Using a polygon with 96 sides, he concluded that $223/71 < \pi < 22/7$. Giving upper and lower bounds was a rather sophisticated approach for the time. Also, if we take his best estimate as the average of his two bounds we obtain 3.1418, an error of about 0.0002. Not bad!

Long before computers were invented, the French mathematicians Buffon (1707-1788) and Laplace (1749-1827) proposed using a stochastic simulation to estimate the value of π.[90] Think about inscribing a circle in a square with sides of length 2, so that the radius, r, of the circle is of length 1.

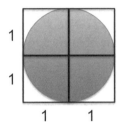

By the definition of π, area $= \pi r^2$. Since r is 1, $\pi =$ area. But what's the area of the circle? Buffon suggested that he could estimate the area of a circle by a dropping a large number of needles (which he argued would follow a random path as they fell) in the vicinity of the square. The ratio of the number of needles with tips lying within the square to the number of needles with tips lying within the circle could then be used to estimate the area of the circle.

If the locations of the needles are truly random, we know that,

$$\frac{needles\ in\ circle}{needles\ in\ square} = \frac{area\ of\ circle}{area\ of\ square}$$

solving for the area of the circle,

$$area\ of\ circle = \frac{area\ of\ square * needles\ in\ circle}{needles\ in\ square}$$

Recall that the area of a 2 by 2 square is 4, so,

$$area\ of\ circle = \frac{4 * needles\ in\ circle}{needles\ in\ square}$$

In general, to estimate the area of some region R

1. Pick an enclosing region, E, such that the area of E is easy to calculate and R lies completely within E.
2. Pick a set of random points that lie within E.
3. Let F be the fraction of the points that fall within R.
4. Multiply the area of E by F.

---

[90] Buffon proposed the idea first, but there was an error in his formulation that was later corrected by Laplace.

If you try Buffon's experiment, you'll soon realize that the places where the needles land are not truly random. Moreover, even if you could drop them randomly, it would take a very large number of needles to get an approximation of π as good as even the *Bible*'s. Fortunately, computers can randomly drop simulated needles at a ferocious rate.

Figure 14.5 contains a program that estimates π using the Buffon-Laplace method. For simplicity, it considers only those needles that fall in the upper right-hand quadrant of the square.

The function `throwNeedles` simulates dropping a needle by first using `random.random` to get a pair of positive Cartesian coordinates (x and y values). It then uses the Pythagorean theorem to compute the hypotenuse of the right triangle with base x and height y. This is the distance of the tip of the needle from the origin (the center of the square). Since the radius of the circle is 1, we know that the needle lies within the circle if and only if the distance from the origin is no greater than 1. We use this fact to count the number of needles in the circle.

The function `getEst` uses `throwNeedles` to find an estimate of π by dropping `numNeedles` needles and averaging the result over `numTrials` trials.

The function `estPi` calls `getEst` with an ever-growing number of needles until `getEst` returns an estimate that, with a confidence of 95%, is within `precision` of the actual value. It does this by calling `throwNeedles` with an ever-larger number of needles, until the standard deviation of the results of `numTrials` trials is no larger than `precision/2.0`. Under the assumption that the errors are normally distributed, this ensures that 95% of the values lie within `precision` of the mean.

```
def throwNeedles(numNeedles):
    inCircle = 0
    for Needles in xrange(1, numNeedles + 1):
        x = random.random()
        y = random.random()
        if (x*x + y*y)**0.5 <= 1.0:
            inCircle += 1
    #Counting needles in one quadrant only, so multiply by 4
    return 4*(inCircle/float(numNeedles))

def getEst(numNeedles, numTrials):
    estimates = []
    for t in range(numTrials):
        piGuess = throwNeedles(numNeedles)
        estimates.append(piGuess)
    sDev = stdDev(estimates)
    curEst = sum(estimates)/len(estimates)
    print 'Est. = ' + str(round(curEst, 5)) +\
          ', Std. dev. = ' + str(round(sDev, 5))\
          + ', Needles = ' + str(numNeedles)
    return (curEst, sDev)

def estPi(precision, numTrials):
    numNeedles = 1000
    sDev = precision
    while sDev >= precision/2.0:
        curEst, sDev = getEst(numNeedles, numTrials)
        numNeedles *= 2
    return curEst
```

Figure 14.5 Estimating π

When we ran estPi(0.01, 100) it printed

```
Est. = 3.14844, Std. dev. = 0.04789, Needles = 1000
Est. = 3.13918, Std. dev. = 0.0355, Needles = 2000
Est. = 3.14108, Std. dev. = 0.02713, Needles = 4000
Est. = 3.14143, Std. dev. = 0.0168, Needles = 8000
Est. = 3.14135, Std. dev. = 0.0137, Needles = 16000
Est. = 3.14131, Std. dev. = 0.00848, Needles = 32000
Est. = 3.14117, Std. dev. = 0.00703, Needles = 64000
Est. = 3.14159, Std. dev. = 0.00403, Needles = 128000
```

As one would expect, the standard deviations decreased monotonically as we increased the number of samples. In the beginning the estimates of the value of π also improved steadily. Some were above the true value and some below, but each increase in numNeedles led to an improved estimate. With 1000 samples per trial, the simulation's estimate was already better than those of the *Bible* and the *Rhind Papyrus*.

Curiously, the estimate got worse when the number of needles went from 8,000 to 16,000, since 3.14135 is further from the true value of π than is 3.14143. However, if we look at the ranges defined by one standard deviation around each of the means, both ranges contain the true value of π, and the range associated with the larger sample size is considerably smaller. Even though the estimate generated with 16,000 samples happens to be further from the actual value of π, we should have more confidence in its accuracy. This is an extremely important notion. It is not sufficient to produce a good answer. We have to have a valid reason to be confident that it is in fact a good answer. And when we drop a large enough number of needles, the small standard deviation gives us reason to be confident that we have a correct answer. Right?

Not exactly. Having a small standard deviation is a necessary condition for having confidence in the validity of the result. It is not a sufficient condition. The notion of a statistically valid conclusion should never be confused with the notion of a correct conclusion.

Each statistical analysis starts with a set of assumptions. The key assumption here is that our simulation is an accurate model of reality. Recall that the design of our Buffon-Laplace simulation started with a little algebra demonstrating how we could use the ratio of two areas to find the value of π. We then translated this idea into code that depended upon a little geometry and the randomness of `random.random`.

Let's see what happens if we get any of this wrong. Suppose, for example, we replace the 4 in the last line of `throwNeedles` by a 2, and again run `estPi(0.01, 100)`. This time it prints

```
Est. = 1.57422, Std. dev. = 0.02394, Needles = 1000
Est. = 1.56959, Std. dev. = 0.01775, Needles = 2000
Est. = 1.57054, Std. dev. = 0.01356, Needles = 4000
Est. = 1.57072, Std. dev. = 0.0084, Needles = 8000
Est. = 1.57068, Std. dev. = 0.00685, Needles = 16000
Est. = 1.57066, Std. dev. = 0.00424, Needles = 32000
```

The standard deviation for a mere 32,000 needles suggests that we should have a fair amount of confidence in the estimate. But what does that really mean? It means that we can be reasonably confident that if we were to draw more samples from the same distribution, we would get a similar value. It says nothing about whether or not this value is close to the actual value of π. A statistically valid conclusion should not be confused with a correct conclusion.

Before believing the results of a simulation, we need to have confidence both that our conceptual model is correct and that we have correctly implemented that model. Whenever possible, one should attempt to validate results against reality. In this case, one could use some other means to compute an approximation to the area of a circle (e.g., physical measurement) and check that the computed value of π is at least in the right neighborhood.

14.5 Some Closing Remarks About Simulation Models

For most of the history of science, theorists used mathematical techniques to construct purely analytical models that could be used to predict the behavior of a system from a set of parameters and initial conditions. This led to the development of important mathematical tools ranging from calculus to probability theory. These tools helped scientists develop a reasonably accurate understanding of the macroscopic physical world.

As the 20th century progressed, the limitations of this approach became increasingly clear. Reasons for this include:

- An increased interest in the social sciences, e.g., economics, led to a desire to construct good models of systems that were not mathematically tractable.

- As the systems to be modeled grew increasingly complex, it seemed easier to successively refine a series of simulation models than to construct accurate analytic models.

- It is often easier to extract useful intermediate results from a simulation than from an analytical model, e.g., to play "what if" games.

- The availability of computers made it feasible to run large-scale simulations. Until the advent of the modern computer in the middle of the 20th century the utility of simulation was limited by the time required to perform calculations by hand.

Simulation attempts to build an experimental device, called a **model**, that will provide useful information about the possible behaviors of the system being modeled. It is important to remember that these models, like all models, are only an approximation of reality. One can never be sure that the actual system will behave in the way predicted by the model. In fact, one can usually be pretty confident that the actual system will not behave exactly as predicted by the model. It is a commonly quoted truism that "all models are wrong, but some are useful."[91]

Simulation models are **descriptive**, not **prescriptive**. They tell how a system works under given conditions; not how to arrange the conditions to make the system work best. A simulation does not optimize, it merely describes. That is not to say that simulation cannot be used as part of an optimization process. For example, simulation is often used as part of a search process in finding an optimal set of parameter settings.

Simulation models can be classified along three dimensions:

- Deterministic versus stochastic,
- Static versus dynamic, and
- Discrete versus continuous.

The behavior of a **deterministic simulation** is completely defined by the model. Rerunning a simulation will not change the outcome. Deterministic simulations are typically used when the system being modeled is too complex to analyze analytically, e.g., the performance of a processor chip. **Stochastic simulations** incorporate randomness in the model. Multiple runs of the same model may generate different values. This random element forces us to generate many outcomes to see the range of possibilities. The question of whether to generate 10 or 1000 or 100,000 outcomes is a statistical question, as discussed earlier.

---

[91] Usually attributed to the statistician George E.P. Box.

In a **static model**, time plays no essential role. The needle-dropping simulation used to estimate π in this chapter is an example of a static simulation. In a **dynamic model**, time, or some analog, plays an essential role. In the series of random walks simulated in Chapter 13, the number of steps taken was used as a surrogate for time.

In a **discrete model**, the values of pertinent variables are enumerable, e.g., they are integers. In a **continuous model**, the values of pertinent variables range over non-enumerable sets, e.g., the real numbers. Imagine analyzing the flow of traffic along a highway. We might choose to model each individual car, in which case we have a discrete model. Alternatively, we might choose to treat traffic as a flow, where changes in the flow can be described by differential equations. This leads to a continuous model. In this example, the discrete model more closely resembles the physical situation (nobody drives half a car, though some cars are half the size of others), but is more computationally complex than a continuous one. In practice, models often have both discrete and continuous components. For example, one might choose to model the flow of blood through the human body using a discrete model for blood (i.e., modeling individual corpuscles) and a continuous model for blood pressure.

15 UNDERSTANDING EXPERIMENTAL DATA

This chapter is all about understanding experimental data. We will make extensive use of plotting to visualize the data, and will return to the topic of what is and what is not a valid statistical conclusion. We will also talk about the interplay between physical and computational experiments.

15.1 The Behavior of Springs

Springs are wonderful things. When they are compressed or stretched by some force, they store energy. When that force is no longer applied they release the stored energy. This property allows them to smooth the ride in cars, help mattresses conform to our bodies, retract seat belts, and launch projectiles.

In 1676 the British physicist Robert Hooke formulated **Hooke's law** of elasticity: *Ut tensio, sic vis*, in English, $F = -kx$. In other words, the force, F, stored in a spring is linearly related to the distance, x, the spring has been compressed (or stretched). (The minus sign indicates that the force exerted by the spring is in the opposite direction of the displacement.) Hooke's law holds for a wide variety of materials and systems, including many biological systems. Of course, it does not hold for an arbitrarily large force. All springs have an **elastic limit**, beyond which the law fails. Those of you who have stretched a Slinky too far know this all too well.

The constant of proportionality, k, is called the **spring constant**. If the spring is stiff (like the ones in the suspension of a car or the limbs of an archer's bow), k is large. If the spring is weak, like the spring in a ballpoint pen, k is small.

Knowing the spring constant of a particular spring can be a matter of some import. The calibrations of both simple scales and atomic force microscopes depend upon knowing the spring constants of components. The mechanical behavior of a strand of DNA is related to the force required to compress it. The force with which a bow launches an arrow is determined by the spring constant of its limbs. And so on.

Generations of physics students have learned to estimate spring constants using an experimental apparatus similar to that pictured here. The basic idea is to estimate the force stored *in* the spring by measuring the displacement caused by exerting a known force *on* the spring.

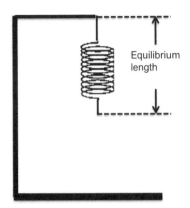 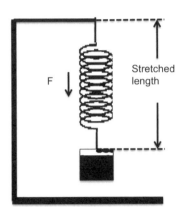

We start with a spring with no weight on it, and measure the distance to the bottom of the spring from the top of the stand. We then hang a known mass on the spring, wait for it to stop moving, and again measure the distance from the bottom of the spring to the top of the stand. The difference between the two distances then becomes the value of *x* in Hooke's law.

We know that the force, *F*, being exerted on the spring is equal to the mass, *m*, multiplied by the acceleration due to gravity, *g* (9.81 m/s² is a pretty good approximation of *g* on this planet), so we substitute *m·g* for *F*. By simple algebra we know that *k = -(m·g)/x*.

Suppose, for example, that *m = 1kg* and *x = 0.1m*, then

$$k = \frac{1kg * 9.81m/s^2}{0.1m} = -\frac{9.81N}{0.1m} = -98.1N/m$$

According to this calculation, it will take *98.1* Newtons[92] of force to stretch the spring one meter.

This would all be well and good if

- We had complete confidence in our ability to conduct this experiment perfectly. In that case, we could take one measurement, perform the calculation, and know that we had found *k*. Unfortunately, experimental science hardly ever works this way, and

- We could be sure that we were operating below the elastic limit of the spring.

A more robust experiment is to hang a series of increasingly heavier weights on the spring, measure the stretch of the spring each time, and plot the results.

---

[92] The Newton, written *N*, is the standard international unit for measuring force. It is the amount of force needed to accelerate a mass of one kilogram at a rate of one meter per second per second. A Slinky, by the way, has a spring constant of approximately *1N/m*.

We ran such an experiment, and typed the results into a file named
`springData.txt`:

```
Distance (m) Mass (kg)
0.0865 0.1
0.1015 0.15
...
0.4416 0.9
0.4304 0.95
0.437 1.0
```

The function in Figure 15.1 reads data from a file such as the one we saved, and
returns lists containing the distances and masses.

```
def getData(fileName):
    dataFile = open(fileName, 'r')
    distances = []
    masses = []
    discardHeader = dataFile.readline()
    for line in dataFile:
        d, m = line.split(' ')
        distances.append(float(d))
        masses.append(float(m))
    dataFile.close()
    return (masses, distances)
```

Figure 15.1 Extracting the data from a file

The function in Figure 15.2 uses `getData` to extract the experimental data from
the file and then plots it.

```
def plotData(inputFile):
    masses, distances = getData(inputFile)
    masses = pylab.array(masses)
    distances = pylab.array(distances)
    forces = masses*9.81
    pylab.plot(forces, distances, 'bo',
               label = 'Measured displacements')
    pylab.title('Measured Displacement of Spring')
    pylab.xlabel('|Force| (Newtons)')
    pylab.ylabel('Distance (meters)')
```

Figure 15.2 Plotting the data

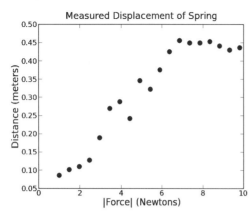

When `plotData('springData.txt')` is run, it produces the plot on the left.

This is not what Hooke's law predicts. Hooke's law tells us that the distance should increase linearly with the mass, i.e., the points should lie on a straight line the slope of which is determined by the spring constant. Of course, we know that when we take real measurements the experimental data are rarely a perfect match for the theory. Measurement error is to be expected, so we should expect the points to lie around a line rather than on it.

Still, it would be nice to see a line that represents our best guess of where the points would have been if we had no measurement error. The usual way to do this is to **fit** a line to the data.

15.1.1 Using Linear Regression to Find a Fit

Whenever we fit any curve (including a line) to data we need some way to decide which curve is the best fit for the data. This means that we need to define an **objective function** that provides a quantitative assessment of how well the curve fits the data. Once we have such a function, finding the best fit can be formulated as finding a curve that minimizes (or maximizes) the value of that function, i.e., as an optimization problem (see Chapters 17 and 18).

The most commonly used objective function is called **least squares**. Let *observed* and *predicted* be vectors of equal length, where *observed* contains the measured points and predicted the corresponding data points on the proposed fit.

The objective function is then defined as:

$$\sum_{i=0}^{len(observed)-1} (observed[i] - predicted[i])^2$$

Squaring the difference between observed and predicted points makes large differences between observed and predicted points relatively more important than small differences. Squaring the difference also discards information about whether the difference is positive or negative.

How might we go about finding the best least-squares fit? One way to do this would be to use a successive approximation algorithm similar to the Newton-Raphson algorithm in Chapter 3. Alternatively, there is an analytic solution that is usually applicable. But we don't have to use either, because PyLab provides a built-in function, `polyfit`, that finds the best least-squares fit.

The call

```
    pylab.polyfit(observedXVals, observedYVals, n)
```

finds the coefficients of a polynomial of degree n that provides a best least-squares fit for the set of points defined by the arrays observedXVals and observedYVals. For example, the call

```
    pylab.polyfit(observedXVals, observedYVals, 1)
```

will find a line described by the polynomial $y = ax + b$, where a is the slope of the line and b the y-intercept. In this case, the call returns an array with two floating point values. Similarly, a parabola is described by the quadratic equation $y = ax^2 + bx + c$. Therefore, the call

```
    pylab.polyfit(observedXVals, observedYVals, 2)
```

returns an array with three floating point values.

The algorithm used by polyfit is called **linear regression**. This may seem a bit confusing, since we can use it to fit curves other than lines. The method is linear in the sense that the value of the dependent variable is a linear function of the independent variables and the coefficients found by the regression. For example, when we fit a quadratic, we get a model of the form $y = ax^2 + bx + c$. In such a model, the value of the dependent variable y is linear in the independent variables x^2, x^1, and x^0 and the coefficients a, b, and c.[93]

The function fitData in Figure 15.3 extends the plotData function in Figure 15.2 by adding a line that represents the best fit for the data. It uses polyfit to find the coefficients a and b, and then uses those coefficients to generate the predicted spring displacement for each force. Notice that there is an asymmetry in the way forces and distance are treated. The values in forces (which are derived from the mass suspended from the spring) are treated as independent, and used to produce the values in the dependent variable predictedDistances (a prediction of the displacements produced by suspending the mass).

The function also computes the spring constant, k. The slope of the line, a, is $\Delta distance/\Delta force$. The spring constant, on the other hand, is $\Delta force/\Delta distance$. Consequently k is the inverse of a.

---

[93] A function is linear if the variables appear only in the first degree, are multiplied by constants, and are combined by addition and subtraction.

```
def fitData(inputFile):
    masses, distances = getData(inputFile)
    distances = pylab.array(distances)
    masses = pylab.array(masses)
    forces = masses*9.81
    pylab.plot(forces, distances, 'bo',
               label = 'Measured displacements')
    pylab.title('Measured Displacement of Spring')
    pylab.xlabel('|Force| (Newtons)')
    pylab.ylabel('Distance (meters)')
    #find linear fit
    a,b = pylab.polyfit(forces, distances, 1)
    predictedDistances = a*pylab.array(forces) + b
    k = 1.0/a
    pylab.plot(forces, predictedDistances,
               label = 'Displacements predicted by\nlinear fit, k = '
               + str(round(k, 5)))
    pylab.legend(loc = 'best')
```

Figure 15.3 Fitting a curve to data

The call
`fitData('springData.txt')`
produces the plot on the right. It
is interesting to observe that very
few points actually lie on the
least-squares fit. This is
plausible because we are trying
to minimize the sum of the
squared errors, rather than
maximize the number of points
that lie on the line. Still, it
doesn't look like a great fit. Let's
try a cubic fit by adding to
`fitData`

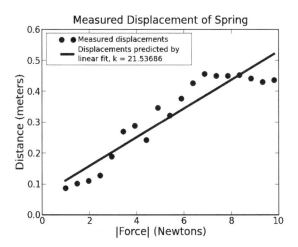

```
#find cubic fit
a,b,c,d = pylab.polyfit(forces, distances, 3)
predictedDistances = a*(forces**3) + b*forces**2 + c*forces + d
pylab.plot(forces, predictedDistances, 'b:', label = 'cubic fit')
```

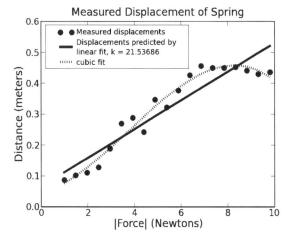

This produces the plot on
the left. The cubic fit looks
like a much better model of
the data, but is it?
Probably not.

In the technical literature,
one frequently sees plots
like this that include both
raw data and a curve fit to
the data. All too often,
however, the authors then

go on to assume that the fitted curve is the description of the real situation, and the raw data merely an indication of experimental error. This can be dangerous.

Recall that we started with a theory that there should be a linear relationship

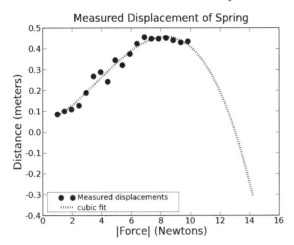

between the x and y values, not a cubic one. Let's see what happens if we use our cubic fit to predict where the point corresponding to 1.5kg would lie. The result is shown in the plot on the left.

Now the cubic fit doesn't look so good. In particular, it seems highly unlikely that by hanging a large weight on the spring we can cause the spring to rise above (the y-value is negative)

the bar from which it is suspended. What we have is an example of **overfitting**. Overfitting typically occurs when a model is excessively complex, e.g., it has too many parameters relative to the amount of data. When this happens, the fit can capture noise in the data rather than meaningful relationships. A model that has been overfit usually has poor predictive power, as seen in this example.

Finger exercise: Modify the code in Figure 15.3 so that it produces the above plot.

Let's go back to the linear fit. For the moment, forget the line and study the raw

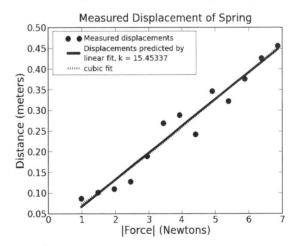

data. Does anything about it seem odd? If we were to fit a line to the rightmost six points it would be nearly parallel to the x-axis. This seems to contradict Hooke's law—until we recall that Hooke's law holds only up to some elastic limit. Perhaps that limit is reached for this spring somewhere around 7N (approximately 0.7kg). Let's see what happens if we eliminate the last six points by replacing the second and third lines of fitData by

```
distances = pylab.array(distances[:-6])
masses = pylab.array(masses[:-6])
```

Eliminating those points certainly makes a difference, e.g., k has dropped dramatically and the linear and cubic fits are almost indistinguishable. But how do we know which of the two linear fits is a better representation of how our spring performs up to its elastic limit? We could use some statistical test to determine which line is a better fit for the data, but that would be beside the point. This is not a question that can be answered by statistics. After all we could throw out all the data except any two points and know that `polyfit` would find a line that would be a perfect fit for those two points. One should never throw out experimental results merely to get a better fit.[94] Here we justified throwing out the rightmost points by appealing to the theory underlying Hooke's law, i.e., that springs have an elastic limit. That justification could not have been appropriately used to eliminate points elsewhere in the data.

15.2 The Behavior of Projectiles

Growing bored with merely stretching springs, we decided to use one of our springs to build a device capable of launching a projectile.[95] We used the device four times to fire a projectile at a target 30 yards (1080 inches) from the launching point. Each time, we measured the height of the projectile at various distances from the launch point. The launching point and the target were at the same height, which we treated as 0.0 in our measurements. The data was stored in a file with the contents

```
Distance  trial1   trial2   trial3   trial4
1080      0.0      0.0      0.0      0.0
1044      2.25     3.25     4.5      6.5
1008      5.25     6.5      6.5      8.75
972       7.5      7.75     8.25     9.25
936       8.75     9.25     9.5      10.5
900       12.0     12.25    12.5     14.75
864       13.75    16.0     16.0     16.5
828       14.75    15.25    15.5     17.5
792       15.5     16.0     16.6     16.75
756       17.0     17.0     17.5     19.25
720       17.5     18.5     18.5     19.0
540       19.5     20.0     20.25    20.5
360       18.5     18.5     19.0     19.0
180       13.0     13.0     13.0     13.0
0         0.0      0.0      0.0      0.0
```

The first column contains distances of the projectile from the target. The other columns contain the height of the projectile at that distance for each of the four trials. All of the measurements are in inches.

The code in Figure 15.4 was used to plot the mean altitude of the projectile against the distance from the point of launch. It also plots the best linear and quadratic fits to the points. (In case you have forgotten the meaning of multiplying a list by an integer, the expression `[0]*len(distances)` produces a list of `len(distances)` 0's.)

---

[94] Which isn't to say that people never do.

[95] A projectile is an object that is propelled through space by the exertion of a force that stops after the projectile is launched. In the interest of public safety, we will not describe the launching device used in this experiment. Suffice it to say that it was awesome.

```
def getTrajectoryData(fileName):
    dataFile = open(fileName, 'r')
    distances = []
    heights1, heights2, heights3, heights4 = [],[],[],[]
    discardHeader = dataFile.readline()
    for line in dataFile:
        d, h1, h2, h3, h4 = line.split()
        distances.append(float(d))
        heights1.append(float(h1))
        heights2.append(float(h2))
        heights3.append(float(h3))
        heights4.append(float(h4))
    dataFile.close()
    return (distances, [heights1, heights2, heights3, heights4])

def processTrajectories(fileName):
    distances, heights = getTrajectoryData(fileName)
    numTrials = len(heights)
    distances = pylab.array(distances)
    #Get array containing mean height at each distance
    totHeights = pylab.array([0]*len(distances))
    for h in heights:
        totHeights = totHeights + pylab.array(h)
    meanHeights = totHeights/len(heights)
    pylab.title('Trajectory of Projectile (Mean of '\
                + str(numTrials) + ' Trials)')
    pylab.xlabel('Inches from Launch Point')
    pylab.ylabel('Inches Above Launch Point')
    pylab.plot(distances, meanHeights, 'bo')
    a,b = pylab.polyfit(distances, meanHeights, 1)
    altitudes = a*distances + b
    pylab.plot(distances, altitudes, 'b', label = 'Linear Fit')
    a,b,c = pylab.polyfit(distances, meanHeights, 2)
    altitudes = a*(distances**2) +  b*distances + c
    pylab.plot(distances, altitudes, 'b:', label = 'Quadratic Fit')
    pylab.legend()
```

Figure 15.4 Plotting the Trajectory of a Projectile

A quick look at the plot[96] on the right makes it quite clear that a quadratic fit is far better than a linear one. (The reason that the quadratic fit is not smooth is that we are only plotting the predicted heights that correspond to the measured heights.) But just how bad a fit is the line and how good is the quadratic fit?

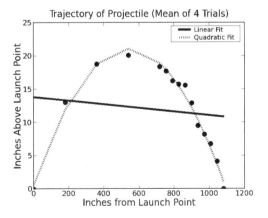

_____

[96] Don't be misled by this plot into thinking that the projectile had a steep angle of ascent. It only looks that way because of the difference in scale between the vertical and horizontal axes on the plot.

15.2.1 Coefficient of Determination

When we fit a curve to a set of data, we are finding a function that relates an independent variable (inches horizontally from the launch point in this example) to a predicted value of a dependent variable (inches above the launch point in this example). Asking about the **goodness of a fit** is equivalent to asking about the accuracy of these predictions. Recall that the fits were found by minimizing the mean square error. This suggests that one could evaluate the goodness of a fit by looking at the mean square error. The problem with that approach is that while there is a lower bound for the mean square error (zero), there is no upper bound. This means that while the mean square error is useful for comparing the relative goodness of two fits to the same data, it is not particularly useful for getting a sense of the absolute goodness of a fit.

We can calculate the absolute goodness of a fit using the **coefficient of determination**, often written as R^2.[97] Let y_i be the ith observed value, p_i be the corresponding value predicted by model, and μ be the mean of the observed values.

$$R^2 = 1 - \frac{\Sigma_i(y_i - p_i)^2}{\Sigma_i(y_i - \mu)^2}$$

By comparing the estimation errors (the numerator) with the variability of the original values (the denominator), R^2 is intended to capture the proportion of variability in a data set that is accounted for by the statistical model provided by the fit. When the model being evaluated is produced by a linear regression, the value of R^2 always lies between 0 and 1. If $R^2 = 1$, the model explains all of the variability in the data. If $R^2 = 0$, there is no relationship between the values predicted by the model and the actual data.

The code in Figure 15.5 provides a straightforward implementation of this statistical measure. Its compactness stems from the expressiveness of the operations on arrays. The expression `(predicted - measured)**2` subtracts the elements of one array from the elements of another, and then squares each element in the result. The expression `(measured - meanOfMeasured)**2` subtracts the scalar value `meanOfMeasured` from each element of the array `measured`, and then squares each element of the results.

```
def rSquared(measured, predicted):
    """Assumes measured a one-dimensional array of measured values
              predicted a one-dimensional array of predicted values
       Returns coefficient of determination"""
    estimateError = ((predicted - measured)**2).sum()
    meanOfMeasured = measured.sum()/float(len(measured))
    variability = ((measured - meanOfMeasured)**2).sum()
    return 1 - estimateError/variability
```

Figure 15.5 Computing R^2

---

[97] There are several different definitions of the coefficient of determination. The definition supplied here is used to evaluate the quality of a fit produced by a linear regression.

When the lines of code

```
print 'RSquare of linear fit =', rSquared(meanHeights, altitudes)
```

and

```
print 'RSquare of quadratic fit =', rSquared(meanHeights, altitudes)
```

are inserted after the appropriate calls to `pylab.plot` in `processTrajectories`, they print

```
RSquared of linear fit = 0.0177433205441
RSquared of quadratic fit = 0.985765369287
```

Roughly speaking, this tells us that less than 2% of the variation in the measured data can be explained by the linear model, but more than 98% of the variation can be explained by the quadratic model.

15.2.2 Using a Computational Model

Now that we have what seems to be a good model of our data, we can use this model to help answer questions about our original data. One interesting question is the horizontal speed at which the projectile is traveling when it hits the target. We might use the following train of thought to design a computation that answers this question:

1. We know that the trajectory of the projectile is given by a formula of the form $y = ax^2 + bx + c$, i.e., it is a parabola. Since every parabola is symmetrical around its vertex, we know that its peak occurs halfway between the launch point and the target; call this value *xMid*. The peak height, *yPeak*, is therefore given by $yPeak = a * xMid^2 + b * xMid + c$.

2. If we ignore air resistance (remember that no model is perfect), we can compute the amount of time it takes for the projectile to fall from *yPeak* to the height of the target, because that is purely a function of gravity. It is given by the equation $t = \sqrt{(2 * yPeak)/g}$.[98] This is also the amount of time it takes for the projectile to travel the horizontal distance from *xMid* to the target, because once it reaches the target it stops moving.

3. Given the time to go from *xMid* to the target, we can easily compute the average horizontal speed of the projectile over that interval. If we assume that the projectile was neither accelerating nor decelerating in the horizontal direction during that interval, we can use the average horizontal speed as an estimate of the horizontal speed when the projectile hits the target.[99]

Figure 15.6 implements this technique for estimating the horizontal velocity of the projectile.

---

[98] This equation can be derived from first principles, but it is easier to just look it up. We found it at `http://en.wikipedia.org/wiki/Equations_for_a_falling_body`.

[99] The vertical component of the velocity is also easily estimated, since it is merely the product of the `g` and `t` in Figure 15.6.

```
def getHorizontalSpeed(a, b, c, minX, maxX):
    """Assumes minX and maxX are distances in inches
       Returns horizontal speed in feet per second"""
    inchesPerFoot = 12.0
    xMid = (maxX - minX)/2.0
    yPeak = a*xMid**2 + b*xMid + c
    g = 32.16*inchesPerFoot #accel. of gravity in inches/sec/sec
    t = (2*yPeak/g)**0.5
    print 'Horizontal speed =', int(xMid/(t*inchesPerFoot)), 'feet/sec'
```

Figure 15.6 Computing the horizontal speed of a projectile

When the line getHorizontalSpeed(a, b, c, distances[-1], distances[0]) is inserted at the end of processTrajectories, it prints

```
Horizontal speed = 136 feet/sec
```

The sequence of steps we have just worked through follows a common pattern.

1. We started by performing an experiment to get some data about the behavior of a physical system.

2. We then used computation to find and evaluate the quality of a model of the behavior of the system.

3. Finally, we used some theory and analysis to design a simple computation to derive an interesting consequence of the model.

15.3 Fitting Exponentially Distributed Data

Polyfit uses linear regression to find a polynomial of a given degree that is the best least-squares fit for some data. It works well if the data can be directly approximated by a polynomial. But this is not always possible. Consider, for example, the simple exponential growth function $y = 2^x$. The code in Figure 15.7 fits a 4th-degree polynomial to the first ten points and plots the results. It uses the function call pylab.arange(10), which returns an array containing the integers 0-9.

```
vals = []
for i in range(10):
    vals.append(2**i)
pylab.plot(vals,'bo', label = 'Actual points')
xVals = pylab.arange(10)
a,b,c,d,e = pylab.polyfit(xVals, vals, 4)
yVals = a*(xVals**4) + b*(xVals**3) + c*(xVals**2)+ d*xVals + e
pylab.plot(yVals, 'bx', label = 'Predicted points', markersize = 20)
pylab.title('Fitting y = 2**x')
pylab.legend()
```

Figure 15.7 Fitting a polynomial curve to an exponential distribution

The code in Figure 15.7 produces the plot

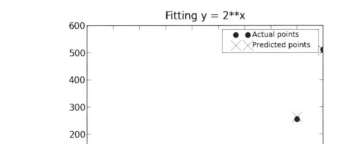

The fit is clearly a good one, for these data points. However, let's look at what the model predicts for 2^{20}. When we add the code

```
pred2to20 = a*(20**4) + b*(20**3) + c*(20**2)+ d*20 + e
print 'Model predicts that 2**20 is roughly', round(pred2to20)
print 'Actual value of 2**20 is', 2**20
```

to the end of Figure 15.7, it prints,

```
Model predicts that 2**20 is roughly 29796.0
Actual value of 2**20 is 1048576
```

Oh dear, despite fitting the data, the model produced by `polyfit` is apparently not a good one. Is it because four was not the right degree? No. It is because no polynomial is a good fit for an exponential distribution. Does this mean that we cannot use `polyfit` to build a model of an exponential distribution? Fortunately, it does not, because we can use `polyfit` to find a curve that fits the original independent values and the log of the dependent values.

Consider the sequence [1, 2, 4, 8, 16, 32, 64, 128, 256, 512]. If we take the log base 2 of each value. we get the sequence [0, 1, 2, 3, 4, 5, 6, 7, 8, 9], i.e., a sequence that grows linearly. In fact, if a function y = f(x), exhibits exponential growth, the log (to any base) of f(x) grows linearly. This can be visualized by plotting an exponential function with a logarithmic y-axis. The code

```
xVals, yVals = [], []
for i in range(10):
    xVals.append(i)
    yVals.append(2**i)
pylab.plot(xVals, yVals)
pylab.semilogy()
```

produces the plot on the right.

The fact that taking the log of an exponential function produces a linear function can be used to construct a

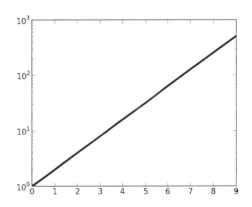

model for an exponentially distributed set of data points, as illustrated by the code in Figure 15.8. We use `polyfit` to find a curve that fits the x values and log of the y values. Notice that we use yet another Python standard library module, `math`, which supplies a `log` function.

```
import math

#define an arbitrary exponential function
def f(x):
    return 3*(2**(1.2*x))

def createExpData(f, xVals):
    """Asssumes f is an exponential function of one argument
              xVals is an array of suitable arguments for f
       Returns array containing results of applying f to the
              elements of xVals"""
    yVals = []
    for i in range(len(xVals)):
        yVals.append(f(xVals[i]))
    return pylab.array(xVals), pylab.array(yVals)

def fitExpData(xVals, yVals):
    """Assumes xVals and yVals arrays of numbers such that
         yVals[i] == f(xVals[i])
       Returns a, b, base such that log(f(x), base) == ax + b"""
    logVals = []
    for y in yVals:
        logVals.append(math.log(y, 2.0)) #get log base 2
    a,b = pylab.polyfit(xVals, logVals, 1)
    return a, b, 2.0

xVals, yVals = createExpData(f, range(10))
pylab.plot(xVals, yVals, 'ro', label = 'Actual values')
a, b, base = fitExpData(xVals, yVals)
predictedYVals = []
for x in xVals:
    predictedYVals.append(base**(a*x + b))
pylab.plot(xVals, predictedYVals, label = 'Predicted values')
pylab.title('Fitting an Exponential Function')
pylab.legend()
#Look at a value for x not in original data
print 'f(20) =', f(20)
print 'Predicted f(20) =', base**(a*20 + b)
```

Figure 15.8 Using polyfit to fit an exponential distribution

When run, this code produces the plot on the right, in which the actual values and the predicted values coincide. Moreover, when the model is tested on a value (20) that was not used to produce the fit, it prints

```
f(20) = 50331648.0
Predicted f(20) = 50331648.0
```

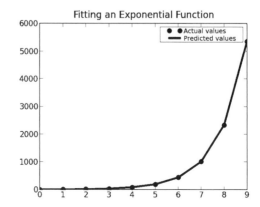

This method of using `polyfit` to find a model for data works when the relationship can be described by an equation of the form $y = base^{ax+b}$. If used on data that cannot be described this way, it will yield erroneous results. To see this, let's try replacing the body of the function f by,

```
return 3*(2**(1.2*x)) + x
```

It now prints,

```
f(20) = 50331668.0
Predicted f(20) = 44846543.4909
```

15.4 When Theory Is Missing

In this chapter we have emphasized the interplay between theoretical, experimental, and computational science. Sometimes, however, we find ourselves with lots of interesting data, but little or no theory. In such cases, we often resort to using computational techniques to develop a theory by building a model that seems to fit the data.

In an ideal world, we would run a controlled experiment (e.g., hang weights from a spring), study the results, and retrospectively formulate a model consistent with those results. We would then run a different **prospective experiment** (e.g., hang different weights from the same spring) and compare the results of that experiment to what the model predicted.

Unfortunately, in many cases it is impossible to run even one controlled experiment. Imagine, for example, building a model designed to shed light on how interest rates affect stock prices. Very few of us are in a position to set interest rates and see what happens. On the other hand there is no shortage of relevant historical data.

In such situations, one can simulate a set of experiments by dividing the existing data into a **training set** and a **holdout set**. Without looking at the holdout set, we build a model that seems to explain the training set. For example, we find a curve that has a reasonable R^2 for the training set. We then test that model on the holdout set. Most of the time the model will fit the training set more closely than it fits the holdout set. But if the model is a good one, it should fit the holdout set reasonably well. If it doesn't, the model should probably be discarded.

How does one choose the training set? We want it to be representative of the data set as a whole. One way to do this is to randomly choose the samples for the training set. If the data set is sufficiently large this often works pretty well.

A related but slightly different way to check a model is to train on many randomly selected subsets of the original data, and see how similar the models are to one another. If they are quite similar, than we can feel pretty good. This approach is known as **cross validation**.

16 LIES, DAMNED LIES, AND STATISTICS

"If you can't prove what you want to prove, demonstrate something else and pretend they are the same thing. In the daze that follows the collision of statistics with the human mind, hardly anyone will notice the difference."[100]

Statistical thinking is a relatively new invention. For most of recorded history things were assessed qualitatively rather than quantitatively. People must have had an intuitive sense of some statistical facts (e.g., that women are usually shorter than men), but they had no mathematical tools that would allow them to proceed from anecdotal evidence to statistical conclusions. This started to change in the middle of the 17th century, most notably with the publication of John Graunt's *Natural and Political Observations Made Upon the Bills of Mortality*. This pioneering work used statistical analysis to estimate the population of London from death rolls, and attempted to provide a model that could be used to predict the spread of plague.

Since that time people have used statistics as much to mislead as to inform. Some have willfully used statistics to mislead; others have merely been incompetent. In this chapter we discuss a few ways in which people can be fooled into drawing inappropriate inferences from statistical data. We trust that you will use this information only for good, i.e., to become a better consumer and a more honest purveyor of statistical information.

16.1 Garbage In Garbage Out (GIGO)

"On two occasions I have been asked [by members of Parliament], 'Pray, Mr. Babbage, if you put into the machine wrong figures, will the right answers come out?' I am not able rightly to apprehend the kind of confusion of ideas that could provoke such a question." – Charles Babbage.

The message here is a simple one. If the input data is seriously flawed, no amount of statistical massaging will produce a meaningful result.

The 1840 United States census showed that insanity among free blacks and mulattoes was roughly ten times more common than among enslaved blacks and mulattoes. The conclusion was obvious. As U.S. Senator (and former Vice President and future Secretary of State) John C. Calhoun put it, "The data on insanity revealed in this census is unimpeachable. From it our nation must conclude that the abolition of slavery would be to the African a curse." Never mind that it was soon clear that the census was riddled with errors. As Calhoun reportedly explained to John Quincy Adams, "there were so many errors they

---

[100] Darrell Huff, *How to Lie with Statistics*, 1954.

balanced one another, and led to the same conclusion as if they were all correct."

Calhoun's (perhaps willfully) spurious response to Adams was based on a classical error, the **assumption of independence**. Were he more sophisticated mathematically, he might have said something like, "I believe that the measurement errors are unbiased and independent of each of other, and therefore evenly distributed on either side of the mean." In fact, later analysis showed that the errors were so heavily biased that no statistically valid conclusions could be drawn.[101]

16.2 Pictures Can Be Deceiving

There can be no doubt about the utility of graphics for quickly conveying information. However, when used carelessly (or maliciously) a plot can be highly misleading. Consider, for example, the following charts depicting housing prices in the U.S. Midwestern states.

 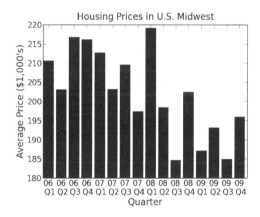

Looking at the chart on the left, it seems as if housing prices were pretty stable from 2006-2009. But wait a minute, wasn't there a collapse of U.S. residential real estate followed by a global financial crisis in late 2008? There was indeed, as shown in the chart on the right.

These two charts show exactly the same data, but convey very different impressions.

The first chart was designed to give the impression that housing prices had been stable. On the y-axis, the designer used a logarithmic scale ranging from the absurdly low average price for a house of $10,000 to the improbably high average price of $1 million. This minimized the amount of space devoted to the area where prices are changing, giving the impression that the changes were relatively small. The chart above and on the right was designed to give the impression that housing prices moved erratically, and then crashed. The

---

[101] We should note that Calhoun was in office over 150 years ago. It goes without saying that no contemporary politician would find ways to abuse statistics to support a position.

designer used a linear scale and a narrow range of prices, so the sizes of the changes were exaggerated.

The code in Figure 16.1 produces the two plots we looked at above and a plot intended to give an accurate impression of the movement of housing prices.

It uses two plotting facilities that we have not yet seen. The call `pylab.bar(quarters, prices, width)` produces a **bar chart** with `width` wide bars. The left edges of the bars are the values of the elements of `quarters` and the heights of the bars are the values of the corresponding elements of `prices`. The call `pylab.xticks(quarters+width/2.0, labels)` describes the labels associated with the bars. The first argument specifies where each label is to be placed and the second argument the text of the labels. The function `yticks` behaves analogously.

```
def plotHousing(impression):
    """Assumes impression a str.  Must be one of 'flat',
        'volatile,' and 'fair'
      Produce bar chart of housing prices over time"""
    f = open('midWestHousingPrices.txt', 'r')
    #Each line of file contains year quarter price
    #for Midwest region of U.S.
    labels, prices = ([], [])
    for line in f:
        year, quarter, price = line.split()
        label = year[2:4] + '\n Q' + quarter[1]
        labels.append(label)
        prices.append(float(price)/1000)
    quarters = pylab.arange(len(labels)) #x coords of bars
    width = 0.8 #Width of bars
    if impression == 'flat':
        pylab.semilogy()
    pylab.bar(quarters, prices, width)
    pylab.xticks(quarters+width/2.0, labels)
    pylab.title('Housing Prices in U.S. Midwest')
    pylab.xlabel('Quarter')
    pylab.ylabel('Average Price ($1,000\'s)')
    if impression == 'flat':
        pylab.ylim(10, 10**3)
    elif impression == 'volatile':
        pylab.ylim(180, 220)
    elif impression == 'fair':
        pylab.ylim(150, 250)
    else:
        raise ValueError

plotHousing('flat')
pylab.figure()
plotHousing('volatile')
pylab.figure()
plotHousing('fair')
```

Figure 16.1 Plotting housing prices

The call `plotHousing('fair')` produces the plot

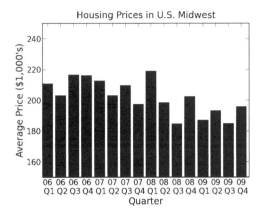

16.3 *Cum Hoc Ergo Propter Hoc*[102]

It has been shown that college students who regularly attend class have higher average grades than students who attend class only sporadically. Those of us who teach these classes would like to believe that this is because the students learn something from the lectures. Of course, it is at least equally likely that those students get better grades because students who are more likely to attend classes are also more likely to study hard.

When two things are correlated,[103] there is a temptation to assume that one has caused the other. Consider the incidence of flu in North America. The number of cases rises and falls in a predictable pattern. There are almost no cases in the summer, the number of cases starts to rise in the early fall, and then starts dropping as summer approaches. Now consider the number of children attending school. There are very few children in school in the summer, enrollment starts to rise in the early fall, and then drops as summer approaches.

The correlation between the opening of schools and the rise in the incidence of flu is inarguable. This has led many to conclude that that going to school is an important causative factor in the spread of flu. That might be true, but one cannot conclude it based simply on the correlation. Correlation does not imply causation! After all, the correlation could be used just as easily to justify the belief that flu outbreaks cause schools to be in session. Or perhaps there is no causal relationship in either direction, and there is some **lurking variable** that

---

[102]Statisticians, like attorneys and physicians, sometimes use Latin for no obvious reason other than to seem erudite. This phrase means, "with this, therefore because of this."

[103] Correlation is a measure of the degree to which two variables move in the same direction. If when x goes up y goes up, the variables are positively correlated. If they move in opposite directions they are negatively correlated. If there is no relationship, the correlation is 0. People's heights are positively correlated with the heights of their parents. The correlation between hours spent playing video games and grade point average is negative.

we have not considered that causes each. In fact, as it happens, the flu virus survives considerably longer in cool dry air than it does in warm wet air, and in North America both the flu season and school sessions are correlated with cooler and dryer weather.

Given enough retrospective data, it is always possible to find two variables that are correlated, as illustrated by the chart on the right.[104] When such correlations are found, the first thing to do is to ask whether there is a plausible theory explaining the correlation.

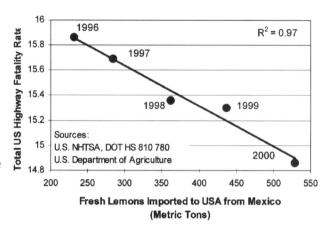

Falling prey to the *cum hoc ergo propter hoc* fallacy can be quite dangerous. At the start of 2002, roughly six million American women were being prescribed hormone replacement therapy (HRT) in the belief that it would substantially lower their risk of cardiovascular disease. That belief was supported by several highly reputable published studies that demonstrated a reduced incidence of cardiovascular death among women using HRT. Many women, and their physicians, were taken by surprise when the *Journal of the American Medical Society* published an article asserting that HRT in fact increased the risk of cardiovascular disease.[105] How could this have happened?

Re-analysis of some of the earlier studies showed that women undertaking HRT were likely to be from groups with better than average diet and exercise regimes. Perhaps the women undertaking HRT were on average more health conscious than the other women in the study, so that taking HRT and improved cardiac health were coincident effects of a common cause.

16.4 Statistical Measures Don't Tell the Whole Story

There are an enormous number of different statistics that can be extracted from a data set. By carefully choosing among these, it is possible to convey a variety of different impressions about the same data. A good antidote is to look at the data set itself.

In 1973, the statistician F.J. Anscombe published a paper containing the table below. It contains the <x, y> coordinates of the points in each of four data sets.

---

[104] Stephen R. Johnson, "The Trouble with QSAR (or How I Learned to Stop Worrying and Embrace Fallacy)," *J. Chem. Inf. Model.*, 2008.

[105] Nelson HD, Humphrey LL, Nygren P, Teutsch SM, Allan JD. Postmenopausal hormone replacement therapy: scientific review. *JAMA.* 2002;288:872-881.

x	y	x	y	x	y	x	y
10.0	8.04	10.0	9.14	10.0	7.46	8.0	6.58
8.0	6.95	8.0	8.14	8.0	6.77	8.0	5.76
13.0	7.58	13.0	8.74	13.0	12.74	8.0	7.71
9.0	8.81	9.0	8.77	9.0	7.11	8.0	8.84
11.0	8.33	11.0	9.26	11.0	7.81	8.0	8.47
14.0	9.96	14.0	8.10	14.0	8.84	8.0	7.04
6.0	7.24	6.0	6.13	6.0	6.08	8.0	5.25
4.0	4.26	4.0	3.10	4.0	5.39	19.0	12.50
12.0	10.84	12.0	9.13	12.0	8.15	8.0	5.56
7.0	4.82	7.0	7.26	7.0	6.42	8.0	7.91
5.0	5.68	5.0	4.74	5.0	5.73	8.0	6.89

These four data sets are statistically similar. They have the same mean value for x (9.0), the same mean value for y (7.5), the same variance for x (10.0), the same variance for y (3.75), and the same correlation between x and y (0.816). Furthermore, if we use linear regression to fit a line to each, we get the same result for each, y = 0.5x + 3.

Does this mean that there is no obvious way to distinguish these data sets from each other? No, one simply needs to plot the data to see that the data sets are not at all alike.

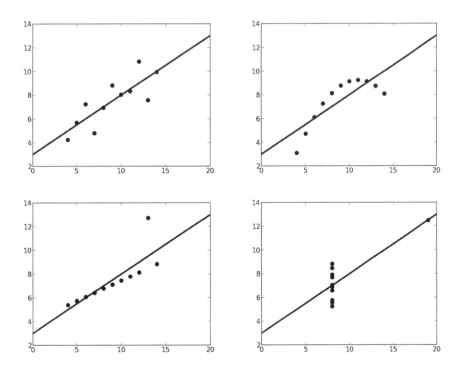

The moral is simple: if possible, always take a look at some representation of the raw data.

16.5 Sampling Bias

During World War II, whenever an Allied plane would return from a mission over Europe the plane would be inspected to see where the flak had impacted. Based upon this data, mechanics reinforced those areas of the planes that seemed most likely to be hit by flak.

What's wrong with this? They did not inspect the planes that failed to return from missions because they had been downed by flak. Perhaps these unexamined planes failed to return precisely because they were hit in the places where the flak would do the most damage. This particular error is called **non-response bias**. It is quite common in surveys. At many universities, for examples, students are asked during one of the lectures late in the term to fill out a form rating the quality of the professor's lectures. Though the results of such surveys are often unflattering, they could be worse. Those students who think that the lectures are so bad that they aren't worth attending are not included in the survey.[106]

As we said earlier, all statistical techniques are based upon the assumption that by sampling a subset of a population we can infer things about the population as a whole. If random sampling is used, we can make precise mathematical statements about the expected relationship of the sample to the entire population. Unfortunately, many studies, particularly in the social sciences, are based on what has been called **convenience** (or **accidental**) **sampling**. This involves choosing samples based on how easy they are to procure. Why do so many psychological studies use populations of undergraduates? Because they are easy to find on college campuses. A convenience sample *might* be representative, but there is no way of knowing whether it actually *is* representative.

The Family Research Institute's Web site contains a table with the following information:

Category	Mean Age at Death	% Died Aged 65+
Heterosexual Married Men	75	80%
Heterosexual Married Women	79	85%
Homosexual Males, AIDS Deaths	39	1%
Homosexual Males, Non-AIDS Deaths	42	9%
Lesbians	44	20%

Table 1: How Long Do Homosexuals Live? [107]

---

[106] The move to online surveys, which allows students who do not attend class to participate in the survey, does not augur well for the egos of professors.

[107] http://www.familyresearchinst.org/2012/01/how-long-do-homosexuals-live/

Pretty scary stuff if your sexual preference is other than heterosexual—until one looks at how the data was compiled. According to the Web site it was based on "6,737 obituaries from 18 U.S. homosexual journals, compared to obituaries from 2 mainstream newspapers."

This method produces a sample that could be non-representative of either the homosexual or non-homosexual population (or both) for a large number of reasons. For example, it seems to infer that someone is gay or lesbian if and only if their obituary appears in a "homosexual journal," and that someone is not gay if their obituary appears in a "mainstream newspaper." It also seems to assume that the deaths for which obituaries appear are representative of all deaths. How does one go about evaluating such a sample? One technique is to compare data compiled from the sample against data compiled elsewhere. For example, one could compare the ratio of gay men to straight men in the obituary study to other studies reporting the relative sizes of those two populations.

16.6 Context Matters

It is easy to read more into the data than it actually implies, especially when viewing the data out of context. On April 29, 2009, CNN reported that, "Mexican health officials suspect that the swine flu outbreak has caused more than 159 deaths and roughly 2,500 illnesses." Pretty scary stuff—until one compares it to the 36,000 deaths attributable annually to the seasonal flu in the U.S.

An often quoted, and accurate, statistic is that most auto accidents happen within 10 miles of home. So what—most driving is done within 10 miles of home. And besides, what does "home" mean in this context? The statistic is computed using the address at which the automobile is registered as "home." Might one reduce the probability of getting into an accident by merely registering one's car in some distant place?

Opponents of government initiatives to reduce the prevalence of guns in the U.S. are fond of quoting the statistic that roughly 99.8% of the firearms in the U.S. will not be used to commit a violent crime in any given year. Does this mean that there is not much gun violence in the U.S? The National Rifle Association reports that that there are roughly 300 million privately owned firearms in the U.S.—0.2% of 300 million is 600,000.

16.7 Beware of Extrapolation

It is all too easy to extrapolate from data. We did that in Chapter 15 when we extended fits derived from linear regression beyond the data upon which the regression was done. Extrapolation should be done only when one has a sound theoretical justification for doing so. One should be especially wary of straight-line extrapolations.

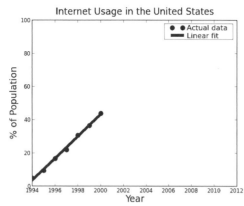

Consider the plot on the left. It shows the growth of Internet usage in the United States from 1994 to 2000. As you can see, a straight line provides a pretty good fit.

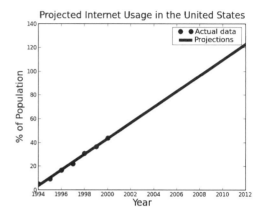

The plot on the right uses this fit to project the percentage of the U.S. population using the Internet in following years. The projection is a bit hard to believe. It seems unlikely that by 2009 everybody in the U.S. was using the Internet, and even less likely that by 2012 more than 120% of the U.S. population was using the Internet.

16.8 The Texas Sharpshooter Fallacy

Imagine that you are driving down a country road in Texas. You see a barn that has six targets painted on it, and a bullet hole at the very center of each target. "Yes sir," says the owner of the barn, "I never miss." "That's right," says his spouse, "there ain't a man in the state of Texas who's more accurate with a paint brush." Got it? He fired the six shots, and then painted the targets around them.

Professor Puzzles Over Students' Chalk Throwing Ability

A classic of the genre appeared in 2001.[108] It reported that a research team at the Royal Cornhill hospital in Aberdeen had discovered that "anorexic women are most likely to have been born in the spring or early summer... Between

---

[108] Eagles, John, et al., "Season of birth in females with anorexia nervosa in Northeast Scotland," *International Journal of Eating Disorders*, 30, 2, September 2001.

March and June there were 13% more anorexics born than average, and 30% more in June itself."

Let's look at that worrisome statistic for those women born in June. The team studied 446 women who had been diagnosed as anorexic, so the mean number of births per month was slightly more than 37. This suggests that the number born in June was 48 (37*1.3). Let's write a short program to see if we can reject the null hypothesis that this occurred purely by chance.

```
def juneProb(numTrials):
    june48 = 0
    for trial in range(numTrials):
      june = 0
      for i in range(446):
          if random.randint(1,12) == 6:
              june += 1
      if june >= 48:
          june48 += 1
    jProb = june48/float(numTrials)
    print 'Probability of at least 48 births in June =', jProb
```

Figure 16.2 Probability of 48 anorexics being born in June

When we ran juneProb(10000) it printed

    Probability of at least 48 births in June = 0.044

It looks as if the probability of at least 48 babies being born in June purely by chance is around 4.5%. So perhaps those researchers in Aberdeen are on to something. Well, they might have been on to something had they started with the hypothesis that more babies who will become anorexic are born in June, and then run a study designed to check that hypothesis.

But that is not what they did. Instead, they looked at the data and then, imitating the Texas sharpshooter, drew a circle around June. The right statistical question to have asked is what is the probability that there was at least one month (out of 12) in which at least 48 babies were born. The program in Figure 16.3 answers that question.

```
def anyProb(numTrials):
    anyMonth48 = 0
    for trial in range(numTrials):
      months = [0]*12
      for i in range(446):
          months[random.randint(0,11)] += 1
      if max(months) >= 48:
          anyMonth48 += 1
    aProb = anyMonth48/float(numTrials)
    print 'Probability of at least 48 births in some month =', aProb
```

Figure 16.3 Probability of 48 anorexics being born in some month

The call `anyProb(10000)` printed

```
Probability of at least 48 births in some month = 0.446
```

It appears that it is not so unlikely after all that the results reported in the study reflect a chance occurrence rather a real association between birth month and anorexia. One doesn't have to come from Texas to fall victim to the Texas Sharpshooter Fallacy.

What we see here is that the statistical significance of a result depends upon the way the experiment was conducted. If the Aberdeen group had started out with the hypothesis that more anorexics are born in June, their result would be worth considering. But if they started off with the hypothesis that there exists a month in which an unusually large proportion of anorexics are born, their result is not very compelling.

What next steps might the Aberdeen group have taken to test their newfound hypothesis? One possibility is to conduct a **prospective study**. In a prospective study, one starts with a set of hypotheses and then gathers data with the potential to either refute or confirm the hypothesis. If the group conducted a new study and got similar results, one might be convinced.

Prospective studies can be expensive and time consuming to perform. In a **retrospective study**, one has to examine existing data in ways that reduce the likelihood of getting misleading results. One common technique, as discussed in Chapter 15, is to split the data into a training set and a holdout set. For example, they could have chosen 446/2 women at random from their data (the training set), and tallied the number of births for each month. They could have then compared that to the number of births each month for the remaining women (the holdout set).

16.9 Percentages Can Confuse

An investment advisor called a client to report that the value of his stock portfolio had risen 16% over the last month. He admitted that there had been some ups and downs over the year, but was pleased to report that the average monthly change was +0.5%. Image the client's surprise when he got his statement for the year, and observed that the value of his portfolio had declined over the year.

He called his advisor, and accused him of being a liar. "It looks to me," he said, "like my portfolio declined by 0.67%, and you told me that it went up by 0.5% a month." "I did not," the financial advisor replied, "I told you that the average monthly change was +0.5%." When he examined his monthly statements, the investor realized that he had not been lied to, just misled. His portfolio went down by 15% in each month during the first half of the year, and then went up by 16% in each month during the second half of the year.

When thinking about percentages, we always need to pay attention to the basis on which the percentage is computed. In this case, the 15% declines were on a higher average basis than the 16% increases.

Percentages can be particularly misleading when applied to a small basis. You might read about a drug that has a side effect of increasing the incidence of some illness by 200%. But if the base incidence of the disease is very low, say one in 1,000,000, you might well decide that the risk of taking the drug was more than counterbalanced by the drug's positive effects.

16.10   Just Beware

It would be easy, and fun, to fill a few hundred pages with a history of statistical abuses. But by now you probably got the message: It's just as easy to lie with numbers as it is to lie with words. Make sure that you understand what is actually being measured and how those "statistically significant" results were computed before you jump to conclusions.

17 KNAPSACK AND GRAPH OPTIMIZATION PROBLEMS

The notion of an optimization problem provides a structured way to think about solving lots of computational problems. Whenever you set about solving a problem that involves finding the biggest, the smallest, the most, the fewest, the fastest, the least expensive, etc., there is a good chance that you can map the problem onto a classic optimization problem for which there is a known computational solution.

In general, an optimization problem has two parts:

1. An **objective function** that is to be maximized or minimized. For example, the airfare between Boston and Istanbul.
2. A **set of constraints** (possibly empty) that must be honored. For example, an upper bound on the travel time.

In this chapter, we introduce the notion of an optimization problem and give a few examples. We also provide some simple algorithms that solve them. In the next chapter, we discuss more efficient ways of solving an important class of optimization problems.

The main things to take away from this chapter are:

- Many problems of real importance can be simply formulated in a way that leads naturally to a computational solution.

- Reducing a seemingly new problem to an instance of a well-known problem allows one to use preexisting solutions.

- Exhaustive enumeration algorithms provide a simple, but often computationally intractable, way to search for optimal solutions.

- A greedy algorithm is often a practical approach to finding a pretty good, but not always optimal, solution to an optimization problem.

- Knapsack problems and graph problems are classes of problems to which other problems can often be reduced.

As usual we will supplement the material on computational thinking with a few bits of Python and some tips about programming.

17.1 Knapsack Problems

It's not easy being a burglar. In addition to the obvious problems (making sure that a home is empty, picking locks, circumventing alarms, dealing with ethical quandaries, etc.), a burglar has to decide what to steal. The problem is that most homes contain more things of value than the average burglar can carry away. What's a poor burglar to do? He needs to find the set of things that provides the most value without exceeding his carrying capacity.

Suppose for example, a burglar who has a knapsack[109] that can hold at most 20 pounds of loot breaks into a house and finds the items in Figure 17.1. Clearly, he will not be able to fit it all in his knapsack, so he needs to decide what to take and what to leave behind.

	Value	Weight	Value/Weight
Clock	175	10	17.5
Painting	90	9	10
Radio	20	4	5
Vase	50	2	25
Book	10	1	10
Computer	200	20	10

Figure 17.1 Table of items

17.1.1 Greedy Algorithms

The simplest way to find an approximate solution to this problem is to use a **greedy algorithm**. The thief would choose the best item first, then the next best, and continue until he reached his limit. Of course, before doing this, the thief would have to decide what "best" should mean. Is the best item the most valuable, the least heavy, or maybe the item with the highest value-to-weight ratio? If he chose highest value, he would leave with just the computer, which he could fence for $200. If he chose lowest weight, he would take, in order, the book, the radio, the vase, and the painting—which would be worth a total of $170. Finally, if he decided that best meant highest value-to-weight ratio, he would start by taking the vase and the clock. That would leave three items with a value-to-weight ratio of 10, but of those only the book would still fit in the knapsack. After taking the book, he would take the remaining item that still fit, the radio. The total value of his loot would be $255.

Though greedy-by-density (value-to-weight ratio) happens to yield the best result for this data set, there is no guarantee that a greedy-by-density algorithm always finds a better solution than greedy by weight or value. More generally, there is no guarantee that any solution to this kind of knapsack problem that is found by a greedy algorithm will be optimal.[110] We will discuss this issue in more detail a bit later.

The code in Figure 17.2 and Figure 17.3 implements all three of these greedy algorithms. In Figure 17.2, we first define class `Item`. Each `Item` has a `name`, `value`, and `weight` attribute.

---

[109] For those of you too young to remember, a "knapsack" is a simple bag that people used to carry on their back—long before "backpacks" became fashionable. If you happen to have been in scouting you might remember the words of the "Happy Wanderer," "I love to go a-wandering, Along the mountain track, And as I go, I love to sing, My knapsack on my back."

[110] There is probably some deep moral lesson to be extracted from this fact, and it is probably not "greed is good."

The only interesting code is the implementation of the function greedy. By introducing the parameter keyFunction, we make greedy independent of the order in which the elements of the list are to be considered. All that is required is that keyFunction defines an ordering on the elements in items. We then use this ordering to produce a sorted list containing the same elements as items. We use the built-in Python function sorted to do this. (We use sorted rather than sort because we want to generate a new list rather than mutate the list passed to the function.) We use the reverse parameter to indicate that we want the list sorted from largest (with respect to keyFunction) to smallest.

```
class Item(object):
    def __init__(self, n, v, w):
        self.name = n
        self.value = float(v)
        self.weight = float(w)
    def getName(self):
        return self.name
    def getValue(self):
        return self.value
    def getWeight(self):
        return self.weight
    def __str__(self):
        result = '<' + self.name + ', ' + str(self.value)\
                 + ', ' + str(self.weight) + '>'
        return result

def value(item):
    return item.getValue()

def weightInverse(item):
    return 1.0/item.getWeight()

def density(item):
    return item.getValue()/item.getWeight()

def buildItems():
    names = ['clock', 'painting', 'radio', 'vase', 'book', 'computer']
    values = [175,90,20,50,10,200]
    weights = [10,9,4,2,1,20]
    Items = []
    for i in range(len(values)):
        Items.append(Item(names[i], values[i], weights[i]))
    return Items
```

Figure 17.2 Building a set of items with orderings

```
def greedy(items, maxWeight, keyFunction):
    """Assumes Items a list, maxWeight >= 0,
        keyFunction maps elements of Items to floats"""
    itemsCopy = sorted(items, key=keyFunction, reverse = True)
    result = []
    totalValue = 0.0
    totalWeight = 0.0
    for i in range(len(itemsCopy)):
        if (totalWeight + itemsCopy[i].getWeight() <= maxWeight:
            result.append(itemsCopy[i])
            totalWeight += itemsCopy[i].getWeight()
            totalValue += itemsCopy[i].getValue()
    return (result, totalValue)

def testGreedy(items, constraint, keyFunction):
    taken, val = greedy(items, constraint, keyFunction)
    print 'Total value of items taken = ', val
    for item in taken:
        print '   ', item

def testGreedys(maxWeight = 20):
    items = buildItems()
    print 'Use greedy by value to fill knapsack of size', maxWeight
    testGreedy(items, maxWeight, value)
    print '\nUse greedy by weight to fill knapsack of size', maxWeight
    testGreedy(items, maxWeight, weightInverse)
    print '\nUse greedy by density to fill knapsack of size', maxWeight
    testGreedy(items, maxWeight, density)
```

Figure 17.3 Using a greedy algorithm to choose items

When `testGreedys()` is executed it prints

```
Use greedy by value to fill knapsack of size 20
Total value of items taken =  200.0
    <computer, 200.0, 20.0>

Use greedy by weight to fill knapsack of size 20
Total value of items taken =  170.0
    <book, 10.0, 1.0>
    <vase, 50.0, 2.0>
    <radio, 20.0, 4.0>
    <painting, 90.0, 9.0>

Use greedy by density to fill knapsack of size 20
Total value of items taken =  255.0
    <vase, 50.0, 2.0>
    <clock, 175.0, 10.0>
    <book, 10.0, 1.0>
    <radio, 20.0, 4.0>
```

What is the algorithmic efficiency of `greedy`? There are two things to consider: the time complexity of the built-in function `sorted`, and the number of times through the `for` loop in the body of `greedy`. The number of iterations of the loop is bounded by the number of elements in `items`, i.e., it is O(n), where n is the length of `items`. However, the worst-case time for Python's built-in sorting function is roughly O(n log n), where n is the length of the list to be sorted[111]. Therefore the running time of greedy is O(n log n).

17.1.2 An Optimal Solution to the 0/1 Knapsack Problem

Suppose we decide that an approximation is not good enough, i.e., we want the best possible solution to this problem. Such a solution is called **optimal**, not surprising since we are solving an optimization problem. As it happens, this is an instance of a classic optimization problem, called the **0/1 knapsack problem**.

The 0/1 knapsack problem can be formalized as follows:

1. Each item is represented by a pair, *<value, weight>*.

2. The knapsack can accommodate items with a total weight of no more than w.

3. A vector, *I*, of length *n*, represents the set of available items. Each element of the vector is an item.

4. A vector, *V*, of length *n*, is used to indicate whether or not each item is taken by the burglar. If V[i] = 1, item I[i] is taken. If V[i] = 0, item I[i] is not taken.

5. Find a V that maximizes

$$\sum_{i=0}^{n-1} V[i]*I[i].value$$

subject to the constraint that

$$\sum_{i=0}^{n-1} V[i]*I[i].weight \le w$$

Let's see what happens if we try to implement this formulation of the problem in a straightforward way:

1. Enumerate all possible combinations of items. That is to say, generate all subsets[112] of the set of items. This is called the power set, and was discussed in Chapter 9.

2. Remove all of the combinations whose weight exceeds the allowed weight.

3. From the remaining combinations choose any one whose value is the largest.

This approach will certainly find an optimal answer. However, if the original set of items is large, it will take a very long time to run, because, as we saw in Chapter 9, the number of subsets grows exceedingly quickly with the number of items.

Figure 17.4 contains a straightforward implementation of this brute-force approach to solving the 0/1 knapsack problem. It uses the classes and functions defined in Figure 17.2 and Figure 17.3, and the function `genPowerset` defined in Figure 9.5.

---

[111] As we discussed in Chapter 10, the time complexity of the sorting algorithm, timsort, used in most Python implementations is O(n log n).

[112] Recall that every set is a subset of itself and the empty set is a subset of every set.

```
def chooseBest(pset, maxWeight, getVal, getWeight):
    bestVal = 0.0
    bestSet = None
    for items in pset:
        itemsVal = 0.0
        itemsWeight = 0.0
        for item in items:
            itemsVal += getVal(item)
            itemsWeight += getWeight(item)
        if itemsWeight <= maxWeight and itemsVal > bestVal:
            bestVal = itemsVal
            bestSet = items
    return (bestSet, bestVal)

def testBest(maxWeight = 20):
    items = buildItems()
    pset = genPowerset(items)
    taken, val = chooseBest(pset, maxWeight, Item.getValue,
                            Item.getWeight)
    print 'Total value of items taken =', val
    for item in taken:
        print item
```

Figure 17.4 Brute-force optimal solution to the 0/1 knapsack problem

The complexity of this implementation is $O(n*2^n)$, where n is the length of items. The function genPowerset returns a list of lists of Items. This list is of length 2^n, and the longest list in it is of length n. Therefore the outer loop in chooseBest will be executed $O(2^n)$ times, and the number of times the inner loop will be executed is bounded by n.

Many small optimizations can be applied to speed this program up. For example, genPowerset could have had the header

```
    def genPowerset(items, constraint, getVal, getWeight)
```

and returned only those combinations that meet the weight constraint. Alternatively, chooseBest could exit the inner loop as soon as the weight constraint is exceeded. While these kinds of optimizations are often worth doing, they don't address the fundamental issue. The complexity of chooseBest will still be $O(n*2^n)$, where n is the length of items, and chooseBest will therefore still take a very long time to run when items is large.

In a theoretical sense, the problem is hopeless. The 0/1 knapsack problem is inherently exponential in the number of items. In a practical sense, however, the problem is far from hopeless, as we will discuss in Chapter 18.

When testBest is run, it prints,
```
  Total value of items taken = 275.0
  <clock, 175.0, 10.0>
  <painting, 90.0, 9.0>
  <book, 10.0, 1.0>
```
Notice that this solution is better than any of the solutions found by the greedy algorithms. The essence of a greedy algorithm is making the best (as defined by

some metric) local choice at each step. It makes a choice that is **locally optimal**. However, as this example illustrates, a series of locally optimal decisions does not always lead to a solution that is **globally optimal**.

Despite the fact that they do not always find the best solution, greedy algorithms are often used in practice. They are usually easier to implement and more efficient to run than algorithms guaranteed to find optimal solutions. As Ivan Boesky once said, "I think greed is healthy. You can be greedy and still feel good about yourself." [113]

There is a variant of the knapsack problem, called the **fractional** (or **continuous**) **knapsack problem**, for which a greedy algorithm is guaranteed to find an optimal solution. Since the items are infinitely divisible, it always makes sense to take as much as possible of the item with the highest remaining value-to-weight ratio. Suppose, for example, that our burglar found only three things of value in the house: a sack of gold dust, a sack of silver dust, and a sack of raisins. In this case, a greedy-by-density algorithm will always find the optimal solution.

17.2 Graph Optimization Problems

Let's think about another kind of optimization problem. Suppose you had a list of the prices of all of the airline flights between each pair of cities in the United States. Suppose also that for all cities, A, B, and C, the cost of flying from A to C by way of B was the cost of flying from A to B plus the cost of flying from B to C. A few questions you might like to ask are:

- What is the smallest number of stops between some pair of cities?

- What is the least expensive airfare between some pair of cities?

- What is the least expensive airfare between some pair of cities involving no more than two stops?

- What is the least expensive way to visit some collection of cities?

All of these problems (and many others) can be easily formalized as graph problems.

A **graph**[114] is a set of objects called **nodes** (or **vertices**) connected by a set of **edges** (or **arcs**). If the edges are unidirectional the graph is called a **directed graph** or **digraph**. In a directed graph, if there is an edge from n1 to n2, we refer to n1 as the **source** or **parent node** and n2 as the **destination** or **child node**.

---

[113] He said this, to enthusiastic applause, in a 1986 commencement address at the University of California at Berkeley Business School. A few months later he was indicted for insider trading, a charge that led to two years in prison and a $100,000,000 fine.

[114] Computer scientists and mathematicians use the word "graph" in the sense used in this book. They typically use the word "plot" to denote the kind of graphs we saw in Chapters 11-16.

Graphs are typically used to represent situations in which there are interesting relations among the parts. The first documented use of graphs in mathematics was in 1735 when the Swiss mathematician Leonhard Euler used what has come to be known as **graph theory** to formulate and solve the **Königsberg bridges problem**.

Königsberg, then the capital of East Prussia, was built at the intersection of two rivers that contained a number of islands. The islands were connected to each other and to the mainland by seven bridges, as shown on the map below. For some reason, the residents of the city were obsessed with the question of whether it was possible to take a walk that crossed each bridge exactly once.

Euler's great insight was that the problem could be vastly simplified by viewing each separate landmass as a point (think "node") and each bridge as a line (think "edge") connecting two of these points. The map of the town could then be represented by the graph to the right of the map. Euler then reasoned that if a walk were to traverse each edge exactly once, it must be the case that each node in the middle of the walk (i.e., any node except the first and last node visited) must have an even number of edges to which it is connected. Since none of the nodes in this graph has an even number of edges, Euler concluded that it is impossible to traverse each bridge exactly once.

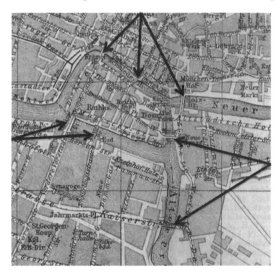

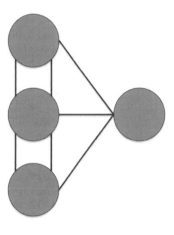

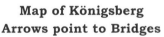

Map of Königsberg
Arrows point to Bridges

Euler's Simplified Map

Of greater interest than the Königsberg bridges problem, or even Euler's theorem (which generalizes his solution to the Königsberg bridges problem), is the whole idea of using graph theory to help understand problems.

For example, only one small extension to the kind of graph used by Euler is needed to model a country's highway system. If a weight is associated with each edge in a graph (or digraph) it is called a **weighted graph**. Using weighted graphs, the highway system can be represented as a graph in which cities are represented by nodes and the highways connecting them as edges, where each edge is labeled with the distance between the two nodes. More generally, one can represent any road map (including those with one-way streets) by a weighted digraph.

Similarly, the structure of the World Wide Web can be represented as a digraph in which the nodes are Web pages and there is an edge from node A to node B if and only if there is a link to page B on page A. Traffic patterns could be modeled by adding a weight to each edge indicating how often is it used.

There are also many less obvious uses of graphs. Biologists use graphs to model things ranging from the way proteins interact with each other to gene expression networks. Physicists use graphs to describe phase transitions. Epidemiologists use graphs to model disease trajectories. And so on.

Figure 17.5 contains classes implementing abstract types corresponding to nodes, weighted edges, and edges.

Having a class for nodes may seem like overkill. After all, none of the methods in class `Node` perform any interesting computation. We introduced the class merely to give us the flexibility of deciding, perhaps at some later point, to introduce a subclass of `Node` with additional properties.

```
class Node(object):
    def __init__(self, name):
        """Assumes name is a string"""
        self.name = name
    def getName(self):
        return self.name
    def __str__(self):
        return self.name

class Edge(object):
    def __init__(self, src, dest):
        """Assumes src and dest are nodes"""
        self.src = src
        self.dest = dest
    def getSource(self):
        return self.src
    def getDestination(self):
        return self.dest
    def __str__(self):
        return self.src.getName() + '->' + self.dest.getName()

class WeightedEdge(Edge):
    def __init__(self, src, dest, weight = 1.0):
        """Assumes src and dest are nodes, weight a float"""
        self.src = src
        self.dest = dest
        self.weight = weight
    def getWeight(self):
        return self.weight
    def __str__(self):
        return self.src.getName() + '->(' + str(self.weight) + ')'\
               + self.dest.getName()
```

Figure 17.5 Nodes and edges

Figure 17.6 contains implementations of the classes `Digraph` and `Graph`. One important decision is the choice of data structure used to represent a `Digraph`. One common representation is an n x n **adjacency matrix**, where n is the number of nodes in the graph. Each cell of the matrix contains information (e.g., weights) about the edges connecting the pair of nodes <i, j>. If the edges are unweighted, each entry is `True` if and only if there is an edge from i to j.

Another common representation is an **adjacency list**, which we use here. Class Digraph has two instance variables. The variable `nodes` is a Python list containing the names of the nodes in the `Digraph`. The connectivity of the nodes is represented using an adjacency list implemented as a dictionary. The variable `edges` is a dictionary that maps each `Node` in the `Digraph` to a list of the children of that `Node`.

Class `Graph` is a subclass of `Digraph`. It inherits all of the methods of `Digraph` except `addEdge`, which it overrides. (This is not the most space-efficient way to implement `Graph`, since it stores each edge twice, once for each direction in the `Digraph`. But it has the virtue of simplicity.)

```python
class Digraph(object):
    #nodes is a list of the nodes in the graph
    #edges is a dict mapping each node to a list of its children
    def __init__(self):
        self.nodes = []
        self.edges = {}
    def addNode(self, node):
        if node in self.nodes:
            raise ValueError('Duplicate node')
        else:
            self.nodes.append(node)
            self.edges[node] = []
    def addEdge(self, edge):
        src = edge.getSource()
        dest = edge.getDestination()
        if not(src in self.nodes and dest in self.nodes):
            raise ValueError('Node not in graph')
        self.edges[src].append(dest)
    def childrenOf(self, node):
        return self.edges[node]
    def hasNode(self, node):
        return node in self.nodes
    def __str__(self):
        result = ''
        for src in self.nodes:
            for dest in self.edges[src]:
                result = result + src.getName() + '->'\
                         + dest.getName() + '\n'
        return result[:-1] #omit final newline

class Graph(Digraph):
    def addEdge(self, edge):
        Digraph.addEdge(self, edge)
        rev = Edge(edge.getDestination(), edge.getSource())
        Digraph.addEdge(self, rev)
```

Figure 17.6 Classes `Graph` and `Digraph`

You might want to stop for a minute and think about why Graph is a subclass of Digraph, rather than the other way around. In many of the examples of subclassing we have looked at, the subclass adds attributes to the superclass. For example, class WeightedEdge added a weight attribute to class Edge.

Here, Digraph and Graph have the same attributes. The only difference is the implementation of the addEdge method. Either could have been easily implemented by inheriting methods from the other, but the choice of which to make the superclass was not arbitrary. In Chapter 8 we stressed the importance of obeying the substitution principle: If client code works correctly using an instance of the supertype, it should also work correctly when an instance of the subtype is substituted for the instance of the supertype.

And indeed if client code works correctly using an instance of Digraph, it will work correctly if an instance of Graph is substituted for the instance of Digraph. The converse is not true. There are many algorithms that work on graphs (by exploiting the symmetry of edges) that do not work on directed graphs.

17.2.1 Some Classic Graph-Theoretic Problems

One of the nice things about formulating a problem using graph theory is that there are well-known algorithms for solving many optimization problems on graphs. Some of the best-known graph optimization problems are:

- **Shortest path**. For some pair of nodes, N1 and N2, find the shortest sequence of edges <s, d> (source node and destination node), such that

    o   The source node in the first edge is N1

    o   The destination node of the last edge is N2

    o   For all edges e1 and e2 in the sequence, if e2 follows e1 in the sequence, the source node of e2 is the destination node of e1.

- **Shortest weighted path**. This is like the shortest path, except instead of choosing the shortest sequence of edges that connects two nodes, we define some function on the weights of the edges in the sequence (e.g., their sum) and minimize that value. This is the kind of problem solved by Mapquest and Google Maps when asked to compute driving directions between two points.

- **Cliques**. Find a set of nodes such that there is a path (or often a path not exceeding a maximum length) in the graph between each pair of nodes in the set.[115]

- **Min cut**. Given two sets of nodes in a graph, a **cut** is a set of edges whose removal eliminates all paths from each node in one set to each node in the other. The minimum cut is the smallest set of edges whose removal accomplishes this.

---

[115] This notion is quite similar to the notion of a social clique, i.e., a group of people who feel closely connected to each other and are inclined to exclude those not in the clique. See, for example, the movie *Heathers*.

17.2.2 The Spread of Disease and Min Cut

Figure 17.7 contains a pictorial representation of a weighted graph generated by the U.S. Centers for Disease Control (CDC) in the course of studying an outbreak of tuberculosis in the United States. Each node represents a person, and each node is labeled by a color[116] indicating whether the person has active TB, tested positive for exposure to TB (i.e., high TST reaction rate), tested negative for exposure to TB, or had not been tested. The edges represent contact between pairs of people. The weights, which are not visible in the picture, indicate whether the contact between people was "close" or "casual."

Figure 17.7 Spread of tuberculosis

There are many interesting questions that can be formalized using this graph. For example,

- Is it possible that all cases stemmed from a single "index" patient? More formally, is there a node, n, such that there is a path from n to every other node in the graph with an active TB label?[117] The answer is "almost." There is path from the node in the middle of the graph to each active TB node except those nodes in the black circle on the right. Interestingly, subsequent investigation revealed that the person in the center of the black circle had previously been a neighbor of the putative index patient, and therefore there should have been a casual contact edge linking the two.

---

[116] To see a color version of this graph, go to page 23 of
http://www.orgnet.com/TB_web.ppt

[117] The edges of the graph do not capture anything related to time. Therefore, the existence of such a node does not mean that the node represents an index patient. However, the absence of such a node would indicate the absence of an index patient. We have a necessary, but not sufficient, condition.

- In order to best limit the continued spread, which uninfected people should be vaccinated? This can be formalized as solving a min cut problem. Let N_A be the set of active TB nodes and N_O be the set of all the other nodes. Each edge in the minimum cut between these two sets will contain one person with known active TB and one person without. The people without known active TB are candidates for vaccination.

17.2.3 Shortest Path: Depth-First Search and Breadth-First Search

Social networks are made up of individuals and relationships between individuals. These are typically modeled as graphs in which the individuals are nodes and the edges relationships. If the relationships are symmetric, the edges are undirected; if the relationships are asymmetric the edges are directed. Some social networks model multiple kinds of relationships, in which case labels on the edges indicate the kind of relationship.

In 1990[118] the playwright John Guare wrote *Six Degrees of Separation.* The slightly dubious premise underlying the play is that "everybody on this planet is separated by only six other people." By this he meant that if one built a social network including every person on the earth using the relation "knows," the shortest path between any two individuals would pass through at most six other nodes.

A less hypothetical question is the distance using the "friend" relation between pairs of people on Facebook. For example, you might wonder if you have a friend who has a friend who has a friend who is a friend of Mick Jagger. Let's think about designing a program to answer such questions.

The friend relation (at least on Facebook) is symmetric, e.g., if Stephanie is a friend of Andrea, Andrea is a friend of Stephanie. We will, therefore, implement the social network using type Graph. We can then define the problem of finding the shortest connection between you and Mick Jagger as:

- For the graph G, find the shortest sequence of nodes, path = [You,...,Mick Jagger], such that

- If n_i and n_{i+1} are consecutive nodes in path, there is an edge in G connecting n_i and n_{i+1}.

Figure 17.8 contains a recursive function that finds the shortest path between two nodes, start and end, in a Digraph. Since Graph is a subclass of Digraph, it will work for our Facebook problem.

The algorithm implemented by DFS is an example of a recursive **depth-first-search (DFS)** algorithm. In general, a depth-first-search algorithm begins by choosing one child of the start node. It then chooses one child of that node and so on, going deeper and deeper until it either reaches the goal node or a node with no children. The search then **backtracks**, returning to the most recent node with children that it has not yet visited. When all paths have been

---

[118] When Mark Zuckerberg was six years old.

explored, it chooses the shortest path (assuming that there is one) from the start to the goal.

The code is a bit more complicated than the algorithm we just described because it has to deal with the possibility of the graph containing cycles. It also avoids exploring paths longer than the shortest path that it has already found.

- The function `search` calls DFS with `path = []` (to indicate that the current path being explored is empty) and `shortest = None` (to indicate that no path from `start` to `end` has yet been found).

- DFS begins by choosing one child of `start`. It then chooses one child of that node and so on, until either it reaches the node `end` or a node with no unvisited children.

  - The check
    ```
    if node not in path
    ```
    prevents the program from getting caught in a cycle.

  - The check
    ```
    if shortest == None or len(path) < len(shortest):
    ```
    is used to decide if it is possible that continuing to search this path might yield a shorter path than the best path found so far.

  - If so, DFS is called recursively. If it finds a path to `end` that is no longer than the best found so far, `shortest` is updated.

  - When the last node on `path` has no children left to visit, the program backtracks to the previously visited node and visits the next child of that node.

- The function returns when all possibly shortest paths from `start` to `end` have been explored.

Figure 17.9 contains some code that runs the code in Figure. The function `testSP` in Figure 17.9 first builds a directed graph like the one pictured on the right, and then searches for a shortest path between node 0 and node 5.

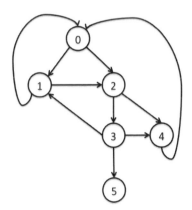

```
def printPath(path):
    """Assumes path is a list of nodes"""
    result = ''
    for i in range(len(path)):
        result = result + str(path[i])
        if i != len(path) - 1:
            result = result + '->'
    return result

def DFS(graph, start, end, path, shortest):
    """Assumes graph is a Digraph; start and end are nodes;
          path and shortest are lists of nodes
       Returns a shortest path from start to end in graph"""
    path = path + [start]
    print 'Current DFS path:', printPath(path)
    if start == end:
        return path
    for node in graph.childrenOf(start):
        if node not in path: #avoid cycles
            if shortest == None or len(path) < len(shortest):
                newPath = DFS(graph, node, end, path, shortest)
                if newPath != None:
                    shortest = newPath
    return shortest

def search(graph, start, end):
    """Assumes graph is a Digraph; start and end are nodes
       Returns a shortest path from start to end in graph"""
    return DFS(graph, start, end, [], None)
```

Figure 17.8 Depth-first-search shortest-path algorithm

```
def testSP():
    nodes = []
    for name in range(6): #Create 6 nodes
        nodes.append(Node(str(name)))
    g = Digraph()
    for n in nodes:
        g.addNode(n)
    g.addEdge(Edge(nodes[0],nodes[1]))
    g.addEdge(Edge(nodes[1],nodes[2]))
    g.addEdge(Edge(nodes[2],nodes[3]))
    g.addEdge(Edge(nodes[2],nodes[4]))
    g.addEdge(Edge(nodes[3],nodes[4]))
    g.addEdge(Edge(nodes[3],nodes[5]))
    g.addEdge(Edge(nodes[0],nodes[2]))
    g.addEdge(Edge(nodes[1],nodes[0]))
    g.addEdge(Edge(nodes[3],nodes[1]))
    g.addEdge(Edge(nodes[4],nodes[0]))
    sp = search(g, nodes[0], nodes[5])
    print 'Shortest path found by DFS:', printPath(sp)
```

Figure 17.9 Test depth-first-search code

When executed, `testSP` produces the output

```
Current DFS path: 0
Current DFS path: 0->1
Current DFS path: 0->1->2
Current DFS path: 0->1->2->3
Current DFS path: 0->1->2->3->4
Current DFS path: 0->1->2->3->5
Current DFS path: 0->1->2->4
Current DFS path: 0->2
Current DFS path: 0->2->3
Current DFS path: 0->2->3->4
Current DFS path: 0->2->3->5
Current DFS path: 0->2->3->1
Current DFS path: 0->2->4
Shortest path found by DFS: 0->2->3->5
```

Notice that after exploring the path 0->1->2->3->4, it backs up to node 3 and explores the path 0->1->2->3->5. After saving that as the shortest successful path so far, it backs up to node 2 and explores the path 0->1->2->4. When it reaches the end of that path (node 4), it backs up all the way to node 0 and investigates the path starting with the edge from 0 to 2. And so on.

The DFS algorithm implemented above finds the path with the minimum number of edges. If the edges have weights, it will not necessarily find the path that minimizes the sum of the weights of the edges. However, it is easily modified to do so.

Of course, there are other ways to traverse a graph than depth-first. Another common approach is **breadth-first search (BFS)**. In a breadth-first traversal one first visits all children of the start node. If none of those is the end node, one visits all children of each of those nodes. And so on. Unlike depth-first search, which is usually implemented recursively, breadth-first search is usually implemented iteratively. BFS explores many paths simultaneously, adding one node to each path on each iteration. Since it generates the paths in ascending order of length, the first path found with the goal as its last node is guaranteed to have a minimum number of edges.

Figure 17.10 contains code that uses a breadth-first search to find the shortest path in a directed graph. The variable `pathQueue` is used to store all of the paths currently being explored. Each iteration starts by removing a path from `pathQueue` and assigning that path to `tmpPath`. If the last node in `tmpPath` is end, `tmpPath` is returned. Otherwise, a set of new paths is created, each of which extends `tmpPath` by adding one of its children. Each of these new paths is then added to `pathQueue`.

```
def BFS(graph, start, end):
    """Assumes graph is a Digraph; start and end are nodes
       Returns a shortest path from start to end in graph"""
    initPath = [start]
    pathQueue = [initPath]
    while len(pathQueue) != 0:
        #Get and remove oldest element in pathQueue
        tmpPath = pathQueue.pop(0)
        print 'Current BFS path:', printPath(tmpPath)
        lastNode = tmpPath[-1]
        if lastNode == end:
            return tmpPath
        for nextNode in graph.childrenOf(lastNode):
            if nextNode not in tmpPath:
                newPath = tmpPath + [nextNode]
                pathQueue.append(newPath)
    return None
```

Figure 17.10 Breadth-first-search shortest path

When the lines

```
        sp = BFS(g, nodes[0], nodes[5])
        print 'Shortest path found by BFS:', printPath(sp)
```

are added at the end of testSP and the function is executed it prints

```
Current DFS path: 0
Current DFS path: 0->1
Current DFS path: 0->1->2
Current DFS path: 0->1->2->3
Current DFS path: 0->1->2->3->4
Current DFS path: 0->1->2->3->5
Current DFS path: 0->1->2->4
Current DFS path: 0->2
Current DFS path: 0->2->3
Current DFS path: 0->2->3->4
Current DFS path: 0->2->3->5
Current DFS path: 0->2->3->1
Current DFS path: 0->2->4
Shortest path found by DFS: 0->2->3->5
Current BFS path: 0
Current BFS path: 0->1
Current BFS path: 0->2
Current BFS path: 0->1->2
Current BFS path: 0->2->3
Current BFS path: 0->2->4
Current BFS path: 0->1->2->3
Current BFS path: 0->1->2->4
Current BFS path: 0->2->3->4
Current BFS path: 0->2->3->5
Shortest path found by BFS: 0->2->3->5
```

Comfortingly, each algorithm found a path of the same length. In this case, they found the same path. However, if a graph contains more than one shortest path between a pair of nodes, DFS and BFS will not necessarily find the same shortest path.

As mentioned above, BFS is a convenient way to search for a path with the fewest edges because the first time a path is found, it is guaranteed to be such a path.

Finger exercise: Consider a digraph with weighted edges. Is the first path found by BFS guaranteed to minimize the sum of the weights of the edges?

18 DYNAMIC PROGRAMMING

Dynamic programming was invented by Richard Bellman in the early 1950s. Don't try to infer anything about the technique from its name. As Bellman described it, the name "dynamic programming" was chosen to hide from governmental sponsors "the fact that I was really doing mathematics... [the phrase dynamic programming] was something not even a Congressman could object to."[119]

Dynamic programming is a method for efficiently solving problems that exhibit the characteristics of overlapping subproblems and optimal substructure. Fortunately, many optimization problems exhibit these characteristics.

A problem has **optimal substructure** if a globally optimal solution can be found by combining optimal solutions to local subproblems. We've already looked at a number of such problems. Merge sort, for example, exploits the fact that a list can be sorted by first sorting sublists and then merging the solutions.

A problem has **overlapping subproblems** if an optimal solution involves solving the same problem multiple times. Merge sort does not exhibit this property. Even though we are performing a merge many times, we are merging different lists each time.

It's not immediately obvious, but the 0/1 knapsack problem exhibits both of these properties. Before looking at that, however, we will digress to look at a problem where the optimal substructure and overlapping subproblems are more obvious.

18.1 Fibonacci Sequences, Revisited

In Chapter 4, we looked at a straightforward recursive implementation of the Fibonacci function, shown here in Figure 18.1.

```
def fib(n):
    """Assumes n is an int >= 0
       Returns Fibonacci of n"""
    if n == 0 or n == 1:
        return 1
    else:
        return fib(n-1) + fib(n-2)
```

Figure 18.1 Recursive implementation of Fibonacci function

---

[119] As quoted in Stuart Dreyfus "Richard Bellman on the Birth of Dynamic Programming," *Operations Research*, vol. 50, no. 1 (2002).

While this implementation of the recurrence is obviously correct, it is terribly inefficient. Try, for example, running fib(120), but don't wait for it to complete. The complexity of the implementation is a bit hard to derive, but it is roughly O(fib(n)). That is, its growth is proportional to the growth in the value of the result, and the growth rate of the Fibonacci sequence is substantial. For example, fib(120) is 8,670,007,398,507,948,658,051,921. If each recursive call took a nanosecond, fib(120) would take about 250,000 years to finish.

Let's try and figure out why this implementation takes so long. Given the tiny amount of code in the body of fib, it's clear that the problem must be the number of times that fib calls itself. As an example, look at the tree of calls associated with the invocation fib(6).

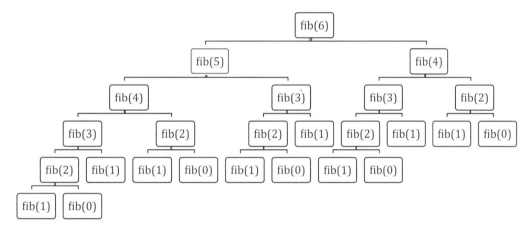

Figure 18.2 Tree of calls for recursive Fibonacci

Notice that we are computing the same values over and over again. For example fib gets called with 3 three times, and each of these calls provokes four additional calls of fib. It doesn't require a genius to think that it might be a good idea to record the value returned by the first call, and then look it up rather than compute it each time it is needed. This is called **memoization**, and is the key idea behind dynamic programming.

Figure 18.3 contains an implementation of Fibonacci based on this idea. The function fastFib has a parameter, memo, that it uses to keep track of the numbers it has already evaluated. The parameter has a default value, the empty dictionary, so that clients of fastFib don't have to worry about supplying an initial value for memo. When fastFib is called with an n > 1, it attempts to look up n in memo. If it is not there (because this is the first time fastFib has been called with that value), an exception is raised. When this happens, fastFib uses the normal Fibonacci recurrence, and then stores the result in memo.

```
def fastFib(n, memo = {}):
    """Assumes n is an int >= 0, memo used only by recursive calls
       Returns Fibonacci of n"""
    if n == 0 or n == 1:
        return 1
    try:
        return memo[n]
    except KeyError:
        result = fastFib(n-1, memo) + fastFib(n-2, memo)
        memo[n] = result
        return result
```

Figure 18.3 Implementing Fibonacci using a memo

If you try running `fastFib`, you will see that it is indeed quite fast: `fib(120)` returns almost instantly. What is the complexity of `fastFib`? It calls `fib` exactly once for each value from 0 to n. Therefore, under the assumption that dictionary lookup can be done in constant time, the time complexity of `fastFib(n)` is O(n).[120]

18.2 Dynamic Programming and the 0/1 Knapsack Problem

One of the optimization problems we looked at in Chapter 17 was the 0/1 knapsack problem. Recall that we looked at a greedy algorithm that ran in n log n time, but was not guaranteed to find an optimal solution. We also looked at a brute-force algorithm that was guaranteed to find an optimal solution, but ran in exponential time. Finally, we discussed the fact that the problem is inherently exponential in the size of the input. In the worst case, one cannot find an optimal solution without looking at all possible answers.

Fortunately, the situation is not as bad as it seems. Dynamic programming provides a practical method for solving most 0/1 knapsack problems in a reasonable amount of time. As a first step in deriving such a solution, we begin with an exponential solution based on exhaustive enumeration. The key idea is to think about exploring the space of possible solutions by constructing a rooted binary tree that enumerates all states that satisfy the weight constraint.

A **rooted binary tree** is an acyclic directed graph in which

- There is exactly one node with no parents. This is called the **root**.
- Each non-root node has exactly one parent.
- Each node has at most two children. A childless node is called a **leaf**.

Each node in the search tree for the 0/1 knapsack problem is labeled with a quadruple that denotes a partial solution to the knapsack problem.

---

[120] Though cute and pedagogically interesting, this is not the best way to implement Fibonacci. There is a simple linear-time iterative implementation.

The elements of the quadruple are:

- A set of items to be taken,

- The list of items for which a decision has not been made,

- The total value of the items in the set of items to be taken (this is merely an optimization, since the value could be computed from the set), and

- The remaining space in the knapsack. (Again, this is an optimization since it is merely the difference between the weight allowed and the weight of all the items taken so far.)

The tree is built top-down starting with the root.[121] One element is selected from the still-to-be-considered items. If there is room for that item in the knapsack, a node is constructed that reflects the consequence of choosing to take that item. By convention, we draw that node as the left child. The right child shows the consequences of choosing not to take that item. The process is then applied recursively until either the knapsack is full or there are no more items to consider. Because each edge represents a decision (to take or not to take an item), such trees are called **decision trees**.[122]

Figure 18.4 is a table describing a set of items. Figure 18.5 is a decision tree for deciding which of those items to take under the assumption that the knapsack has a maximum weight of 5.

Name	Value	Weight
a	6	3
b	7	3
c	8	2
d	9	5

Figure 18.4 Table of items with values and weights

---

[121] It may seem odd to put the root of a tree at the top, but that is the way that mathematicians and computer scientists usually draw them. Perhaps it is evidence that those folks do not spend enough time contemplating nature.

[122] Decision trees, which need not be binary, provide a structured way to explore the consequences of making a series of sequential decisions. They are used extensively in many fields.

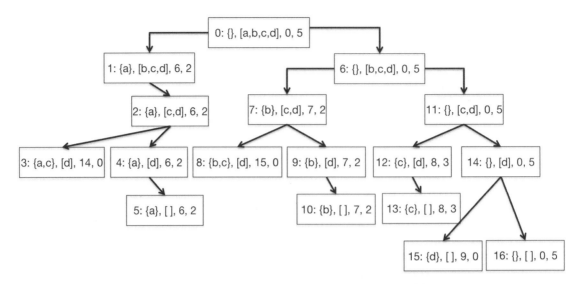

Figure 18.5 Decision tree for knapsack problem

The root of the tree (node 0) has a label <{}, [a,b,c,d], 0, 5>, indicating that no items
have been taken, all items remain to be considered, the value of the items taken
is 0, and a weight of 5 is still available. Node 1 indicates that a has been taken,
[b,c,d] remain to be considered, the value of the items taken is 6, and the
knapsack can hold another 2 pounds. There is no node to the left of node 1,
since item b, which weighs 3 pounds, would not fit in the knapsack.

In Figure 18.5, the numbers that precede the colon in each node indicate one
order in which the nodes could be generated. This particular ordering is called
left-first depth-first. At each node we attempt to generate a left node. If that is
impossible, we attempt to generate a right node. If that too is impossible, we
back up one node (to the parent) and repeat the process. Eventually, we find
ourselves having generated all descendants of the root, and the process halts.
When the process halts, each combination of items that could fit in the
knapsack has been generated, and any leaf node with the greatest value
represents an optimal solution. Notice that for each leaf node, either the second
element is the empty list (indicating that there are no more items to consider
taking) or the fourth element is 0 (indicating that there is no room left in the
knapsack).

Unsurprisingly (especially if you read the previous chapter), the natural
implementation of a depth-first tree search is recursive. Figure 18.6 contains
such an implementation. It uses class `Item` from Figure 17.2. The function
`maxVal` returns two values, the set of items chosen and the total value of those
items. It is called with two arguments, corresponding to the second and fourth
elements of the labels of the nodes in the tree:

- `toConsider`. Those items that nodes higher up in the tree (corresponding
  to earlier calls in the recursive call stack) have not yet considered.

- `avail`. The amount of space still available.

Notice that the implementation of `maxVal` does not build the decision tree and then look for an optimal node. Instead, it uses the local variable `result` to record the best solution found so far.

```
def maxVal(toConsider, avail):
    """Assumes toConsider a list of items, avail a weight
       Returns a tuple of the total weight of a solution to the
         0/1 knapsack problem and the items of that solution"""
    if toConsider == [] or avail == 0:
        result = (0, ())
    elif toConsider[0].getWeight() > avail:
        #Explore right branch only
        result = maxVal(toConsider[1:], avail)
    else:
        nextItem = toConsider[0]
        #Explore left branch
        withVal, withToTake = maxVal(toConsider[1:],
                                     avail - nextItem.getWeight())
        withVal += nextItem.getValue()
        #Explore right branch
        withoutVal, withoutToTake = maxVal(toConsider[1:],
                                           avail)
        #Choose better branch
        if withVal > withoutVal:
            result = (withVal, withToTake + (nextItem,))
        else:
            result = (withoutVal, withoutToTake)
    return result

def smallTest():
    names = ['a', 'b', 'c', 'd']
    vals = [6, 7, 8, 9]
    weights = [3, 3, 2, 5]
    Items = []
    for i in range(len(vals)):
        Items.append(Item(names[i], vals[i], weights[i]))
    val, taken = maxVal(Items, 5)
    for item in taken:
        print item
    print 'Total value of items taken =', val
```

Figure 18.6 Using a decision tree to solve a knapsack problem

When `smallTest` (which uses the values in Figure 18.4) is run it prints a result indicating that node 8 in Figure 18.5 is an optimal solution:

```
<c, 8.0, 3.0>
<b, 7.0, 2.0>
Total value of items taken = 15.0
```

If you run this code on any of the examples we have looked at, you will find that it produces an optimal answer. In fact, it will always produce an optimal answer, if it gets around to producing any answer at all.

The code in Figure 18.7 makes it convenient to test `maxVal`. It randomly generates a list of `Items` of a specified size. Try `bigTest(10)`. Now try `bigTest(40)`. After you get tired of waiting for it to return, stop it and ask yourself what is going on.

```
def buildManyItems(numItems, maxVal, maxWeight):
    items = []
    for i in range(numItems):
        items.append(Item(str(i),
                          random.randint(1, maxVal),
                          random.randint(1, maxWeight)))
    return items

def bigTest(numItems):
    items = buildManyItems(numItems, 10, 10)
    val, taken = maxVal(items, 40)
    print 'Items Taken'
    for item in taken:
        print item
    print 'Total value of items taken =', val
```

Figure 18.7 Testing the decision tree-based implementation

Let's think about the size of the tree we are exploring. Since at each level of the tree we are deciding to keep or not keep one item, the maximum depth of the tree is `len(items)`. At level 0 we have only one node, at level 1 up to two nodes, at level 2 up to four nodes, at level 3 up to eight nodes. At level 39 we have up to 2^{39} nodes. No wonder it takes a long time to run!

What should we do about this? Let's start by asking whether this program has anything in common with our first implementation of Fibonacci. In particular, is there optimal substructure and are there overlapping subproblems?

Optimal substructure is visible both in Figure 18.5 and in Figure 18.6. Each parent node combines the solutions reached by its children to derive an optimal solution for the subtree rooted at that parent. This is reflected in Figure 18.6 by the code following the comment `#Choose better branch`.

Are there also overlapping subproblems? At first glance, the answer seems to be "no." At each level of the tree we have a different set of available items to consider. This implies that if common subproblems do exist, they must be at the same level of the tree. And indeed at each level of the tree each node has the same set of items to consider taking. However, we can see by looking at the labels in Figure 18.5 that each node at a level represents a different set of choices about the items considered higher in the tree.

Think about what problem is being solved at each node. The problem being solved is finding the optimal items to take from those left to consider, given the remaining available weight. The available weight depends upon the total weight of the items taken, but not on which items are taken or the total value of the items taken. So, for example, in Figure 18.5, nodes 2 and 7 are actually solving the same problem: deciding which elements of [c,d] should be taken, given that the available weight is 2.

The code in Figure 18.8 exploits the optimal substructure and overlapping subproblems to provide a dynamic programming solution to the 0/1 knapsack problem. An extra parameter, memo, has been added to keep track of solutions to subproblems that have already been solved. It is implemented using a dictionary with a key constructed from the length of toConsider and the available weight. The expression len(toConsider) is a compact way of representing the items still to be considered. This works because items are always removed from the same end (the front) of the list toConsider.

```python
def fastMaxVal(toConsider, avail, memo = {}):
    """Assumes toConsider a list of items, avail a weight
          memo used only by recursive calls
       Returns a tuple of the total weight of a solution to the
          0/1 knapsack problem and the items of that solution"""
    if (len(toConsider), avail) in memo:
        result = memo[(len(toConsider), avail)]
    elif toConsider == [] or avail == 0:
        result = (0, ())
    elif toConsider[0].getWeight() > avail:
        #Explore right branch only
        result = fastMaxVal(toConsider[1:], avail, memo)
    else:
        nextItem = toConsider[0]
        #Explore left branch
        withVal, withToTake =\
                 fastMaxVal(toConsider[1:],
                            avail - nextItem.getWeight(), memo)
        withVal += nextItem.getValue()
        #Explore right branch
        withoutVal, withoutToTake = fastMaxVal(toConsider[1:],
                                                avail, memo)
        #Choose better branch
        if withVal > withoutVal:
            result = (withVal, withToTake + (nextItem,))
        else:
            result = (withoutVal, withoutToTake)
    memo[(len(toConsider), avail)] = result
    return result
```

Figure 18.8 Dynamic programming solution to knapsack problem

Figure 18.9 shows the number of calls made when we ran the code on problems of various sizes.

len(Items)	Number of items selected	Number of calls
4	4	31
8	6	337
16	9	1,493
32	12	3,650
64	19	8,707
128	27	18.306
256	40	36,675

Figure 18.9 Performance of dynamic programming solution

The growth is hard to quantify, but it is clearly far less than exponential.[123] But how can this be, since we know that the 0/1 knapsack problem is inherently exponential in the number of items? Have we found a way to overturn fundamental laws of the universe? No, but we have discovered that computational complexity can be a subtle notion.[124]

The running time of fastMaxVal is governed by the number of distinct <toConsider, avail> pairs generated. This is because the decision about what to do next depends only upon the items still available and the total weight of the items already taken.

The number of possible values of toConsider is bounded by len(items).

The number of possible values of avail is more difficult to characterize. It is bounded from above by the maximum number of distinct totals of weights of the items that the knapsack can hold. If the knapsack can hold at most n items (based on the capacity of the knapsack and the weights of the available items), avail can take on at most 2^n different values. In principle, this could be a rather large number. However, in practice, it is not usually so large. Even if the knapsack has a large capacity, if the weights of the items are chosen from a reasonably small set of possible weights, many sets of items will have the same total weight, greatly reducing the running time.

This algorithm falls into a complexity class called **pseudo polynomial**. A careful explanation of this concept is beyond the scope of this book. Roughly speaking, fastMaxVal is exponential in the number of bits needed to represent the possible values of avail.

---

[123] Since 2^{128} = 340,282,366,920,938,463,463,374,607,431,768,211,456

[124] OK, "discovered" may be too strong a word. People have known this for a long time. You probably figured it out around Chapter 9.

To see what happens when the the values of `avail` are chosen from a considerably larger space, change the call to `fastMaxVal` in Figure 18.7 to

```
val, taken = fastMaxVal(items, 1000)
```

Finding a solution now takes 1,802,817 calls of `fastMaxVal` when the number of items is 256.

To see what happens when the weights are chosen from an enormous space, we can choose the possible weights from the positive reals rather than the positive integers. To do this, replace the line,

```
items.append(Item(str(i),
                random.randint(1, maxVal),
                random.randint(1, maxWeight)))
```

in `buildManyItems` by the line

```
items.append(Item(str(i),
                random.randint(1, maxVal),
                random.randint(1, maxWeight)*random.random()))
```

Don't hold your breath waiting for this last test to finish. Dynamic programming may be a miraculous technique in the common sense of the word,[125] but it is not capable of performing miracles in the liturgical sense.

18.3 Dynamic Programming and Divide-and-Conquer

Like divide-and-conquer algorithms, dynamic programming is based upon solving independent subproblems and then combining those solutions. There are, however, some important differences.

Divide-and-conquer algorithms are based upon finding subproblems that are substantially smaller than the original problem. For example, merge sort works by dividing the problem size in half at each step. In contrast, dynamic programming involves solving problems that are only slightly smaller than the original problem. For example, computing the 19th Fibonacci number is not a substantially smaller problem than computing the 20th Fibonacci number.

Another important distinction is that the efficiency of divide-and-conquer algorithms does not depend upon structuring the algorithm so that the same problems are solved repeatedly. In contrast, dynamic programming is efficient only when the number of distinct subproblems is significantly smaller than the total number of subproblems.

---

[125] Extraordinary and bringing welcome consequences.

19 A QUICK LOOK AT MACHINE LEARNING

The amount of digital data in the world has been growing at a rate that defies human comprehension. The world's data storage capacity has doubled about every three years since the 1980s. During the time it will take you to read this chapter, approximately 10^{18} bits of data will be added to the world's store. It's not easy to relate to a number that large. One way to think about it is that 10^{18} Canadian pennies would have a surface area roughly twice that of the earth.

Of course, more data does not always lead to more useful information. Evolution is a slow process, and the ability of the human mind to assimilate data has, alas, not doubled every three years. One approach that the world is using to attempt to exploit what has come to be known as "big data" is **statistical machine learning**.

Machine learning is hard to define. One of the earliest definitions was proposed by the American electrical engineer and computer scientist Arthur Samuel,[126] who defined it as a "Field of study that gives computers the ability to learn without being explicitly programmed." Of course, in some sense, every useful program learns something. For example, an implementation of Newton's method learns the roots of a polynomial.

Humans learn things in two ways—memorization and generalization. We use memorization to accumulate individual facts. In England, for example, primary school students might learn a list of English monarchs. Humans use generalization to deduce new facts from old facts. A student of political science, for example, might observe the behavior of a large number of politicians and generalize to conclude that *all* politicians are likely to make decisions intended to enhance their chances of staying in office.

When computer scientists speak about machine learning, they most often mean the field of writing programs that automatically learn to make useful inferences from implicit patterns in data. For example, linear regression (see Chapter 15) learns a curve that is a model of a collection of examples. That model can then be used to make predictions about previously unseen examples.

In general, machine learning involves observing a set of examples that represent incomplete information about some statistical phenomenon, and then attempting to infer something about the process that generated those examples. The examples are frequently called **training data**.

---

[126] Samuel is probably best known as the author of program that played checkers. The program, which he started working on in the 1950s and continued to work on into the 1970s, was impressive for its time, though not particularly good by modern standards. However, while working on it Samuel invented several techniques that are still used today. Among other things, Samuel's checker-playing program was quite possibly the first program ever written that improved based upon "experience."

Suppose, for example, you were given the following two sets of people:

```
A: {Abraham Lincoln, George Washington, Charles de Gaulle}
B: {Benjamin Harrison, James Madison, Louis Napoleon}
```

Now, suppose that you were provided with the following partial descriptions of each of them:

```
Abraham Lincoln: American, President, 193 cm tall
George Washington: American, President, 189 cm tall
Benjamin Harrison: American, President, 168 cm tall
James Madison: American, President, 163 cm tall
Louis Napoleon: French, President, 169 cm tall
Charles de Gaulle: French, President, 196 cm tall
```

Based on this incomplete information about these historical figures, you might infer that the process that assigned these examples to the set labeled A or the set labeled B involved separating tall presidents from shorter ones.

The incomplete information is typically called a **feature vector**. Each element of the vector describes some aspect (i.e., feature) of the example.

There are a large number of different approaches to machine learning, but all try to learn a model that is a generalization of the provided examples. All have three components:

- A representation of the model,

- An objective function for assessing the goodness of the model, and

- An optimization method for learning a model that minimizes or maximizes the value of the objective function.

Broadly speaking, machine learning algorithms can be thought of as either supervised or unsupervised.

In **supervised learning**, we start with a set of feature vector/label pairs.[127] The goal is to derive from these examples a rule that predicts the label associated with a previously unseen feature vector. For example, given the sets A and B, a learning algorithm might infer that all tall presidents should be labeled A and all short presidents labeled B. When asked to assign a label to

```
Thomas Jefferson: American, President, 189 cm.
```

it would then choose label A.

Supervised machine learning is broadly used in practice for such tasks as detecting fraudulent use of credit cards and recommending movies to people. The best algorithms are quite sophisticated, and understanding them requires a level of mathematical sophistication well beyond that assumed for this book. Consequently, we will not cover them here.

---

[127] Much of the machine learning literature uses the word "class" rather than "label." Since we use the word "class" for something else in this book, we will stick to using "label" for this concept.

In **unsupervised learning**, we are given a set of feature vectors but no labels. The goal of unsupervised learning is to uncover latent structure in the set of feature vectors. For example, given the set of presidential feature vectors, an unsupervised learning algorithm might separate the presidents into tall and short, or perhaps into American and French.

The most popular unsupervised learning techniques are designed to find clusters of similar feature vectors. Geneticists, for example, use clustering to find groups of related genes. Many popular clustering methods are surprisingly simple. We will present the most widely used algorithm later in this chapter. First, however, we want to say a few words about feature extraction.

19.1 Feature Vectors

The concept of **signal-to-noise ratio** (**SNR**) is used in many branches of engineering and science. The precise definition varies across applications, but the basic idea is simple. Think of it as the ratio of useful input to irrelevant input. In a restaurant, the signal might be the voice of your dinner date, and the noise the voices of the other diners.[128] If we were trying to predict which students would do well in a programming course, previous programming experience and mathematical aptitude would be part of the signal, but gender merely noise. Separating the signal from the noise is not always easy. And when it is done poorly, the noise can be a distraction that obscures the truth in the signal.

The purpose of feature extraction is to separate those features in the available data that contribute to the signal from those that are merely noise. Failure to do an adequate job of this introduces two kinds of problems:

1. Irrelevant features can lead to a bad model. The danger of this is particularly high when the dimensionality of the data (i.e., the number of different features) is large relative to the number of samples.

2. Irrelevant features can greatly slow the learning process. Machine learning algorithms are often computationally intensive, and complexity grows with both the number of examples and the number of features.

The goal of feature extraction is to reduce the vast amount of information that might be available in examples to information from which it will be productive to generalize. Imagine, for example, that your goal is to learn a model that will predict whether a person likes to drink wine. Some attributes, e.g., age and the nation in which they live, are likely to be relevant. Other attributes, e.g., whether they are left-handed, are less likely to be relevant.

Feature extraction is difficult. In the context of supervised learning, one can try to select those features that are correlated with the labels of the examples. In

---

[128] Unless your dinner date is exceedingly boring. In which case, your dinner date's conversation becomes the noise, and the conversation at the next table the signal.

unsupervised learning, the problem is harder. Typically, we choose features based upon our intuition about which features might be relevant to the kinds of structure we would like to find.

Consider Figure 19.1, which contains a table of feature vectors and the label (reptile or not) with which each vector is associated.

Name	Egg-laying	Scales	Poisonous	Cold-blooded	# Legs	Reptile
Cobra	True	True	True	True	0	Yes
Rattlesnake	True	True	True	True	0	Yes
Boa constrictor	False	True	False	True	0	Yes
Alligator	True	True	False	True	4	Yes
Dart frog	True	False	True	False	4	No
Salmon	True	True	False	True	0	No
Python	True	True	False	True	0	Yes

Figure 19.1 Name, features and labels for assorted animals

A supervised machine learning algorithm (or a human) given only the information about cobras cannot do much more than to remember the fact that a cobra is a reptile. Now, let's add the information about rattlesnakes. We can begin to generalize, and might infer the rule that an animal is a reptile if it lays eggs, has scales, is poisonous, is cold-blooded, and has no legs.

Now, suppose we are asked to decide if a boa constrictor is a reptile. We might answer "no," because a boa constrictor is neither poisonous nor egg-laying. But this would be the wrong answer. Of course, it is hardly surprising that attempting to generalize from two examples might lead us astray. Once we include the boa constrictor in our training data, we might formulate the new rule that an animal is a reptile if it is has scales, is cold-blooded, and is legless. In doing so, we are discarding the features `egg-laying` and `poisonous` as irrelevant to the classification problem.

If we use the new rule to classify the alligator, we conclude incorrectly that since it has legs it is not a reptile. Once we include the alligator in the training data we reformulate the rule to allow reptiles to have either none or four legs. When we look at the dart frog, we correctly conclude that it is not a reptile, since it is not cold-blooded. However, when we use our current rule to classify the salmon, we incorrectly conclude that a salmon is a reptile. We can add yet more complexity to our rule, to separate salmon from alligators, but it's a losing battle. There is no way to modify our rule so that it will correctly classify both salmon and pythons—since the feature vectors of these two species are identical.

This kind of problem is more common than not in machine learning. It is quite rare to have feature vectors that contain enough information to classify things perfectly. In this case, the problem is that we don't have enough features. If we had included the fact that reptile eggs have amnios,[129] we could devise a rule that separates reptiles from fish. Unfortunately, in most practical applications of machine learning it is not possible to construct feature vectors that allow for perfect discrimination.

Does this mean that we should give up because all of the available features are mere noise? No. In this case the features `scales` and `cold-blooded` are necessary conditions for being a reptile, but not sufficient conditions. The rule has scales and is cold-blooded will not yield any **false negatives**, i.e., any animal classified as a non-reptile will indeed not be a reptile. However, it will yield some **false positives**, i.e., some of the animals classified as reptiles will not be reptiles.

19.2 Distance Metrics

In Figure 19.1 we described animals using four binary features and one integer feature. Suppose we want to use these features to evaluate the similarity of two animals, e.g., to ask, is a boa constrictor more similar to a rattlesnake or to a dart frog?[130]

The first step in doing this kind of comparison is converting the features for each animal into a sequence of numbers. If we say `True` = 1 and `False` = 0, we get the following feature vectors:

```
Rattlesnake: [1,1,1,1,0]
Boa constrictor: [0,1,0,1,0]
Dart frog: [1,0,1,0,4]
```

There are many different ways to compare the similarity of vectors of numbers. The most commonly used metrics for comparing equal-length vectors are based on the **Minkowski distance**:

$$distance(V1, V2, p) = \left(\sum_{i=1}^{len} abs(V1_i - V2_i)^p\right)^{1/p}$$

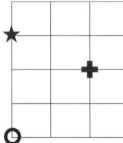

The parameter p defines the kinds of paths that can be followed in traversing the distance between the vectors $V1$ and $V2$. This can be mostly easily visualized if the vectors are of length two, and represent Cartesian coordinates. Consider the picture on the left. Is the circle in the bottom left corner closer to the cross or to the star? It depends. If we can travel in a straight line, the cross is closer. The Pythagorean Theorem tells us that the cross is the square root of 8 units from the circle, about 2.8 units, whereas we can

---

[129] Amnios are protective outer layers that allow eggs to be laid on land rather than in the water.

[130] This question is not quite as silly as it sounds. A naturalist and a toxicologist (or someone looking to enhance the effectiveness of a blow dart) might give different answers to this question.

easily see that the star is 3 units from the circle. These distances are called
Euclidean distances, and correspond to using the Minkowski distance with p = 2.
But imagine that the lines in the picture correspond to streets, and that one has
to stay on the streets to get from one place to another. In that case, the star
remains 3 units from the circle, but the cross is now 4 units away. These
distances are called **Manhattan distances**,[131] and correspond to using the
Minkowski distance with p = 1.

Figure 19.2 contains an implementation of the Minkowski distance.

```
def minkowskiDist(v1, v2, p):
    """Assumes v1 and v2 are equal-length arrays of numbers
       Returns Minkowski distance of order p between v1 and v2"""
    dist = 0.0
    for i in range(len(v1)):
        dist += abs(v1[i] - v2[i])**p
    return dist**(1.0/p)
```

Figure 19.2 Minkowski distance

Figure 19.3 contains class `Animal`. It defines the distance between two animals
as the Euclidean distance between the feature vectors associated with the
animals.

```
class Animal(object):
    def __init__(self, name, features):
        """Assumes name a string; features a list of numbers"""
        self.name = name
        self.features = pylab.array(features)

    def getName(self):
        return self.name

    def getFeatures(self):
        return self.features

    def distance(self, other):
        """Assumes other an animal
           Returns the Euclidean distance between feature vectors
               of self and other"""
        return minkowskiDist(self.getFeatures(),
                             other.getFeatures(), 2)
```

Figure 19.3 Class `Animal`

Figure 19.4 contains a function that compares a list of animals to each other,
and produces a table showing the pairwise distances.

---

[131] Manhattan Island is the most densely populated borough of New York City. On most
of the island, the streets are laid out in a grid, so using the Minkowski distance with p = 1
provides a good approximation of the distance one has to travel to walk from one place
(say the Museum of Modern Art at 53rd Street and 6th Avenue) to another (say the
American Folk Art Museum at 66th Street and 9th, also called Columbus Avenue). Driving
in Manhattan is a totally different story.

```python
def compareAnimals(animals, precision):
    """Assumes animals is a list of animals, precision an int >= 0
       Builds a table of Euclidean distance between each animal"""
    #Get labels for columns and rows
    columnLabels = []
    for a in animals:
        columnLabels.append(a.getName())
    rowLabels = columnLabels[:]
    tableVals = []
    #Get distances between pairs of animals
    #For each row
    for a1 in animals:
        row = []
        #For each column
        for a2 in animals:
            if a1 == a2:
                row.append('--')
            else:
                distance = a1.distance(a2)
                row.append(str(round(distance, precision)))
        tableVals.append(row)
    #Produce table
    table = pylab.table(rowLabels = rowLabels,
                        colLabels = columnLabels,
                        cellText = tableVals,
                        cellLoc = 'center',
                        loc = 'center',
                        colWidths = [0.2]*len(animals))
    table.scale(1, 2.5)
    pylab.axis('off') #Don't display x and y-axes
    pylab.savefig('distances')
```

Figure 19.4 Build table of distances between pairs of animals

The code uses a PyLab plotting facility that we have not previously used: `table`.

The `table` function produces a plot that (surprise!) looks like a table. The keyword arguments `rowLabels` and `colLabels` are used to supply the labels (in this example the names of the animals) for the rows and columns. The keyword argument `cellText` is used to supply the values appearing in the cells of the table. In the example, `cellText` is bound to `tableVals`, which is a list of lists of strings. Each element in `tableVals` is a list of the values for the cells in one row of the table. The keyword argument `cellLoc` is used to specify where in each cell the text should appear, and the keyword argument `loc` is used to specify where in the figure the table itself should appear. The last keyword parameter used in the example is `colWidths`. It is bound to a list of floats giving the width (in inches) of each column in the table. The code `table.scale(1, 2.5)` instructs PyLab to leave the horizontal width of the cells unchanged, but to increase the height of the cells by a factor of 2.5 (so the tables look prettier).

If we run the code

```
rattlesnake = Animal('rattlesnake', [1,1,1,1,0])
boa = Animal('boa\nconstrictor', [0,1,0,1,0])
dartFrog = Animal('dart frog', [1,0,1,0,4])
animals = [rattlesnake, boa, dartFrog]
compareAnimals(animals, 3)
```

it produces a figure containing the table

	rattlesnake	boa constrictor	dart frog
rattlesnake	--	1.414	4.243
boa constrictor	1.414	--	4.472
dart frog	4.243	4.472	--

As you probably expected, the distance between the rattlesnake and the boa constrictor is less than that between either of the snakes and the dart frog. Notice, by the way, that the dart frog does seem to be a bit closer to the rattlesnake than to the boa.

Now, let's add to the bottom of the above code the lines

```
alligator = Animal('alligator', [1,1,0,1,4])
animals.append(alligator)
compareAnimals(animals, 3)
```

It produces the table

	rattlesnake	boa constrictor	dart frog	alligator
rattlesnake	--	1.414	4.243	4.123
boa constrictor	1.414	--	4.472	4.123
dart frog	4.243	4.472	--	1.732
alligator	4.123	4.123	1.732	--

Perhaps you're surprised that the alligator is considerably closer to the dart frog than to either the rattlesnake or the boa constrictor. Take a minute to think about why.

The feature vector for the alligator differs from that of the rattlesnake in two places: whether it is poisonous and the number of legs. The feature vector for the alligator differs from that of the dart frog in three places: whether it is poisonous, whether it has scales, and whether it is cold-blooded. Yet according to our distance metric the alligator is more like the dart frog than like the rattlesnake. What's going on?

The root of the problem is that the different features have different ranges of values. All but one of the features range between 0 and 1, but the number of legs ranges from 0 to 4. This means that when we calculate the Euclidean distance the number of legs gets disproportionate weight. Let's see what happens if we turn the feature into a binary feature, with a value of 0 if the animal is legless and 1 otherwise.

	rattlesnake	boa constrictor	dart frog	alligator
rattlesnake	--	1.414	1.732	1.414
boa constrictor	1.414	--	2.236	1.414
dart frog	1.732	2.236	--	1.732
alligator	1.414	1.414	1.732	--

This looks a lot more plausible.

Of course, it is not always convenient to use only binary features. In Section 19.7 we will present a more general approach to dealing with differences in scale among features.

19.3 Clustering

Clustering can be defined as the process of organizing objects into groups whose members are similar in some way. A key issue is defining the meaning of "similar."

Consider the plot on the right, which shows the height, weight, and whether or not they are wearing a striped shirt for 13 people.

If we want to cluster people by height, there are two obvious clusters—delimited by the dotted horizontal line. If we want to cluster people by weight there are two different obvious clusters—delimited by the solid vertical line. If we want to cluster people based on their shirt, there is yet a third clustering—delimited by the angled dotted arrows. Notice, by the way, that this last division is not linear, i.e., we cannot separate the people wearing striped shirts from the others using a single straight line.

Clustering is an optimization problem. The goal is to find a set of clusters that optimizes an objective function, subject to some set of constraints. Given a distance metric that can be used to decide how close two examples are to each other, we need to define an objective function that

- Minimizes the distance between examples in the same clusters, i.e., minimizes the dissimilarity of the examples within a cluster.

As we will see later, the exact definition of the objective function can greatly influence the outcome.

A good measure of how close the examples within a single cluster, c, are to each other is variance. To compute the variance of the examples within a cluster, we first compute the mean of the feature vectors of all the examples in the cluster. If V is a list of feature vectors each of which is an array of numbers, the mean (more precisely the Euclidean mean) is the value of the expression `sum(V)/float(len(V))`. Given the mean and a metric for computing the distance between feature vectors, the **variance** of a cluster is

$$variance(c) = \sqrt[2]{\sum_{e \in c} distance(mean(c), e)^2}$$

Notice that the variance is not normalized by the size of the cluster, so clusters with more points are likely to look less cohesive according to this measure. If one wants to compare the coherence of two clusters of different sizes, one needs to divide the variance of each by the size of the cluster.

The definition of variance within a single cluster, c, can be extended to define a dissimilarity metric for a set of clusters, C:

$$dissimilarity(C) = \sum_{c \in C} variance(c)$$

Notice that since we don't divide the variance by the size of the cluster, a large incoherent cluster increases the value of *dissimilarity(C)* more than a small incoherent cluster does.

So, is the optimization problem to find a set of clusters, C, such that *dissimilarity(C)* is minimized? Not exactly. It can easily be minimized by putting each example in its own cluster. We need to add some constraint. For example, we could put a constraint on the distance between clusters or require that the maximum number of clusters is *k*.

In general, solving this optimization problem is computationally prohibitive for most interesting problems. Consequently, people rely on greedy algorithms that provide approximate solutions. Later in this chapter, we present one such algorithm, k-means clustering. But first we will introduce some abstractions that are useful for implementing that algorithm (and other clustering algorithms as well).

19.4 Types Example and Cluster

Class `Example` will be used to build the samples to be clustered. Associated with each example is a name, a feature vector, and an optional label. The `distance` method returns the Euclidean distance between two examples.

```
class Example(object):

    def __init__(self, name, features, label = None):
        #Assumes features is an array of numbers
        self.name = name
        self.features = features
        self.label = label

    def dimensionality(self):
        return len(self.features)

    def getFeatures(self):
        return self.features[:]

    def getLabel(self):
        return self.label

    def getName(self):
        return self.name

    def distance(self, other):
        return minkowskiDist(self.features, other.getFeatures(), 2)

    def __str__(self):
        return self.name +':'+ str(self.features) + ':' + str(self.label)
```

Figure 19.5 Class `Example`

Class `Cluster`, Figure 19.6, is slightly more complex. Think of a cluster as a set of examples. The two interesting methods in `Cluster` are `computeCentroid` and `variance`. Think of the **centroid** of a cluster as its center of mass. The method `computeCentroid` returns an example with a feature vector equal to the Euclidean mean of the feature vectors of the examples in the cluster. The method `variance` provides a measure of the coherence of the cluster.

```
class Cluster(object):

    def __init__(self, examples, exampleType):
        """Assumes examples is a list of example of type exampleType"""
        self.examples = examples
        self.exampleType = exampleType
        self.centroid = self.computeCentroid()

    def update(self, examples):
        """Replace the examples in the cluster by new examples
           Return how much the centroid has changed"""
        oldCentroid = self.centroid
        self.examples = examples
        if len(examples) > 0:
            self.centroid = self.computeCentroid()
            return oldCentroid.distance(self.centroid)
        else:
            return 0.0

    def members(self):
        for e in self.examples:
            yield e

    def size(self):
        return len(self.examples)

    def getCentroid(self):
        return self.centroid

    def computeCentroid(self):
        dim = self.examples[0].dimensionality()
        totVals = pylab.array([0.0]*dim)
        for e in self.examples:
            totVals += e.getFeatures()
        centroid = self.exampleType('centroid',
                            totVals/float(len(self.examples)))
        return centroid

    def variance(self):
        totDist = 0.0
        for e in self.examples:
            totDist += (e.distance(self.centroid))**2
        return totDist**0.5

    def __str__(self):
        names = []
        for e in self.examples:
            names.append(e.getName())
        names.sort()
        result = 'Cluster with centroid '\
                + str(self.centroid.getFeatures()) + ' contains:\n  '
        for e in names:
            result = result + e + ', '
        return result[:-2]
```

Figure 19.6 Class Cluster

19.5 K-means Clustering

K-means clustering is probably the most widely used clustering method.[132] Its goal is to partition a set of examples into k clusters such that

1. Each example is in the cluster whose centroid is the closest centroid to that example, and

2. The dissimilarity of the set of clusters is minimized.

Unfortunately, finding an optimal solution to this problem on a large dataset is computationally intractable. Fortunately, there is an efficient greedy algorithm[133] that can be used to find a useful approximation. It is described by the pseudocode

```
randomly choose k examples as initial centroids
while true:
    1) create k clusters by assigning each example to closest centroid
    2) compute k new centroids by averaging the examples in each cluster
    3) if none of the centroids differ from the previous iteration:
        return the current set of clusters
```

The complexity of step 1 is $O(k*n*d)$, where k is the number of clusters, n is the number of examples, and d the time required to compute the distance between a pair of examples. The complexity of step 2 is $O(n)$, and the complexity of step 3 is $O(k)$. Hence, the complexity of a single iteration is $O(k*n*d)$. If the examples are compared using the Minkowski distance, d is linear in the length of the feature vector.[134] Of course, the complexity of the entire algorithm depends upon the number of iterations. That is not easy to characterize, but suffice it to say that it is usually small.

One problem with the k-means algorithm is that it is nondeterministic—the value returned depends upon the initial set of randomly chosen centroids. If a particularly unfortunate set of initial centroids is chosen, the algorithm might settle into a local optimum that is far from the global optimum. In practice, this problem is typically addressed by running k-means multiple times with randomly chosen initial centroids. We then choose the solution with the minimum dissimilarity of clusters.

Figure 19.7 contains a straightforward translation of the pseudocode describing k-means into Python. It uses `random.sample(examples, k)` to get the initial centroids. This invocation returns a list of k randomly chosen distinct elements from the list `examples`.

---

[132] Though k-means clustering is probably the most commonly used clustering method, it is not the most appropriate method in all situations. Two other widely used methods, not coverd in this book, are hierarchical clustering and EM-clustering.

[133] The most widely used k-means algorithm is attributed to James McQueen, and was first published in 1967. However, other approaches to k-means clustering were used as early as the 1950s.

[134] Unfortunately, in many applications we need to use a distance metric, e.g., earth-movers distance or dynamic-time-warping distance, that have a higher computational complexity.

```
def kmeans(examples, exampleType, k, verbose):
    """Assumes examples is a list of examples of type exampleType,
         k is a positive int, verbose is a Boolean
       Returns a list containing k clusters. If verbose is
          True it prints result of each iteration of k-means"""
    #Get k randomly chosen initial centroids
    initialCentroids = random.sample(examples, k)

    #Create a singleton cluster for each centroid
    clusters = []
    for e in initialCentroids:
        clusters.append(Cluster([e], exampleType))

    #Iterate until centroids do not change
    converged = False
    numIterations = 0
    while not converged:
        numIterations += 1
        #Create a list containing k distinct empty lists
        newClusters = []
        for i in range(k):
            newClusters.append([])

        #Associate each example with closest centroid
        for e in examples:
            #Find the centroid closest to e
            smallestDistance = e.distance(clusters[0].getCentroid())
            index = 0
            for i in range(1, k):
                distance = e.distance(clusters[i].getCentroid())
                if distance < smallestDistance:
                    smallestDistance = distance
                    index = i
            #Add e to the list of examples for the appropriate cluster
            newClusters[index].append(e)

        #Upate each cluster; check if a centroid has changed
        converged = True
        for i in range(len(clusters)):
            if clusters[i].update(newClusters[i]) > 0.0:
                converged = False
        if verbose:
            print 'Iteration #' + str(numIterations)
            for c in clusters:
                print c
            print '' #add blank line
    return clusters
```

Figure 19.7 K-means clustering

Figure 19.8 contains a function, trykmeans, that calls kmeans multiple times and selects the result with the lowest dissimilarity.

```
def dissimilarity(clusters):
    totDist = 0.0
    for c in clusters:
        totDist += c.variance()
    return totDist

def trykmeans(examples, exampleType, numClusters, numTrials,
              verbose = False):
    """Calls kmeans numTrials times and returns the result with the
        lowest dissimilarity"""
    best = kmeans(examples, exampleType, numClusters, verbose)
    minDissimilarity = dissimilarity(best)
    for trial in range(1, numTrials):
        clusters = kmeans(examples, exampleType, numClusters, verbose)
        currDissimilarity = dissimilarity(clusters)
        if currDissimilarity < minDissimilarity:
            best = clusters
            minDissimilarity = currDissimilarity
    return best
```

Figure 19.8 Finding the best k-means clustering

19.6 A Contrived Example

Figure 19.9 contains code that generates, plots, and clusters examples drawn
from two distributions.

The function genDistributions generates a list of n examples with two-
dimensional feature vectors. The values of the elements of these feature vectors
are drawn from normal distributions.

The function plotSamples plots the feature vectors of a set of examples. It uses
another PyLab plotting feature that we have not yet seen: the function annotate
is used to place text next to points on the plot. The first argument is the text,
the second argument the point with which the text is associated, and the third
argument the location of the text relative to the point with which it is associated.

The function contrivedTest uses genDistributions to create two distributions of
ten examples each with the same standard deviation but different means, plots
the examples using plotSamples, and then clusters them using trykmeans.

```
def genDistribution(xMean, xSD, yMean, ySD, n, namePrefix):
    samples = []
    for s in range(n):
        x = random.gauss(xMean, xSD)
        y = random.gauss(yMean, ySD)
        samples.append(Example(namePrefix+str(s), [x, y]))
    return samples

def plotSamples(samples, marker):
    xVals, yVals = [], []
    for s in samples:
        x = s.getFeatures()[0]
        y = s.getFeatures()[1]
        pylab.annotate(s.getName(), xy = (x, y),
                       xytext = (x+0.13, y-0.07),
                       fontsize = 'x-large')
        xVals.append(x)
        yVals.append(y)
    pylab.plot(xVals, yVals, marker)

def contrivedTest(numTrials, k, verbose):
    random.seed(0)
    xMean = 3
    xSD = 1
    yMean = 5
    ySD = 1
    n = 10
    d1Samples = genDistribution(xMean, xSD, yMean, ySD, n, '1.')
    plotSamples(d1Samples, 'b^')
    d2Samples = genDistribution(xMean+3, xSD, yMean+1, ySD, n, '2.')
    plotSamples(d2Samples, 'ro')
    clusters = trykmeans(d1Samples + d2Samples, Example, k,
                         numTrials, verbose)
    print 'Final result'
    for c in clusters:
        print '', c
```

Figure 19.9 A test of k-means

When executed, the call contrivedTest(1, 2, True) produced the plot in Figure 19.10.

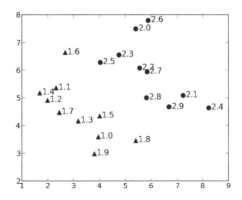

Figure 19.10 Examples from two distributions

and printed

```
Iteration 1
 Cluster with centroid [ 4.57800047  5.35921276] contains:
  1.0, 1.1, 1.2, 1.3, 1.4, 1.5, 1.6, 1.7, 1.8, 2.0, 2.1, 2.2, 2.3,
2.4, 2.5, 2.6, 2.7, 2.8, 2.9
 Cluster with centroid [ 3.79646584  2.99635148] contains:
  1.9

Iteration 2
 Cluster with centroid [ 4.80105783  5.73986393] contains:
  1.1, 1.2, 1.4, 1.5, 1.6, 2.0, 2.1, 2.2, 2.3, 2.4, 2.5, 2.6, 2.7,
2.8, 2.9
 Cluster with centroid [ 3.75252146  3.74468698] contains:
  1.0, 1.3, 1.7, 1.8, 1.9

Iteration 3
 Cluster with centroid [ 5.6388835   6.02296994] contains:
  1.6, 2.0, 2.1, 2.2, 2.3, 2.4, 2.5, 2.6, 2.7, 2.8, 2.9
 Cluster with centroid [ 3.19452848  4.28541384] contains:
  1.0, 1.1, 1.2, 1.3, 1.4, 1.5, 1.7, 1.8, 1.9

Iteration 4
 Cluster with centroid [ 5.93613865  5.96069975] contains:
  2.0, 2.1, 2.2, 2.3, 2.4, 2.5, 2.6, 2.7, 2.8, 2.9
 Cluster with centroid [ 3.14170883  4.52143963] contains:
  1.0, 1.1, 1.2, 1.3, 1.4, 1.5, 1.6, 1.7, 1.8, 1.9

Iteration 5
 Cluster with centroid [ 5.93613865  5.96069975] contains:
  2.0, 2.1, 2.2, 2.3, 2.4, 2.5, 2.6, 2.7, 2.8, 2.9
 Cluster with centroid [ 3.14170883  4.52143963] contains:
  1.0, 1.1, 1.2, 1.3, 1.4, 1.5, 1.6, 1.7, 1.8, 1.9

Final result
 Cluster with centroid [ 5.93613865  5.96069975] contains:
  2.0, 2.1, 2.2, 2.3, 2.4, 2.5, 2.6, 2.7, 2.8, 2.9
 Cluster with centroid [ 3.14170883  4.52143963] contains:
  1.0, 1.1, 1.2, 1.3, 1.4, 1.5, 1.6, 1.7, 1.8, 1.9
```

Notice that the initial (randomly chosen) centroids led to a highly skewed clustering in which a single cluster contained all but one of the points. By the fifth iteration, however, the centroids had moved to places such that the points from the two distributions were cleanly separated into two clusters. Given that a straight line can be used to separate the points generated from the first distribution from those generated by from the second distribution, it is not terribly surprising that k-means converged on this clustering.

When we tried 40 trials rather than 1, by calling `contrivedTest(40, 2, False)`, it printed

```
Final result
 Cluster with centroid [ 6.07470389  5.67876712] contains:
  1.8, 2.0, 2.1, 2.2, 2.3, 2.4, 2.5, 2.6, 2.7, 2.8, 2.9
 Cluster with centroid [ 3.00314359  4.80337227] contains:
  1.0, 1.1, 1.2, 1.3, 1.4, 1.5, 1.6, 1.7, 1.9
```

This indicates that the solution found using 1 trial, despite perfectly separating the examples by the distribution from which they were chosen, was not as good (with respect to minimizing the objective function) as one of the solutions found using 40 trials.

Finger exercise: Draw lines on Figure 19.10 to show the separations found by our two attempts to cluster the points. Do you agree that the solution found using 40 trials is better than the one found using 1 trial?

One of the key issues in using k-means clustering is choosing k. Consider the points in the plot on the right, which were generated using `contrivedTest2`, Figure 19.11. This function generates and clusters points from three overlapping Gaussian distributions.

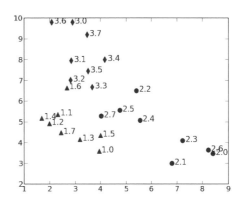

```
def contrivedTest2(numTrials, k, verbose):
    random.seed(0)
    xMean = 3
    xSD = 1
    yMean = 5
    ySD = 1
    n = 8
    d1Samples = genDistribution(xMean,xSD, yMean, ySD, n, '1.')
    plotSamples(d1Samples, 'b^')
    d2Samples = genDistribution(xMean+3,xSD,yMean, ySD, n, '2.')
    plotSamples(d2Samples, 'ro')
    d3Samples = genDistribution(xMean, xSD, yMean+3, ySD, n, '3.')
    plotSamples(d3Samples, 'gd')
    clusters = trykmeans(d1Samples + d2Samples + d3Samples,
                         Example, k, numTrials, verbose)
    print 'Final result'
    for c in clusters:
        print '', c
```

Figure 19.11 Generating points from three distributions

The invocation `contrivedTest2(40, 2, False)` prints

```
Final result
 Cluster with centroid [ 7.66239972  3.55222681] contains:
  2.0, 2.1, 2.3, 2.6
 Cluster with centroid [ 3.36736761  6.35376823] contains:
  1.0, 1.1, 1.2, 1.3, 1.4, 1.5, 1.6, 1.7, 2.2, 2.4, 2.5, 2.7, 3.0,
3.1, 3.2, 3.3, 3.4, 3.5, 3.6, 3.7
```

The invocation `contrivedTest2(40, 3, False)` prints

```
Final result
  Cluster with centroid [ 7.66239972  3.55222681] contains:
    2.0, 2.1, 2.3, 2.6
  Cluster with centroid [ 3.10687385  8.46084886] contains:
    3.0, 3.1, 3.2, 3.4, 3.5, 3.6, 3.7
  Cluster with centroid [ 3.50763348  5.21918636] contains:
    1.0, 1.1, 1.2, 1.3, 1.4, 1.5, 1.6, 1.7, 2.2, 2.4, 2.5, 2.7, 3.3
```

And the invocation `contrivedTest2(40, 6, False)` prints

```
Final result
  Cluster with centroid [ 7.66239972  3.55222681] contains:
    2.0, 2.1, 2.3, 2.6
  Cluster with centroid [ 2.80974427  9.60386549] contains:
    3.0, 3.6, 3.7
  Cluster with centroid [ 3.70472053  4.04178035] contains:
    1.0, 1.3, 1.5
  Cluster with centroid [ 2.10900238  4.99452866] contains:
    1.1, 1.2, 1.4, 1.7
  Cluster with centroid [ 4.92742554  5.60609442] contains:
    2.2, 2.4, 2.5, 2.7
  Cluster with centroid [ 3.27637435  7.28932247] contains:
    1.6, 3.1, 3.2, 3.3, 3.4, 3.5
```

The last clustering is the tightest fit, i.e., the clustering has the lowest dissimilarity. Does this mean that it is the "best" fit? Recall that when we looked at linear regression in Section 15.1.1, we observed that by increasing the degree of the polynomial we got a more complex model that provided a tighter fit to the data. We also observed that when we increased the degree of the polynomial we ran the risk of finding a model with poor predictive value—because it overfit the data.

Choosing the right value for k is exactly analogous to choosing the right degree polynomial for a linear regression. By increasing k, we can decrease dissimilarity, at the risk of overfitting. (When k is equal to the number of examples to be clustered, the dissimilarity is zero!) If we have some information about how the examples to be clustered were generated, e.g., chosen from m distributions, we can use that information to choose k. Absent such information, there are a variety of heuristic procedures for choosing k. Going into them is beyond the scope of this book.

19.7 A Less Contrived Example

Different species of mammals have different eating habits. Some species (e.g., elephants and beavers) eat only plants, others (e.g., lions and tigers) eat only meat, and some (e.g., pigs and humans) eat anything they can get into their mouths. The vegetarian species are called herbivores, the meat eaters are called carnivores, and those species that eat both are called omnivores.

Over the millennia, evolution (or some other mysterious process) has equipped species with teeth suitable for consumption of their preferred foods. That raises the question of whether clustering mammals based on their dentition produces clusters that have some relation to their diets.

The table on the right shows the contents of a file listing some species of mammals, their dental formulas (the first 8 numbers), their average adult weight in pounds,[135] and a code indicating their preferred diet. The comments at the top describe the items associated with each mammal, e.g., the first item following the name is the number of top incisors.

Figure 19.12 contains a function, `readMammalData`, for reading a file formatted in this way and processing the contents of the file to produce a set of examples representing the information in the file. It first processes the header information at the start of the file to get a count of the number of features to be associated with each example. It then uses the lines corresponding to each species to build three lists:

- `speciesNames` is a list of the names of the mammals.

```
#Name
#top incisors
#top canines
#top premolars
#top molars
#bottom incisors
#bottom canines
#bottom premolars
#bottom molars
#weight
#Label: 0=herbivore, 1=carnivore, 2=omnivore
Badger,3,1,3,1,3,1,3,2,10,1
Bear,3,1,4,2,3,1,4,3,278,2
Beaver,1,0,2,3,1,0,1,3,20,0
Brown bat,2,1,1,3,3,1,2,3,0.5,1
Cat,3,1,3,1,3,1,2,1,4,1
Cougar,3,1,3,1,3,1,2,1,63,1
Cow,0,0,3,3,3,1,2,1,400,0
Deer,0,0,3,3,4,0,3,3,200,0
Dog,3,1,4,2,3,1,4,3,20,1
Fox,3,1,4,2,3,1,4,3,5,1
Fur seal,3,1,4,1,2,1,4,1,200,1
Grey seal,3,1,3,2,2,1,3,2,268,1
Guinea pig,1,0,1,3,1,0,1,3,1,0
Elk,0,1,3,3,3,1,3,3,500,0
Human,2,1,2,3,2,1,2,3,150,2
Jaguar,3,1,3,1,3,1,2,1,81,1
Kangaroo,3,1,2,4,1,0,2,4,55,0
Lion,3,1,3,1,3,1,2,1,175,1
Mink,3,1,3,1,3,1,3,2,1,1
Mole,3,1,4,3,3,1,4,3,0.75,1
Moose,0,0,3,3,4,0,3,3,900,0
Mouse,1,0,0,3,1,0,0,3,0.3,2
Porcupine,1,0,1,3,1,0,1,3,3,0
Pig,3,1,4,3,3,1,4,3,50,2
Rabbit,2,0,3,3,1,0,2,3,1,0
Raccoon,3,1,4,2,3,1,4,2,40,2
Rat,1,0,0,3,1,0,0,3,.75,2
Red bat,1,1,2,3,3,1,2,3,1,1
Sea lion,3,1,4,1,2,1,4,1,415,1
Skunk,3,1,3,1,3,1,3,2,2,2
Squirrel,1,0,2,3,1,0,1,3,2,2
Woodchuck,1,0,2,3,1,0,1,3,4,2
Wolf,3,1,4,2,3,1,4,3,27,1
```

- `labelList` is a list of the labels associated with the mammals.

- `featureVals` is a list of lists. Each element of `featureVals` contains the list of values, one for each mammal, for a single feature. The value of the expression `featureVals[i][j]` is the ith feature of the jth mammal.

---

[135] We included the information about weight because the author has been told on more than one occasion that there is a relationship between his weight and his eating habits.

The last part of `readMammalData` uses the values in `featureVals` to create a list of
feature vectors, one for each mammal. (The code could be simplified by not
constructing `featureVals` and instead directly constructing the feature vectors
for each mammal. We chose not to do that in anticipation of an enhancement to
`readMammalData` that we make later in this section.)

```
def readMammalData(fName):
    dataFile = open(fName, 'r')
    numFeatures = 0
    #Process lines at top of file
    for line in dataFile: #Find number of features
        if line[0:6] == '#Label': #indicates end of features
            break
        if line[0:5] != '#Name':
            numFeatures += 1
    featureVals = []

    #Produce featureVals, speciesNames, and labelList
    featureVals, speciesNames, labelList = [], [], []
    for i in range(numFeatures):
        featureVals.append([])

    #Continue processing lines in file, starting after comments
    for line in dataFile:
        dataLine = string.split(line[:-1], ',') #remove newline; then split
        speciesNames.append(dataLine[0])
        classLabel = float(dataLine[-1])
        labelList.append(classLabel)
        for i in range(numFeatures):
            featureVals[i].append(float(dataLine[i+1]))

    #Use featureVals to build list containing the feature vectors
    #for each mammal
    featureVectorList = []
    for mammal in range(len(speciesNames)):
        featureVector = []
        for feature in range(numFeatures):
            featureVector.append(featureVals[feature][mammal])
        featureVectorList.append(featureVector)
    return featureVectorList, labelList, speciesNames
```

Figure 19.12 Read and process file

The function testTeeth in Figure 19.13 uses `trykmeans` to cluster the examples
built by the other function, `buildMammalExamples`, in Figure 19.13. It then
reports the number of herbivores, carnivores, and omnivores in each cluster.

```
def buildMammalExamples(featureList, labelList, speciesNames):
    examples = []
    for i in range(len(speciesNames)):
        features = pylab.array(featureList[i])
        example = Example(speciesNames[i], features, labelList[i])
        examples.append(example)
    return examples

def testTeeth(numClusters, numTrials):
    features, labels, species = readMammalData('dentalFormulas.txt')
    examples = buildMammalExamples(features, labels, species)
    bestClustering =\
                trykmeans(examples, Example, numClusters, numTrials)
    for c in bestClustering:
        names = ''
        for p in c.members():
            names += p.getName() + ', '
        print '\n', names[:-2] #remove trailing comma and space
        herbivores, carnivores, omnivores = 0, 0, 0
        for p in c.members():
            if p.getLabel() == 0:
                herbivores += 1
            elif p.getLabel() == 1:
                carnivores += 1
            else:
                omnivores += 1
        print herbivores, 'herbivores,', carnivores, 'carnivores,',\
            omnivores, 'omnivores'
```

Figure 19.13 Clustering animals

When we executed the code `testTeeth(3, 20)` it printed

```
Cow, Elk, Moose, Sea lion
3 herbivores, 1 carnivores, 0 omnivores

Badger, Cougar, Dog, Fox, Guinea pig, Jaguar, Kangaroo, Mink, Mole,
Mouse, Porcupine, Pig, Rabbit, Raccoon, Rat, Red bat, Skunk, Squirrel,
Woodchuck, Wolf
4 herbivores, 9 carnivores, 7 omnivores

Bear, Deer, Fur seal, Grey seal, Human, Lion
1 herbivores, 3 carnivores, 2 omnivores
```

So much for our conjecture that the clustering would be related to the eating habits of the various species. A cursory inspection suggests that we have a clustering totally dominated by the weights of the animals. The problem is that the range of weights is much larger than the range of any of the other features. Therefore, when the Euclidean distance between examples is computed, the only feature that truly matters is weight.

We encountered a similar problem in Section 19.2 when we found that the distance between animals was dominated by the number of legs. We solved the problem there by turning the number of legs into a binary feature (legged or legless). That was fine for that data set, because all of the animals happened to have either zero or four legs. Here, however, there is no way to binarize weight without losing a great deal of information.

This is a common problem, which is often addressed by scaling the features so that each feature has a mean of 0 and a standard deviation of 1, as done by the function scaleFeatures in Figure 19.14.

```
def scaleFeatures(vals):
    """Assumes vals is a sequence of numbers"""
    result = pylab.array(vals)
    mean = sum(result)/float(len(result))
    result = result - mean
    sd = stdDev(result)
    result = result/sd
    return result
```

Figure 19.14 Scaling attributes

To see the effect of scaleFeatures, let's look at the code below.

```
v1, v2 = [], []
for i in range(1000):
    v1.append(random.gauss(100, 5))
    v2.append(random.gauss(50, 10))
v1 = scaleFeatures(v1)
v2 = scaleFeatures(v2)
print 'v1 mean =', round(sum(v1)/len(v1), 4),\
      'v1 standard deviation', round(stdDev(v1), 4)
print 'v2 mean =', round(sum(v2)/len(v2), 4),\
      'v1 standard deviation', round(stdDev(v2), 4)
```

The code generates two normal distributions with different means (100 and 50) and different standard deviations (5 and 10). It then scales each and prints the means and standard deviations of the results. When run, it prints

```
v1 mean = -0.0 v1 standard deviation 1.0
v2 mean = 0.0 v1 standard deviation 1.0¹³⁶
```

It's easy to see why the statement result = result - mean ensures that the mean of the returned array will always be close to 0[137]. That the standard deviation will always be 1 is not obvious. It can be shown by a long and tedious chain of algebraic manipulations, which we will not bore you with.

Figure 19.15 contains a version of readMammalData that allows scaling of features. The new version of the function testTeeth in the same figure shows the result of clustering with and without scaling.

---

[136] A normal distribution with a mean of 0 and a standard deviation of 1 is called a **standard normal distribution**.

[137] We say "close," because floating point numbers are only an approximation to the reals and the result will not always be exactly 0.

```
def readMammalData(fName, scale):
    """Assumes scale is a Boolean.  If True, features are scaled"""

    #start of code is same as in previous version

    #Use featureVals to build list containing the feature vectors
    #for each mammal scale features, if needed
    if scale:
        for i in range(numFeatures):
            featureVals[i] = scaleFeatures(featureVals[i])

    #remainder of code is the same as in previous version

def testTeeth(numClusters, numTrials, scale):
    features, labels, species =\
            readMammalData('dentalFormulas.txt', scale)
    examples = buildMammalExamples(features, labels, species)

    #remainder of code is the same as in the previous version
```

Figure 19.15 Code that allows scaling of features

When we execute the code

```
print 'Cluster without scaling'
testTeeth(3, 20, False)
print '\nCluster with scaling'
testTeeth(3, 20, True)
```

it prints

```
Cluster without scaling

Cow, Elk, Moose, Sea lion
3 herbivores, 1 carnivores, 0 omnivores

Badger, Cougar, Dog, Fox, Guinea pig, Jaguar, Kangaroo, Mink, Mole,
Mouse, Porcupine, Pig, Rabbit, Raccoon, Rat, Red bat, Skunk, Squirrel,
Woodchuck, Wolf
4 herbivores, 9 carnivores, 7 omnivores

Bear, Deer, Fur seal, Grey seal, Human, Lion
1 herbivores, 3 carnivores, 2 omnivores

Cluster with scaling

Cow, Deer, Elk, Moose
4 herbivores, 0 carnivores, 0 omnivores

Guinea pig, Kangaroo, Mouse, Porcupine, Rabbit, Rat, Squirrel,
Woodchuck
4 herbivores, 0 carnivores, 4 omnivores

Badger, Bear, Cougar, Dog, Fox, Fur seal, Grey seal, Human, Jaguar,
Lion, Mink, Mole, Pig, Raccoon, Red bat, Sea lion, Skunk, Wolf
0 herbivores, 13 carnivores, 5 omnivores
```

The clustering with scaling does not perfectly partition the animals based upon their eating habits, but it is certainly correlated with what the animals eat. It does a good job of separating the carnivores from the herbivores, but there is no obvious pattern in where the omnivores appear. This suggests that perhaps features other than dentition and weight might be needed to separate omnivores from herbivores and carnivores.[138]

19.8 Wrapping Up

In this chapter, we've barely scratched the surface of machine learning. We've tried to give you a taste of the kind of thinking involved in using machine learning—in the hope that you will find ways to pursue the topic on your own.

The same could be said about many of the other topics presented in this book. We've covered a lot more ground than is typical of introductory computer science courses. You probably found some topics less interesting than others. But we do hope that you encountered at least a few topics you are looking forward to learning more about.

---

[138] Eye position might be a useful feature, since both omnivores and carnivores typically have eyes in the front of their head, whereas the eyes of herbivores are typically located more towards the side. Among the mammals, only mothers of humans have eyes in the back of their head.

PYTHON 2.7 QUICK REFERENCE

Common operations on numerical types

i+j is the sum of i and j.

i-j is i minus j.

i*j is the product of i and j.

i//j is integer division.

i/j is i divided by j. In Python 2.7, when i and j are both of type int, the result is also an int, otherwise the result is a float.

i%j is the remainder when the int i is divided by the int j.

ij** is i raised to the power j.

x += y is equivalent to x = x + y. *= and -= work the same way.

Comparison and Boolean operators

x == y returns True if x and y are equal.

x != y returns True if x and y are not equal.

<, >, <=, >= have their usual meanings.

a and b is True if both a and b are True, and False otherwise.

a or b is True if at least one of a or b is True, and False otherwise.

not a is True if a is False, and False if a is True.

Common operations on sequence types

seq[i] returns the ith element in the sequence.

len(seq) returns the length of the sequence.

seq1 + seq2 concatenates the two sequences.

n*seq returns a sequence that repeats seq n times.

seq[start:end] returns a slice of the sequence.

e in seq tests whether e is contained in the sequence.

e not in seq tests whether e is not contained in the sequence.

for e in seq iterates over the elements of the sequence.

Common string methods

s.count(s1) counts how many times the string s1 occurs in s.

s.find(s1) returns the index of the first occurrence of the substring s1 in s; -1 if s1 is not in s.

s.rfind(s1) same as find, but starts from the end of s.

s.index(s1) same as find, but raises an exception if s1 is not in s.

s.rindex(s1) same as index, but starts from the end of s.

s.lower() converts all uppercase letters to lowercase.

s.replace(old, new) replaces all occurrences of string old with string new.

s.rstrip() removes trailing white space.

s.split(d) Splits s using d as a delimiter. Returns a list of substrings of s.

Common list methods

`L.append(e)` adds the object e to the end of L.

`L.count(e)` returns the number of times that e occurs in L.

`L.insert(i, e)` inserts the object e into L at index i.

`L.extend(L1)` appends the items in list L1 to the end of L.

`L.remove(e)` deletes the first occurrence of e from L.

`L.index(e)` returns the index of the first occurrence of e in L.

`L.pop(i)` removes and returns the item at index i. Defaults to -1.

`L.sort()` has the side effect of sorting the elements of L.

`L.reverse()` has the side effect of reversing the order of the elements in L.

Common operations on dictionaries

`len(d)` returns the number of items in d.

`d.keys()` returns a list containing the keys in d.

`d.values()` returns a list containing the values in d.

`k in d` returns True if key k is in d.

`d[k]` returns the item in d with key k. Raises KeyError if k is not in d.

`d.get(k, v)` returns d[k] if k in d, and v otherwise.

`d[k] = v` associates the value v with the key k. If there is already a value associated with k, that value is replaced.

`del d[k]` removes element with key k from d. Raises KeyError if k is not in d.

`for k in d` iterates over the keys in d.

Comparison of common non-scalar types

Type	Type of Index	Type of element	Examples of literals	Mutable
str	int	characters	'', 'a', 'abc'	No
tuple	int	any type	(), (3,), ('abc', 4)	No
list	int	any type	[], [3], ['abc', 4]	Yes
dict	Hashable objects	any type	{}, {'a':1}, {'a':1, 'b':2.0}	Yes

Common input/output mechanisms

```
raw_input(msg) prints msg and then returns value entered as a string.
print s1, …, sn prints strings s1, …, sn with a space between each.
open('fileName', 'w') creates a file for writing.
open('fileName', 'r') opens an existing file for reading.
open('fileName', 'a') opens an existing file for appending.
fileHandle.read() returns a string containing contents of the file.
fileHandle.readline() returns the next line in the file.
fileHandle.readlines() returns a list containing lines of the file.
fileHandle.write(s) write the string s to the end of the file.
fileHandle.writelines(L) Writes each element of L to the file.
fileHandle.close() closes the file.
```

INDEX

init, 94
_lt_ built-in method, 98
name built-in method, 183
str, 95

abs built-in function, 20
abstract data type. *See* data abstraction
abstraction, 43
abstraction barrier, 91, 140
acceleration due to gravity, 208
algorithm, 2
aliasing, 61, 66
   testing for, 73
al-Khwarizmi, Muhammad ibn Musa, 2
American Folk Art Museum, 267
annotate, PyLab plotting, 276
Anscombe, F.J., 226
append method, 61
approximate solutions, 25
arange function, 218
arc of graph, 240
Archimedes, 201
arguments, 35
array type, 148
   operators, 216
assert statement, 90
assertions, 90
assignment statement, 11
   multiple, 13, 57
   mutation versus, 58
   unpacking multiple returned values, 57

Babbage, Charles, 222
Bachelier, Louis, 179
backtracking, 246, 247
bar chart, 224
baseball, 174
Bellman, Richard, 252
Benford's law, 173
Bernoulli, Jacob, 156
Bernoulli's theorem, 156
Bible, 200
big O notation. *See* computational
  complexity

binary feature, 270
binary number, 122, 154
binary search, 128
binary search debugging technique, 80
binary tree, 254
binding, of names, 11
bisection search, 27, 28
bit, 29
bizarre looking plot, 145
black-box testing. *See* testing, black-box
blocks of code, 15
Boesky, Ivan, 240
Boolean expression, 11
   compound, 15
   short-circuit evaluation, 49
Box, George E.P., 205
branching programs, 14
breadth-first search (BFS), 249
break statement, 23
Brown, Rita Mae, 79
Brown, Robert, 179
Brownian motion, 179
Buffon, 201
bug, 76
   covert, 77
   intermittent, 77
   origin of word, 76
   overt, 77
   persistent, 77
built-in functions
   abs, 20
   help, 41
   id, 60
   input, 18
   isinstance, 101
   len, 17
   list, 63
   map, 65
   max, 35
   min, 57
   range, 23
   raw_input, 18
   round, 31
   sorted, 131, 136, 236
   sum, 110

type, 10
  xrange, 24, 197
byte, 1

C++, 91
Cartesian coordinates, 180, 266
case-sensitivity, 12
causal nondeterminism, 152
centroid, 272
child node, 240
Church, Alonzo, 36
Church-Turing thesis, 3
Chutes and Ladders, 191
class variable, 95, 99
classes, 91–112
  init method, 94
  name method, 183
  str method, 95
  abstract, 109
  attribute, 94
  attribute reference, 93
  class variable, 95, 99
  data attribute, 94, 95
  defining, 94
  definition, 92
  dot notation, 94
  inheritance, 99
  instance, 94
  instance variable, 95
  instantiation, 93, 94
  isinstance function, 101
  isinstance vs. type, 102
  method attribute, 93
  overriding attributes, 99
  printing instances, 95
  self, 94
  subclass, 99
  superclass, 99
  type hierarchy, 99
  type vs. isinstance, 102
client, 42, 105
close method for files, 53
CLU, 91
clustering, 270
coefficient of variation, 163, 165
command. *See* statement
comment in programs, 12
compiler, 7

complexity classes, 118, 123–24
computation, 2
computational complexity, 16, 113–24
  amortized analysis, 131
  asymptotic notation, 116
  average-case, 114
  best-case, 114
  big O notation, 117
  Big Theta notation, 118
  constant, 16, 118
  expected-case, 114
  exponential, 118, 121
  inherently exponential, 239
  linear, 118, 119
  logarithmic, 118
  log-linear, 118, 120
  lower bound, 118
  polynomial, 118, 120
  pseudo polynomial, 260
  quadratic, 120
  rules of thumb for expressing, 117
  tight bound, 118
  time-space tradeoff, 140, 199
  upper bound, 114, 117
  worst-case, 114
concatenation (+)
  append, vs., 62
  lists, 62
  sequence types, 16
  tuples, 56
conceptual complexity, 113
conjunct, 48
Copenhagen Doctrine, 152
copy standard library module, 63
correlation, 225
craps, 195
cross validation, 221

data abstraction, 92, 95–96, 179
datetime standard library module, 96
debugging, 41, 53, 70, 76–83, 90
  stochastic programs, 157
decimal numbers, 29
decision tree, 254–56
decomposition, 43
decrementing function, 21, 130
deepcopy function, 63
default parameter values, 37

defensive programming, 77, 88, 90

dental formula, 281

depth-first search (DFS), 246

destination node, 240

deterministic program, 153

dict type, 67–69

  adding an element, 69

  allowable keys, 69

  deleting an element, 69

  keys, 67

  keys method, 67, 69

  values method, 69

dictionary. *See* dict type

Dijkstra, Edsger, 70

dimensionality, of data, 264

disjunct, 48

dispersion, 165

dissimilarity metric, 271

distributions, 160

  bell curve. *See* distributions, normal

  Benford's, 173

  empirical rule for normal, 169

  Gaussian. *See* distributions, normal

  memoryless property, 171

  normal, 169, 168–70, 202

  uniform, 137, 170

divide-and-conquer algorithms, 132, 261

divide-and-conquer problem solving, 49

docstring, 41

don't pass line, 195

dot notation, 48, 52, 94

Dr. Pangloss, 70

dynamic programming, 252–61

dynamic-time-warping, 274

earth-movers distance, 274

edge of a graph, 240

efficient programs, 125

Einstein, Albert, 70, 179

elastic limit of springs, 213

elif, 15

else, 14, 15

encapsulation, 105

ENIAC, 193

error bars, 169

escape character, 53

Euclid, 172

Euclidean distance, 267

Euclidean mean, 271

Euler, Leonhard, 241

except block, 85

exceptions, 84–90

  built-in

    AssertionError, 90

    IndexError, 84

    NameError, 84

    TypeError, 84

    ValueError, 84

  built-in class, 87

  handling, 84–87

  raising, 84

  try–except, 85

  unhandled, 84

exhaustive enumeration algorithms, 21, 22, 26, 234, 254

  square root algorithm, 26, 116

exponential decay, 172

exponential growth, 172

expression, 9

extend method, 62

extending a list, 62

factorial, 45, 115, 120

  iterative implementation, 45, 115

  recursive implementation, 45

false negative, 266

false positive, 266

feature extraction, 264

feature vector, 263

Fibonacci poem, 47

Fibonacci sequence, 45, 252–54

  dynamic programming implementation, 253

  recursive implementation, 46

file system, 53

files, 53–55, 54

  appending, 54

  close method, 53

  file handle, 53

  open function, 53

  reading, 54

  write method, 53

writing, 53
first-class values, 64, 86
fitting a curve to data, 210–14
    coefficient of determination (R^2), 216
    exponential with polyfit, 218
    least-squares objective function, 210
    linear regression, 211
    objective function,, 210
    overfitting, 213
    polyfit, 211
fixed-program computers, 2
float type. *See* floating point
floating point, 9, 30, 29–31
    exponent, 30
    precision, 30
    reals vs., 29
    rounded value, 30
    rounding errors, 31
    significant digits, 30
floppy disk, 142
flow of control, 3
for loop, 54
for statement
    generators, 107
Franklin, Benjamin, 50
function, 35
    actual parameter, 35
    arguments, 35
    as object, 64–65
    as parameter, 135
    call, 35
    class as parameter, 183
    default parameter values, 37
    defining, 35
    invocation, 35
    keyword argument, 36, 37
    positional parameter binding, 36

gambler's fallacy, 157
Gaussian distribution. *See* distributions,
    normal
generalization, 262
generator, 107
geometric distribution, 172
geometric progression, 172
glass-box testing. *See* testing, glass-box
global optimum, 240
global statement, 51

global variable, 50, 75
graph, 240–51
    adjacency list representation, 243
    adjacency matrix representation, 243
    breadth-first search (BFS), 249
    depth-first search (DFS), 246
    digraph, 240
    directed graph, 240
    edge, 240
    graph theory, 241
    node, 240
    problems
        cliques, 244
        min cut, 244, 246
        shortest path, 244, 246–51
        shortest weighted path, 244
    weighted, 241
Graunt, John, 222
gravity, acceleration due to, 208
greedy algorithm, 235
guess-and-check algorithms, 2, 22

halting problem, 3
Hamlet, 77
hand simulation, 19
hashing, 69, 137–40
    collision, 137, 138
    hash buckets, 138
    hash function, 137
    hash tables, 137
    probability of collisions, 177
help built-in function, 41
helper functions, 48, 129
Heron of Alexandria, 1
higher-order functions, 65
higher-order programming, 64
histogram, 166
Hoare, C.A.R., 135
holdout set, 221, 232
Holmes, Sherlock, 82
Hooke's law, 207, 213
Hopper, Grace Murray, 76
hormone replacement therapy, 226
housing prices, 223
Huff, Darrell, 222

id built-in function, 60
IDLE, 13

edit menu, 13
    file menu, 13
if statement, 15
immutable type, 58
import statement, 52
in operator, 66
indentation of code, 15
independent events, 154
indexing for sequence types, 17
indirection, 127
induction, 132
inductive definition, 45
inferential statistics, 155
information hiding, 105, 106
input, 18
input built-in function, 18
    raw_input vs., 18
instance, of a class, 93
integrated development environment
    (IDE), 13
interface, 91
interpreter, 3, 7
Introduction to Algorithms, 125
isinstance built-in function, 101
iteration, 18
    for loop, 23
    over integers, 23
    over lists, 61

Java, 91
Juliet, 12
Julius Caesar, 50

Kennedy, Joseph, 81
key, on a plot. *See* plotting in PyLab,
    legend function
keyword argument, 36
keywords, 12
k-means clustering, 274–86
knapsack problem, 234–40
    0/1, 238
    brute-force solution, 238
    dynamic programming solution, 254–
      61
    fractional (or continuous), 240
Knight Capital Group, 78

knowledge, declarative vs. imperative, 1
Knuth, Donald, 117
Königsberg bridges problem, 241

label keyword argument, 146
lambda abstraction, 36
Lampson, Butler, 128
Laplace, Pierre-Simon, 201
law of large numbers, 156, 157
leaf, of tree, 254
least squares fit, 210, 212
len built-in function, 17
length, for sequence types, 17
Leonardo of Pisa, 46
lexical scoping, 38
library, standard Python, see also
    standard libarbary modules, 53
linear regression, 211, 262
Liskov, Barbara, 103
list built-in function, 63
list comprehension, 63
list type, 58–62
    + (concatenation) operator, 62
    cloning, 63
    comprehension, 63
    copying, 63
    indexing, 126
    internal representation, 127
literals, 4, 288
local optimum, 240
local variable, 38
log function, 220
logarithm, base of, 118
logarithmic axis, 124
logarithmic scaling, 159
loop, 18
loop invariant, 131
lt operator, 133
lurking variable, 225

machine code, 7
machine learning
    supervised, 263
    unsupervised, 264
Manhattan distance, 267
Manhattan Project, 193

many-to-one mapping, 137

map built-in function, 65

MATLAB, 141

max built-in function, 35

memoization, 253

memoryless property, 171

method invocation, 48, 94

min built-in function, 57

Minkowski distance, 266, 269, 274

modules, 51–53, 51, 74, 91

Moksha-patamu, 191

Molière, 92

Monte Carlo simulation, 193–204

Monty Python, 13

mortgages, 108, 146

multi-line statements, 22

multiple assignment, 12, 13, 57
    return values from functions, 58

mutable type, 58

mutation versus assignment, 58

name space, 37

names, 12

nan (not a number), 88

nanosecond, 22

National Rifle Association, 229

natural number, 45

nested statements, 15

newline character, 53

Newton's method. *See* Newton-Raphson
    method

Newtonian mechanics, 152

Newton-Raphson method, 32, 33, 126,
    210

Nixon, Richard, 56

node of a graph, 240

nondeterminism, causal vs. predictive,
    152

None, 9, 110

non-scalar type, 56

normal distribution. *See* distributions,
    normal
    standard, xiii, 284

not in operator, 66

null hypothesis, 174, 231

numeric operators, 10

numeric types, 9

NumPy, 148

O notation. *See* computational complexity

O(1). *See* computational complexity,
    constant

Obama, Barack, 44

object, 9–11
    class, 99
    first-class, 64
    mutable, 58

object equality, 60
    value equality vs., 81

objective function, 210, 263, 270

object-oriented programming, 91

open function for files, 53

operator precedence, 10

operator standard library module, 133

operators, 9
    -, on arrays, 148
    -, on numbers, 10
    *, on arrays, 148
    *, on numbers, 10
    *, on sequences, 66
    **, on numbers, 10
    *=, 25
    /, on numbers, 10
    //, on numbers, 10
    %, on numbers, 10
    +, on numbers, 10
    +, on sequences, 66
    +=, 25
    -=, 25
    Boolean, 11
    floating point, 10
    in, on sequences, 66
    infix, 4
    integer, 10
    not in, on sequences, 66
    overloading, 16

optimal solution, 238

optimal substructure, 252, 258

optimization problem, 210, 234, 263, 270
    constraints, 234
    objective function, 234

order of growth, 117

overfitting, 213, 280

overlapping subproblems, 252, 258

overloading of operators, 16

palindrome, 48

parallel random access machine, 114

parent node, 240

Pascal, Blaise, 194

pass line, 195

pass statement, 101

paths through specification, 72

Peters, Tim, 136

pi (π), estimating by simulation, 200–204

Pingala, 47

Pirandello, 43

plotting in PyLab, 141–46, 166–68, 190

    annotate, 276

    bar chart, 224

    current figure, 143

    default settings, 146

    figure function, 141

    format string, 144

    histogram, 166

    keyword arguments, 145

    label keyword argument, 146

    labels for plots, 146

    legend function, 146

    markers, 189

    plot function, 141

    rc settings, 145

    savefig function, 143

    semilogx function, 159

    semilogy function, 159

    show function, 142

    style, 187

    tables, 268

    title function, 144

    windows, 141

    xlabel function, 144

    xticks, 224

    ylabel function, 144

    yticks, 224

png file extension, 142

point of execution, 36

point, in typography, 145

pointer, 127

polyfit, 210

    fitting an exponential, 218

polymorphic function, 86

polynomial, 32

coefficient, 32

    degree, 32

polynomial fit, 211

pop method, 62

popping a stack, 39

portable network graphics format, 142

power set, 122, 238

predictive nondeterminism, 152

print statement, 18

probabilities, 154

program, 8

programming language, 3, 7

    compiled, 7

    high-level, 7

    interpreted, 7

    low-level, 7

    semantics, 5

    static semantics, 4

    syntax, 4

prompt, shell, 10

prospective experiment, 221

prospective study, 232

PyLab, see also plotting, 141

    arange function, 218

    array, 148

    polyfit, 211

    user's guide, 141

Pythagorean theorem, 180, 202

Python, 7, 35

Python 3, versus 2.7, 8, 9, 18, 24

Python statement, 8

quantum mechanics, 152

rabbits, 46

raise statement, 87

random access machine, 114

random module, 153, 172

    choice, 153

    gauss, 170

    random, 153

    sample, 274

    seed, 157

    uniform, 170

random walk, 179–92

    biased, 186

range built-in function, 23
    Python 2 vs. 3, 24
raw_input built-in function, 18
    input vs., 18
recurrence, 46
recursion, 44
    base case, 44
    recursive (inductive) case, 44
regression testing, 76
regression to the mean, 157
reload statement, 53
remove method, 62
representation invariant, 95
representation-independence, 95
reserved words in Python, 12
retrospective study, 232
return on investment (ROI), 196
return statement, 35
reverse method, 62
reverse parameter, 236
Rhind Papyrus, 200
root, 254
root of polynomial, 32
round built-in function, 31
R-squared, 216

sample function, 274
sampling
    accuracy, 159
    bias, 228
    confidence, 160, 162
Samuel, Arthur, 262
scalar type, 9
scaling features, 284
scoping, 37
    lexical, 38
    static, 38
script, 8
search algorithms, 126–30
    binary Search, 128, 129
    bisection search, 28
    breadth-first search (BFS), 249
    depth-first search (DFS), 246
    linear search, 114, 126
search space, 126
self, 94
semantics, 5
sequence types, 17, *See* str, tuple, list

shell, 8
shell prompt, 10
short-circuit evaluation of Boolean
    expressions, 49
side effect, 61, 62
signal-to-noise ratio, 264
significant digits, 30
simulation
    coin flipping, 155–65
    deterministic, 205
    Monte Carlo, 193–204
    multiple trials, 156
    random walks, 179–92
    smoke test, 184
    stochastic, 205
    typical structure, 196
simulation model, 155, 205
    continuous, 206
    discrete, 206
    dynamic, 206
    static, 206
    summary of, 204–6
slicing, for sequence types, 17
SmallTalk, 91
smoke test, 184
Snakes and Ladders, 191
SNR, 264
social networks, 246
software quality assurance, 75
sort built-in method, 98, 131
sort method, 62, 136
    key parameter, 136
    reverse parameter, 136
sorted built-in function, 131, 136, 236
sorting algorithms, 131–37
    in-place, 134
    merge sort, 120, 134, 252
    quicksort, 135
    stable sort, 137
    timsort, 136
source code, 7
source node, 240
space complexity, 120, 135
specification, 41–44
    assumptions, 42, 129
    docstring, 41
    guarantees, 42
split function for strings, 135

spring constant, 207
SQA, 75
square root, 25, 26, 27, 32
stable sort, 137
stack, 39
stack frame, 38
standard deviation, 160, 169, 198
 relative to mean, 163
standard library modules
 copy, 63
 datetime, 96
 math, 220
 operator, 133
 random, 153
 string, 135
standard normal distribution, 284
statement, 8
statements
 assert, 90
 assignment (=), 11
 break, 23, 24
 conditional, 14
 for loop, 23, 54
 global, 51
 if, 15
 import, 52
 import *, 52
 pass, 101
 print statement, 18
 raise, 87
 reload, 53
 return, 35
 try–except, 85
 while loop, 19
 yield, 107
static scoping, 38
static semantic checking, 5, 106
static semantics, 4
statistical machine learning, 262
statistical sin, 222–33
 assuming independence, 223
 confusing correlation and causation, 225
 convenience (accidental) sampling, 228
 Cum Hoc Ergo Propter Hoc, 225
 deceiving with pictures, 223

 extrapolation, 229
 Garbage In Garbage Out (GIGO), 222
 ignoring context, 229
 non-response bias, 228
 reliance on measures, 226
 Texas sharpshooter fallacy, 230
statistically valid conclusion, 204
statistics
 coefficient of variation, 165
 confidence interval, 165, 168, 169
 confidence level, 168
 correctness vs., 204
 correlation, 225
 error bars, 169
 null hypothesis, 174
 p-value, 174
 testing for, 174
step (of a computation), 114
stochastic process, 153
stored-program computer, 3
str
 * operator, 16
 + operator, 16
 built-in methods, 66
 concatenation (+), 16
 escape character, 53, 100
 indexing, 17
 len, 17
 newline character, 53
 slicing, 17
 substring, 17
straight-line programs, 14
string standard library module, 135
string type. *See* str
stubs, 75
substitution principle, 103, 244
substring, 17
successive approximation, 32, 210
sum built-in function, 110
supervised learning, 263
symbol table, 38, 52
syntax, 4

table lookup, 199–200, 253
tables, in PyLab, 268
termination

of loop, 19, 21
    of recursion, 130
testing, 70–76
    black-box, 71, 73
    boundary conditions, 72
    glass-box, 71, 73–74
    integration testing, 74
    partitioning inputs, 71
    path-complete, 73
    regression testing, 76
    test functions, 41
    test suite, 71
    unit testing, 74
Texas sharpshooter fallacy, 230
total ordering, 27
training data, 262
training set, 221, 232
translating text, 68
tree, 254
    decision tree, 254–56
    leaf node, 254
    left-first depth-first enumeration, 256
    root, of tree, 254
    rooted binary tree, 254
try block, 85
try-except statement, 85
tuple, 56–58
Turing Completeness, 4
Turing machine, universal, 3
Turing-complete programming language,
    34
type, 9, 91
    cast, 18
    conversion, 18, 147
type built-in function, 10
type checking, 17
type type, 92
types
    bool, 9
    dict. *See* dict type
    float, 9

instancemethod, 92
int, 9
list. *See* list type
None, 9
str. *See* str
tuple, 56
type, 92

U.S. citizen, definition of natural-born, 44
Ulam, Stanislaw, 193
unary function, 65
uniform distribution. *See* distributions,
    uniform
unsupervised learning, 264

value, 9
value equality vs. object equality, 81
variable, 11
    choosing a name, 12
variance, 160, 271
versions, 8
vertex of a graph, 240
von Neumann, John, 133
von Rossum, Guido, 8

while loop, 19
whitespace characters, 135
Wing, Jeannette, 103
word size, 127
World Series, 174
wrapper functions, 129
write method for files, 53

xrange built-in function, 24, 197
xticks, 224

yield statement, 107
yticks, 224

zero-based indexing, 17